MAORI

Selected works by Michael King

Moko: Maori Tattooing in the Twentieth Century (1972)

Face value: A study in Maori portraiture (1975)

Te Puea (1977)

Tihe mauri ora: Aspects of Maoritanga (1978)

Te Ao Hurihuri: Aspects of Maoritanga (1979)

Being Maori (1981)

New Zealanders at War (1981)

A place to stand: A history of Turangawaewae marae (1981)

Whina: A Biography of Whina Cooper (1983)

Te Puea Herangi: From darkness to light (1984)

Being Pakeha: An Encounter with New Zealand and the Maori Renaissance (1985)

Kawe korero: A guide to reporting Maori activities (1985)

New Zealand (1987)

Apirana Ngata: E tipu e rea (1988)

Moriori: A People Rediscovered (1989)

A Land Apart: The Chatham Islands of New Zealand (1990)

Pakeha: The quest for identity in New Zealand (1991)

Frank Sargeson: A Life (1995)

Nga iwi o te motu: One thousand years of Maori history (1997)

Being Pakeha Now: Reflections and recollections of a white native (1999)

Wrestling with the Angel: A Life of Janet Frame (2000)

Tread Softly For You Tread on My Life (2001)

An Inward Sun: The World of Janet Frame (2002)

At the Edge of Memory: A family story (2002)

Penguin History of New Zealand (2003)

MAORI

A Photographic and Social History

Revised Edition

MICHAEL KING

RAUPO

He aha te mea nui?
He tangata, he tangata, he tangata

What is the most important thing in the world?
It is people, people, people

from an Aupouri chant

A RAUPO BOOK
Published by the Penguin Group
Penguin Group (NZ), 67 Apollo Drive, Rosedale,
North Shore 0632, New Zealand (a division of Pearson New Zealand Ltd)

Penguin Books Ltd, Registered Offices: 80 Strand, London, WC2R 0RL, England

Originally published by Reed Publishing (NZ) Ltd 1983
Paperback edition 1984; reprinted 1989, 1991, 1994
Revised edition 1996; reprinted 2000, 2003, 2004, 2005 (3 times)

First published by Penguin Group (NZ) 2008
9 10 8

Printed in China through Bookbuilders, Hong Kong

ISBN: 978 0 14 301088 3

A catalogue record for this book is available
from the National Library of New Zealand.

www.penguin.co.nz

Contents

For James Clendon Henare
to remember

Author's Note

The photographs in this book show *how* things were in the recent Maori past; and the text explores *why* such things were. Both are assembled here in the belief that the past holds keys to understanding the present, that nations do not know where they are or where they are heading until they know where they have been. A considerable part of the history of New Zealand has been and will continue to be a history of relations between predominantly two people and two cultures. As the area of overlap between those people grows even larger, it is imperative that both sides understand each other. This means largely that non-Maoris need to know more about Maori experience, because Maoris in New Zealand are almost all, of necessity, bicultural people; most Pakehas are not.

Much that non-Maoris find difficult to grasp about Maori behaviour becomes comprehensible with a knowledge of the past. The intensity of Maori family, hapu and tribal competitiveness, for example, is both a factor in Maori vitality and survival, and a source of the sometimes bitter quarrelling that often prevents Maori individuals and tribes from acting in concert (as in the case of the Sealords deal designed to settle Maori fisheries claims). Or there are the examples of accusations of Pakeha racism in New Zealand. These are far more readily understood when they are seen as the result of policies which brought Maoris into urban and suburban New Zealand in the wake of World War Two, without preparing either Maori or Pakeha populations for the frictions that were an inevitable effect of such a move.

I trust that this book will help preserve evidence of Maori experience for Maori posterity, and that it will give non-Maoris a more informed respect for Maori lifestyles, values and institutions. Because it is the lack of such respect in the past that has caused an under-valuation of Maori ingredients in the national life and brought about conditions that caused difficulties in the 1980s and 1990s. It is not too late to correct some of the mistakes of the past by giving Maori language, culture and history a more emphatic place in the national equation, and by restoring Maori resources seized illegally or unfairly by agencies of the Crown since 1840. This would not be — as some have suggested — a case of turning back the clock; rather it is one of setting it, belatedly, to the correct time.

The note on which the book finishes is one of Maori assertiveness and protest. I had some reservations about this. There was far more going on of a positive and cooperative nature in New Zealand race relations in the 1990s than photographs of protests over the National Government's Fiscal Envelope proposals would suggest. Nevertheless Maori protest against the in-built cultural bias of New Zealand institutions and national ceremonials is likely to be the most noticeable feature of the country's race relations in the 1990s, and it is the debate and reassessment that follows such protest that is most likely to bring about further social change.

In combination, the text and illustrations in this book constitute a wider overview of Maori life and race relations in New Zealand than any published previously. For example, earlier books on Maoris (with the exception of those by Herries Beattie) largely overlook South Island Maoris, as if they had become extinct or were so assimilated with Europeans as to be indistinguishable from Pakeha. I have tried to rectify such omissions and to give the indigenous South Islanders the representation they deserve. I have also drawn attention to the activities of kupapa tribes (those who cooperated with the Crown in the wars of the nineteenth century) since they too were largely ignored by some earlier historians.

The book considers briefly the origins of Polynesian and Maori culture, and then in more detail looks at developments within Maori society, and at Maori-Pakeha contact, conflict and cooperation. Photographs and text investigate Maori appearance, dress, settlements, dwellings, domestic activities, gatherings and ceremonial. They also highlight features of continuity and of change. While social history is the predominant emphasis, attention has also been paid to national politics where politics underlie social changes; and to leadership, because leadership was a far more visible and more potent component in the life of Maori communities than it was in those of non-Maoris.

The photographs are for the most part arranged thematically within chronological sections. While a purely chronological presentation would have been preferable it was not practicable. In the first place it was not always possible to establish exactly when (or even where) photographs were taken; and secondly acculturation proceeded at different rates in different parts of the country, with widely varying but simultaneous consequences. These factors favoured a more thematic arrangement.

It will also be apparent that the photographs selected are not of an even technical standard. Some are superbly sharp prints by professionals; others are re-photographed from buckled snapshots in family albums; and there is much in between these extremes. They have been included not so much for photographic excellence as for what they say about the time and place in which they were taken. Where possible I have tried to communicate with the people in the pictures reproduced, or with their descendants. In many instances, however, I could identify neither the subjects nor the locality with certainty. I would welcome hearing from people who could shed light on such matters.

The general policy adopted towards Maori words is to use in Maori expressions that Maori speakers of English would render in Maori. Such expressions are becoming part of New Zealand English (as distinct from 'the Queen's English') and should not be italicised as exotic or 'foreign'. The word 'Pakeha', of course, denotes non-Maori New Zealanders and is often though by no means always synonomous with 'European'. I have tended to use 'European' in reference to people and influences that came directly from Europe. I have preferred to call non-Maori New Zealanders 'Pakeha' because it is an indigenous term that no longer has pejorative connotations. Maori plurals are given in Maori (without an 's') except where long-standing usage favours the English form.

Acknowledgements to the many people who have helped with this project and to major sources of information can be found at the back of the book.

MICHAEL KING

INTRODUCTION

Maoris and Photography

This book is a social *and* photographic history, meaning that illustrations are as important as text. They are not decoration, they are historical documents. Their content conveys textures of Maori life in the nineteenth and twentieth centuries; and their style frequently reveals European attitudes to Maoris. As a basis for understanding and analysing such photographs, it is useful to consider some information about the introduction of photography to New Zealand and about Maori attitudes to it and uses of it.

The process of photographing people was in use in Europe from 1839. It did not reach New Zealand until the late 1840s. The first method used in the then British colony was the daguerreotype, named after its inventor Louis Daguerre. This required lengthy exposures (at first some 10 to 15 minutes, later five to 30 seconds), was expensive (up to 10 shillings to two guineas per picture) and resulted in a single positive image which could only be seen from certain angles and could not be duplicated. Early daguerreotype photography in New Zealand did not extend far beyond controlled conditions in makeshift studios outside the homes of wealthier European settlers. Hence the number of Maori portraits from this time is few and their range narrow.* The wet-plate process introduced in the mid-1850s allowed greater versatility, however. While (again) long exposures and studio-type conditions were preferred, it was possible for the photographer to carry his equipment and chemicals about with him into the field. The process was more versatile and became cheaper than daguerreotype photography. Maoris were still photographed more often in towns, but photographers began to move out into Maori communities from the late 1850s. Multiple prints were made from the resulting wet-plate negatives and hence more pictures went into circulation and more survived.

In effect, therefore, Maori exposure to photography dates from the late 1850s and early 1860s.** And it was from this time that Maori attitudes to the practice began to form. Almost from the outset those attitudes were ambivalent. In most cases the results of photography generated respect, in some instances even awe and fear. Uninitiated to the mysteries of physics and chemistry, Maoris were unlikely at this time to understand the process. But they were well aware of its dramatic consequences: a person's image — his or her most intimate characteristic — could be captured at a given moment, frozen, reproduced, circulated and retained for posterity, even after the subject was dead.

Some early models appear nonchalant about all this. To people close to European life, such as Mohi Te Ngu of Auckland, photography seems to have been simply one further example of European technological prowess, to which they were already accustomed. A few others face the camera confidently, even defiantly. To many Maoris, however, photography was a source of anxiety; and to others still, something positively sinister. Photographers as far apart as Alfred Burton (in 1885) and George Bourne (in 1908) reported that Maoris called them or

---

* J. N. Crombie of Auckland took daguerreotypes of Maoris to send to Europe, the only Maori photograph of this type known to have survived is that of the Barrett sisters reproduced on page 7.

** Individual Maoris might have been photographed outside New Zealand before this time, but this has yet to be established. Two alleged candidates pictured in Boston in 1850 turned out to be Hawaiians.

their cameras 'taipo' or goblins.* This resulted in part from the apparent magic of the process, and in part from a fear that cameras had the power to suck out a person's mauri or life force. The latter notion appears to have been based on the view that you could not transfer a person's image from one place to another without in some way diminishing the subject. The rumour spread in some Maori communities that sickness or death would result from exposure to the camera. And the fact that — inevitably — a few people did die within a short time of being photographed added impetus to that fear.

And yet at the same time there was widespread interest in and eventual acceptance in most areas of the *results* of photography, even if reservations about the process lingered. By the very fact that images of people *were* personal and were regarded as holding at least something of the life force, developed prints were valued enormously by those who knew the subjects, especially after those subjects had died. In this context it should be noted that the role of Maoris in photography was far from that of simply passive subjects. Workbooks of the Wanganui photographers Alfred Martin and Frank Denton show that from the 1890s Maoris were actively commissioning pictures for their own, for family and for ceremonial use. Like his contemporaries, Denton kept a selection of 'Maori beauties' and 'old time warriors' for the Pakeha and tourist market. But he was also a conventional portrait photographer and sufficiently accepted in this role by Maoris for them to become a significant proportion of his customers. In addition to sittings for portraits, commissions from Maoris included photographs of functions, group pictures on special occasions, and copying earlier photographs taken by other photographers.

About the same time as this growth of Maori interest in portrait photography the custom spread of placing photographs of dead people and their pre-deceased relatives around bodies at tangis. These pictures would then be addressed in oratory and lament as if they were living presences. The parallel custom grew of hanging such portraits on the interior walls of meeting houses. This was an elaboration of the concept of meeting houses as ancestral spirits and representations of genealogies to which the tribe or hapu was connected. Houses were named after ancestors, the rafters were said to represent ancestral ribs, and poupou or upright slabs were often carved or painted with ancestral figures. The placing of photographs of recently deceased relatives within such an environment was entirely consistent with earlier usages. It was a classic example of Maori accomodation of features of Western technology into a framework of Maori values, with a consequent strengthening of those values.

Photographs also came to be used in the twentieth century in tangis where the body was not present (where it could not be recovered, for example); in kawe mate, the ritual 'carrying' of a death around a number of marae; in hahunga or exhumation ceremonies which continued into the 1950s; and at the unveiling of headstones. These last were an adaptation of the pre-European exhumation ceremonies in which bones were removed from the ground years after death, scraped, and then placed in a cave or subsequent burial place. It was a ritual for completing the process of mourning and the acceptance of death. In the twentieth century these functions were transferred to reburials, and to a ceremony centred on the unveiling of headstones. As in the case of tangis, photographs came to be used to recall the presence of the persons concerned.

The twentieth century further complicated Maori attitudes to photography by raising the spectre of commercialisation. Publication of Maori photographs, particularly in pictorial magazines and postcards, became far more extensive. The practice of sending postcards to friends, especially cards regarded as picturesque or amusing, had begun in the late nineteenth century but became a craze from about 1902. In 1909 alone nine million cards passed through the New Zealand postal system, and this at a time when the total population of the country had only just reached one million. Maoris rapidly became favourite subjects for these cards, as they had been for the earlier *cartes de visite*. Maori images were circulated widely within New Zealand and posted overseas as an 'exotic' feature of New Zealand life. It was a reason for further photographing Maoris and for re-issuing earlier prints. The Burton Brothers business in Dunedin, by then called Muir and Moodie, changed its name yet again to The Great Post Card Emporium.

Several categories of Maori pictures acquired especial popularity at this time and in turn influenced the taking of new photographs: nostalgic depictions of 'old-time' Maoris, last in a line of noble warriors and tohungas (this category corresponded to the contemporaneous oil portraits of Charles Frederick Goldie); re-enactments of pre-European Maori scenes in allegedly period costume; scenes of country idylls aping those of London photographic salons; madonna-like Maori women; alluring maidens; depictions of erotic but innocent 'noble savages'; cute renditions of children; and coon humour cards which portrayed Maoris as simple foolish folk, unable to cope with the complexities of Western civilisation. All these were a more telling reflection of European attitudes than of the features of Maori life. They showed little or nothing of the squalor and the vitality that more commonly characterised Maori communities at this time.

Pictorial magazines such as the *Auckland Weekly News* — in addition to covering some Maori functions in a documentary

<hr>

* 'Taipo' is a curious word. Europeans used it believing it to be Maori, Maoris used it under the impression that it was English. It was possibly a mis-rendering by Europeans of the Maori word 'tipua', which meant 'demon' or 'object of terror'.

fashion* — also published Maori studies based on the popular categories. The coon pictures in particular reached new heights of technical achievement and offensiveness in the work of the Northwood brothers of Northland. The most damaging effect of these photographs arose from the fact that few Europeans encountered Maoris in their daily lives. Their experience of them and their attitudes towards them tended to be conditioned by the photographic images they saw. So that stereotypes which arose from ignorance or prejudice tended to feed further negative stereotypes and lead to subsequent instances of prejudice.

Publication on this scale added further elements of reservation in the minds of Maori subjects. The more sophisticated (in things European), such as Apirana Ngata, found patronising and negatively prejudiced photographs offensive. The more traditionally oriented feared that their image and consequently the mana and the tapu of their life force might be exploited commercially, to generate the sale of cards and magazines and consequently to put money in the pockets of photographers and publishers. There was a growing feeling among such Maoris in the twentieth century that money was noa or profane; and that if tapu things were exchanged for it, the result would be injurious for the Maoris concerned, leading at best to the loss of spiritual powers and at worst to accidents, sickness or death.

The injurious consequences were believed to be even more likely if photographic images appeared on articles that were themselves profane in Maori terms, especially those associated with food: tea-towels, biscuit tins, table mats, dining-room walls. Such juxtapositions constituted obscenities in Maori terms. There was the additional complication that the most appealing candidates for commercial photography were often men and women with moko — and the subjects themselves regarded moko as their most tapu feature, as the thing about themselves that should be least exposed to a commercial transaction.

All these attitudes persisted in varying degrees — especially among the elderly — into the 1990s. Anybody who took or attempted to take photographs of Maoris over a period of time encountered them. They were apparent in the continuing refusal of some people to be photographed (the president of the Ratana Church told a professional photographer in 1972 that she had no right to record her image); and in the enormous respect that some Maoris showed towards existing photographs — addressing them, crying over them, using them at tangis and giving them a revered placed in living rooms and meeting houses. Some photographers working with Maoris were asked to observe the conventions of tapu when handling portraits, the head still being regarded as the most tapu part of a person: to keep them away from cooked food, kitchens and dining rooms; and — generally — to treat them with respect, as something more than merely photographic prints. Frequently photographers encountered suspicion or even abuse in the course of taking photographs, only to be asked for the resulting prints, especially in cases where the subject had subsequently died.

An additional Maori reservation about photography arose in the middle of the twentieth century from differences in Maori and Pakeha lifestyles. Because Maoris *looked* different from the non-Maori majority and because they often dressed and behaved differently, they remained a favourite target for photographers. The differences tended to be accentuated by the fact that Maoris lived predominantly in rural Maori communities, insulated geographically and socially from most Pakeha. (This was one of the factors that had led to the negative stereotypes and coon humour.) By the 1950s, however, Maoris were moving into towns and cities in increasing numbers. Maoris and Europeans were beginning to interact on a wide front for the first time since the earliest days of European colonisation — in the work place, the market-place and city suburbs. A worthy determination grew on the part of the Maori leaders and liberal Europeans to break down negative racial and cultural stereotypes so as to make Maoris more welcome in places where they had not been seen previously.

The result was a growing feeling that Maoris should assimilate with Europeans, should submerge or eliminate aspects of their lifestyle that made them obtrusively different from non-Maoris and hence potential sources of offence in Pakeha situations. This was accompanied by an increasing sensitivity on the part of many Maori leaders to what was published about Maoris. All these attitudes came to a head and created a public controversy in 1964 with the publication by the Department of Education of *Washday at the Pa*, with photographs and text by Ans Westra.

This bulletin for primary schools was prepared by Miss Westra in the course of a five-month working trip on the East Coast of the North Island. It portrayed a day in the life of a Maori family who lived in a rather (by Pakeha standards) rundown house in Ruatoria. That same family was about to move into a State rental house in Gisborne, and this too was shown in the original booklet. It was, perhaps, a slightly sentimentalised picture of rural Maori life. But, as everybody agreed subsequently, the photographs were based on fact, they were artistically excellent, and they were characterised by warmth and intimacy. Though the family had no washing machine, electric stove or flush toilet, that was the way many Maoris still lived in the early 1960s and certainly not unhappily (the 1961 census showed 29.9 percent of Maoris had no hot water service, 38.1 percent relied on a wood or coal range for

* Some of these documentary photographs were used by Pakeha artists to draw or paint so-called 'scenes from Maori life'; for example, some of the work of Walter Wright in the early 1900s.

cooking, and 44.4 percent had no flush toilet).

Distribution of the booklet to schools brought strong objections from the Maori Women's Welfare League, other Maoris, and some Pakeha community leaders. The major complaints were that the conditions shown were not 'typical' of Maori life, that they created the impression that Maoris were second-class citizens, and that they would expose Maori children to ridicule in schools. The New Zealand Maori Council newsletter commented: 'The real Maori of the future is not the one living in an old shanty in some remote pa; it is not the one whose children run round in ragged clothes and whose wife does the washing in the backyard. The real Maori is the one who lives down the road and goes to work on the same bus as you; whose son is the local bandleader; whose daughter beat your girl at school last year. These are the Maoris whom the Pakeha has to get to know, the people with whom race relations will be tested.' The Anglican Dean of Dunedin, the Very Rev. P. E. Sutton, added that the booklet was 'hardly encouraging' of the efforts to improve Maori welfare. He thought the inference would be drawn that Maoris lived in lower standard houses than other New Zealanders, and that this would make it more difficult for Pakehas to accept Maoris in the cities. At the direction of the Minister of Education the booklet was withdrawn from schools and from public sale and guillotined. It was republished subsequently by a private company after two others had turned it down.

In the following decade the pendulum of Maori and general public opinion swung away from the extremes revealed in this controversy. There was now, however, greater sensitivity towards publication of what could be regarded as racist expressions, and Maori fears of exploitation persisted. In 1982 Waitangi Day protesters tried to prevent a photographer from using her camera on the ground that she was taking professional and commercial advantage of their activities. Generally, though, there was by this time a greater interest in and acceptance of Maori values, practices and lifestyles on the part of most Pakehas. And there was a corresponding and growing unwillingness on the part of many Maoris to compromise these things simply to fit in with European preconceptions. Slowly but steadily the notion that Maoris were allowed to be Maori in their own country gained acceptance in Pakeha quarters, although some individuals continued to dispute this in the 1990s.

This book focuses largely on the 140-odd years for which there are photographic representations of Maori life, the 1850s to the 1990s. This happens to be the period in which Maoris underwent more intense social and technological change than at any other time in 1000 years of previous history. It is also the period in which the Maori race and culture came closest to being erased from history. Bearing in mind the treatment by Europeans and consequent demise of groups such as the Tasmanian Aboriginals, it is interesting to speculate why Maoris should have better survived the 'fatal impact' of the industrialised West than coloured races in other colonised countries. They retained a large (though greatly reduced) share of their lands; they were paid for much of what they relinquished; they conserved and indeed strengthened many aspects of their culture; and they were by the 1980s taking a confident and forceful part in the national life. If credit is to be assigned for survival on this scale in the face of rampant cultural and technological imperialism, then most of it must go to Maoris themselves for their adaptability and their resilience; and to the fact that when the feelings of Europeans were running highest against Maoris during the wars of the 1860s, annihilation of the adversary was clearly impossible because of the vast and rugged areas of the North Island controlled by armed Natives. The fact that Te Kooti Rikirangi was able to attack settlements and then escape again and again into the hills, defying capture for 15 years until his eventual pardon, had wider significance. It meant simply that large tracts of the country were ungovernable without Maori cooperation. It was not a situation that would allow genocide.

Nevertheless part of the credit for Maori survival must go to their allies among the European settlers. The growth of European pre-eminence in New Zealand was always tempered in some degree by the exercise of liberal and humanitarian consciences. This was by no means apparent on the part of all Europeans; but it was true of a sufficient number to demand a just accounting for race relations policies. This acted as a brake on the more unscrupulous agents of white supremacy, even when those agents seemed to control the organs of settler government.

And in this context, part of the credit for fostering humanitarian feelings for Maoris among Europeans must go to the advent of photography. In case anybody doubted it, especially anybody not in regular association with them, photographs emphasised that Maoris *were* human. And they were humans capable of displaying — in photography as in life — grace, beauty, dignity, courage, as well as a capacity to suffer pain and degradation. Photography gave Maoris real faces in the eyes of their adversaries at a time when they could have been reduced to mere stereotypes of enemies and 'savages'.

A large number of Europeans in New Zealand and in Britain had their admiration for Maoris stirred and intensified by the widespread distribution of *cartes de visite* of Maori subjects. This was one of the major reasons for the popularity of the *cartes*, and their dispersal served to give such feelings wider currency. In the 1860s the sender of a set of them wrote to the recipient:'I cannot name [the Maoris] but chose them for their great beauty of countenance etc. Among the men there are some noble heads worthy of better deeds than have befallen to their lot [sic].

However, they are a fair sample of the Noble Race.' Romantic as such notions might have been, they were a strong ingredient in the impulse of sympathy for Maoris among Europeans. Indeed one photo-historian, William Main, has gone so far as to suggest that photography of Maoris at the time of the New Zealand Wars might have helped to swing settler sympathies against the policies of their own government.

This book is in part, then, a photographic record of years of upheaval and Maori cultural survival in spite of upheaval. It is not a Maori photographic history in the sense of revealing Maori views of themselves and of New Zealand. Relatively few Maoris have pursued an interest in photography and few pictures in this volume (apart from some by Hakaraia Pahewa, Ihaia Te Ahu and John Miller) are by Maoris. Nor is it a history of photography of Maoris; projects of this kind have already been undertaken by photo-historians. Nor is it a history of photographers of Maoris. It is not concerned with the identity and styles of those who wielded cameras, except where these factors are relevant to chronology and to an elucidation of content.

Two major qualifications should be noted in relation to Maori photographs, however. One is that Maori society is not and never has been a single coherent entity. Throughout Maori history — before European contact and after — Maori society has presented a mottled pattern of sub-tribal, tribal and regional variations. If such phenomena as 'Maori society' or 'the Maori' ever come into existence, it would only be at some future time when urbanisation, detribalisation and some outside threat to identity thoroughly mixed and homogenised Maori ingredients. Preferences and trends in the 1990s suggest that such an outcome is unlikely. Even the kotahitanga movements of so-called Maori nationalism were not pervasive. The most durable of them had tribal and regional foundations, and this made them in the long term unacceptable to or remote from Maoris in other places.

In this book the term 'Maori' simply denotes a person of New Zealand Polynesian descent; it does not imply that what a group of people was doing in Rotorua in 1890 corresponded to what another group — also Maori — was doing in Otago at the same time. Both within Maori society and in Maori responses to the European presence, Maori history is characterised by regional variety and experimentation. (It can equally be said, of course, that while Pakeha New Zealanders shared a range of language, beliefs and values, their response to the Maori presence also varied from place to place and from individual to individual. Such variations were especially marked in changes of personnel within government administration.)

The second major qualification is that, as noted, most photographs in New Zealand have been taken by Pakeha. By that fact they become culturally loaded statements. The very presence of a camera operated by a European affected and altered the appearance, arrangement and behaviour of those being photographed. While it is popularly believed that the camera does not lie, it has to be remembered that photographs are more artificial constructions than they are mirrors of reality. Inevitably the values and the beliefs of photographers and the conventions of European art and photography affected the presentation of Maoris in photographs. Certain motifs and compositions recur. Some activities central to the day-to-day workings of Maori communal life are entirely absent because they did not fit notions of what was photogenic, because they would not represent Maoris in contexts that a Pakeha audience would recognise, or because it would have been technically difficult to record them. In the early days of the medium it was necessary to photograph people standing absolutely still for long exposures, and outdoor pictures were easier to take than indoor ones; consequently there are few household interiors among the older prints.

These factors often combined to make historical photographs as infuriatingly though inadvertently concealing as they are revealing. They show selected public moments in Maori lives as arranged by the photographer. There are a plethora of nineteenth century Maori pictures of people standing outside their dwellings, often in their most formal clothing. Sometimes the prints include odds and ends that hint at the technology of the subjects' lives — kettles, cooking fires, blankets; and sometimes domestic animals and toys. To learn about the more intimate aspects of Maori lives, however, how much one would like to see *inside* their dwellings, and to see *them* inside, preparing food, eating, drinking, talking, sleeping, waking. And how much one welcomes the few photographs in which people seem alive rather than statuesque. The greatest cause for regret, perhaps, is that in the earlier years there were no Maori photographers who might have taken such pictures unobtrusively.

The very existence of some kinds of photographs and the absence of others unbalances the historical record: excellent prints from Alfred Burton's King Country trip in 1885, for example, but few from other regions whose communities and individuals were undergoing different degrees of acculturation at the same period; an over-supply of Rotorua pictures because of the wraith-like attractions of steam, the visibility of Maoris for the tourist trade and the ready supply of Maori props; the popularity of the Wanganui River and Urewera communities in the early years of the twentieth century on account of the limited contact of their inhabitants with Europeans. One wonders too whether the garments shown in pictures were those worn conventionally for the place and situation described, or whether they were affected for the photographer (Alfred Burton is one who appears to have carried garments with which to clothe female Maori models).

These limitations aside, however, and these necessary qualifications made, photographs are nonetheless documents. They can be, in Cartier-Bresson's term, 'decisive moments' when a complexity of visual factors resolve themselves into single images, and images which are true of particular times, places and circumstances. They give us an opportunity to do what it is impossible to do for periods earlier than the 1830s: to look upon the actual faces of the protagonists of history — famous, infamous and unknown. At best, in known contexts and intelligently interpreted, photographs may speak to witnesses down through the years — of appearance, of lifestyle, of domestic and communal technology; and, more compellingly, of particular character and experience and of common humanity.

Maoris in Photography

This daguerreotype of the Barrett sisters is one of the earliest known photographs of Maoris in New Zealand. Caroline (left) and Sarah were daughters of the publican and former whaler Dicky Barrett and his wife Rawinia Waikaiua of Ngati Te Whiti. So seriously did Barrett take his obligations to his Maori kinsfolk that he took part in the tribal wars, helping Taranaki fend off Waikato attacks in 1832. This picture is believed to have been taken in New Plymouth in 1852. The scarcity of daguerreotypes and photographers in New Zealand meant that few portraits of Maoris date from this time and even fewer taken in what might be called Maori circumstances.

The establishment of photographic studios in the main settlements and the arrival of cameras capable of making multiple *cartes de visite* cheaply and easily allowed the combination of potentially commercial subjects with a viable process. It produced a flow of Maori portraits from the early 1860s. Some such as this unidentified woman captured by the American Photographic Company in Auckland look as if they have been brought in off the street. The anxiety displayed in every feature by this subject suggests she found the experience traumatic. But such palpable tension is part of the drama and the success of the portrait.

These women — emphatically alive, but possibly no more confident than the previous subject — have been wrapped in blankets, persuaded to squat down and made to hold baskets in an effort to make them more 'Maori'. The effect is achieved though the blankets probably conceal European clothing and the baskets look more like studio props than artifacts in use. The American Photographic Company location is betrayed by the linoleum of the studio floor. The company appears to have operated in Auckland from 1869 to 1876.

Some early subjects were far from unwilling. This style of portrait became a favourite with makers and collectors of *cartes*. They reflect the readiness of some Maoris — often those visiting settlements for major hui or for meetings of the Native Land Court — to enter studios and pose. These men are strong characters and in no way intimidated by the experience. Their appearance, complimented by the distinctively New Zealand moko or facial tattoo, ensured a ready market for the *cartes* at home and abroad. Settlers particularly sought photographs they could send home to emphasise what they regarded as the exotic nature of the country, and what one called 'the great beauty of countenance' of its native inhabitants. The man at left is Te Kora, the one on the right is not identified.

Mohi Te Ngu was a photographer's dream. He enjoyed affecting a variety of costumes and apparently liked posturing for the camera. His face — sometimes serious, sometimes amused, sometimes quizzical — provided a satisfying range of expressions. He lived in Auckland and was greatly liked by Europeans for whom he worked, such as Sir William and Lady Martin, though he was somewhat a figure of fun. His employers felt he had blotted his copybook, however, when he supported the Maori King Movement during the Waikato War. His moko may have been touched up for this picture.

Maori studio subjects frequently appear in formal European attire that is ill-fitting and seems borrowed for the occasion, or at least for the visit to town that led to it. Most clothing worn by Maoris in their day-to-day lives from the late 1850s consisted of cast-off European garments. This chief was posing for posterity to commemorate an event of enormous importance to his race and his tribe, Ngati Apakura. He is Wiremu Toetoe Tumohe and he had just returned from a year in Europe, in 1859 and 1860. With another Maori he had been taken to Trieste on the Austrian naval vessel *Novara* and then spent some months working in the State Printing House in Vienna. He returned to New Zealand with a press that was later used by the Maori King Movement to print the newspaper *Te Hokioi*, which the Government regarded as subversive. Such experiences abroad made Maoris generally more aware of the outside world and especially more aware of the potential power of Europeans to swamp Maoris culturally and numerically.

Further variety in costume and arrangement is provided by these studio portraits. That on the left is from a *carte* of a Moriori girl taken in the Chatham Islands in 1866. It is the less successful; the clothes do not fit well, suggesting they did not belong to the subject, and the positioning of both the arm at left and the bunch of roses is awkward. The woman at right who is not identified seems confident and comfortable, and looks as if she belongs to the garments and hat that she wears.

This *carte* was commissioned by the family concerned, not by the photographer. Taken in Invercargill in the late 1880s it shows Cissie Bradshaw of Bluff (standing), her sister, and two of the sister's children. The Bradshaw women were granddaughters of Hinekino Te Horo, a Poutini Ngai Tahu chieftainess of Arahura. The extent to which her descendants intermarried with Europeans and became involved in local trade indicated a greater degree of cultural integration than that seen over the same period in the North Island. The family remained, however, persistently Maori in their loyalties and identification.

Another and later South Island Maori portrait, that of Dick Webb and Te Whe Robinson-Clough, photographed in a Christchurch studio. These Canterbury Maoris appear very much at home — confident in themselves, and in the presence of the camera and photographer. From the 1890s Maoris had so accepted the social role of photography that they were commissioning photographers to take portraits for family and ceremonial use. It was also from this time that such commissioned portraits began to make their appearance at tangis.

Idyllicised rural scenes (this one printed in 1905) were favourites of later postcard makers, influenced by contemporary styles in Europe and Britain. Such cards tended to represent Maoris as peasant folk living happy uncomplicated lives, or as amusing country bumpkins.

Understandably, perhaps, they reflected nothing of either the suffering or the vitality also being experienced in Maori communities at the turn of the century. The postcard craze reached its height in New Zealand in 1909.

The photographs of Frank Denton of Wanganui, also taken at the turn of the century, come within the rural idyll tradition. Denton was influenced especially by the London Photographic Salon and by his ambition to exhibit there. He tended to imitate the conventions of the Pictorial Movement of that time, particularly the use of 'natural' studio backdrops. Although this photograph suggests a healthy outdoor life for its subjects, it is in fact a cleverly manipulated studio setting. Focus and lighting disguise an artificial backdrop and the apparent fence top is an upturned carving, another studio prop. It is interesting that however idealised they might have been, Denton's portraits were popular with Maoris and many of his printing orders came from Maori customers.

This photograph from a lantern slide is redolent of frontier life — it suggests the difficult establishment and retention of civilisation in harsh natural surroundings. It is one of a series depicting scenes from New Zealand life. As one historian has noted, it has echoes of the hard and barren life of the American West, with which it was contemporary, and its subjects even look Indian or Eskimo in feature and clothing.

Elderly Maori men with facial tattoo became increasingly popular as photographic subjects as their number diminished. Because no tattooing was done on men after the 1860s, they were scarce by the early 1900s and all dead by the late 1920s. They were especially favoured by photographers and painters who wanted to depict what they regarded as the fading nobility of the old-time Maori, even though such highly sentimentalised portraits bore no relation to conditions in contemporary Maori communities, where the population was increasing and Maori culture waxing rather than waning. Here an unidentified photographer plucks out whiskers to expose and highlight moko patterns.

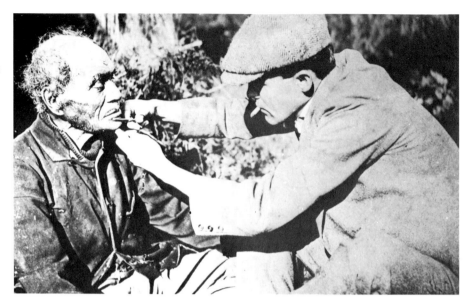

Wharekauri Tahuna was one of Charles Frederick Goldie's favourite subjects for his popular oil portraits. The chief's features and expressions perfectly matched the artist's view of what was worthy of record and poignant in Maori life. Two of the best-known portraits of Wharekauri are characteristically titled 'The Last of the Tohungas' and 'A Noble Relic of a Noble Race'. Born in the early 1800s he was a rangatira and tohunga of the Ngati Manawa hapu of Tuhoe. He took part in tribal warfare and cannibalism in his prime. When he died at Galatea in 1908, he was believed to be the last Maori with a fully tattooed face. Other men with partial tattoo lived on in Waikato and the Urewera into the 1920s.

Early in the twentieth century anthropologists and ethnologists began to make use of photography to illustrate aspects of pre-European Maori life as they envisaged them. This one taken by C. M. Phillips at Rotorua shows a model in a flax kilt about to hurl a spear on a kotaha or sling stick. According to one historian, the posture was suggested to the photographer by classical statuary.

Another and far less successful reconstruction of pre-European Maori life, this one in the interests of photographic art rather than ethnology. A studio picture, it shows a model in a korowai cloak holding a carved wooden club known as a patu wahaika. He rests his hand precariously on a fence crudely thrown together with manuka and string. His eyes fix on some imaginary point suggested by the photographer. The total effect is insipïd and unconvincing, especially in contrast with the previous picture.

15

This unlikely depiction of Maori community life was one of a number staged at the model village at Whakarewarewa by the Government Tourist Department. They were aimed specifically at the tourist market. The combination of Maori life and thermal activity made 'Whaka' a mecca for visitors from the late nineteenth century. The Ngati Whakaue and Tuhourangi community that lived in the settlement adjacent to the model village traditionally acted as guides. In this picture the subjects are dressed in contemporary concert party costume, not pre-European Maori clothing. The women in the foreground are making flax baskets and the one at the back weaving a cloak.

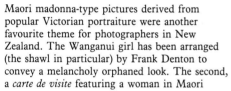

Maori madonna-type pictures derived from popular Victorian portraiture were another favourite theme for photographers in New Zealand. The Wanganui girl has been arranged (the shawl in particular) by Frank Denton to convey a melancholy orphaned look. The second, a *carte de visite* featuring a woman in Maori costume and a peacock feather, has a Spanish flavour. The third is Ana Rupene of Ngati Maru in the Hauraki district, the best-known of Maori mother-and-child pictures; distributed widely by Foy Brothers of Thames, it was also the subject of a large number of near-identical portraits by the Bohemian artist Gottfried Lindauer.

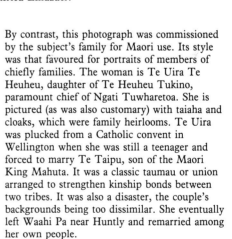

By contrast, this photograph was commissioned by the subject's family for Maori use. Its style was that favoured for portraits of members of chiefly families. The woman is Te Uira Te Heuheu, daughter of Te Heuheu Tukino, paramount chief of Ngati Tuwharetoa. She is pictured (as was also customary) with taiaha and cloaks, which were family heirlooms. Te Uira was plucked from a Catholic convent in Wellington when she was still a teenager and forced to marry Te Taipu, son of the Maori King Mahuta. It was a classic taumau or union arranged to strengthen kinship bonds between two tribes. It was also a disaster, the couple's backgrounds being too dissimilar. She eventually left Waahi Pa near Huntly and remarried among her own people.

Many madonna-type portraits featured women with moko — another theme sought by postcard collectors. Unlike male tattooing, the practice of marking women on the chin continued up to the 1950s, and was revived in the 1990s. This Arawa woman, a guide at Whakarewarewa, was done with a chisel which left a deep groove on the lips and chin. The technique was abandoned after World War One because of the pain it caused and the risk of infection. Later tattooing was done with needles, which left only a coloured pattern. In the last years of practice it came to signify not so much hereditary rank as accomplishment in the female arts and crafts — a kind of diploma for achievement. By the 1970s surviving women with moko were a source of great prestige for their communities and tribes and were made to take a prominent place in ceremonial functions.

Another ploy popular with Victorian photographers was to invest their young female subject with a *gamine* appearance, for the delectation of European customers. This portrait of Matira Rawiri of the Hauraki tribes achieves the effect with the inclusion of a jew's harp. This instrument was popular among Maoris in the nineteenth century because of its versatility and the relative ease with which it could be played. It was often included in early payments for land when such payments were being made in kind rather than cash.

Portraits of alluring maidens with such titles as 'A Maori Belle' and 'Black But Beautiful' were the most popular category in the postcard trade. All commercial photographers at the turn of the century kept a wide range of them. Most had a decidedly and calculatedly erotic quality. The subject here is Maggie Papakura, of Tuhourangi, another guide at Whakarewarewa. Her beauty, intelligence and commanding presence gave her a reputation of almost mythic proportions in the 1890s when this portrait was made. In 1901 she conducted the Duke and Duchess of York (later King George V and Queen Mary) over the thermal area. In 1911 she led a Maori concert party to their Coronation in London and renewed an acquaintance with an Oxfordshire landowner, Colonel R.C. Staples-Brown. Against the wishes of Staples-Brown's family they married and Maggie Papakura of Whakarewarewa lived the life of a country squire's wife at Oddington until her death in 1930. She enrolled for a Bachelor of Science degree at Oxford University in 1926 and the resulting study — *The Old Time Maori* — was published after her death. Her son from a previous union married another famous Rotorua identity, Guide Rangi.

Reclining poses were also favoured for Maori belles in 'native' costume. This striking one dating from the early years of the century employs a flax mat, a canoe prow and a taiaha as additional props. Two piupius are used to create the effect of a single garment over a dress.

By no means did all such contrivances work. This one — surprisingly from the studio of the experienced Iles Brothers of Thames — is a catastrophe. The subject is too thick-set to appear alluring, her korowai is crumpled awkwardly, her pose is obtrusively artificial. The studio backdrop is cluttered by a ridiculous quantity of props.

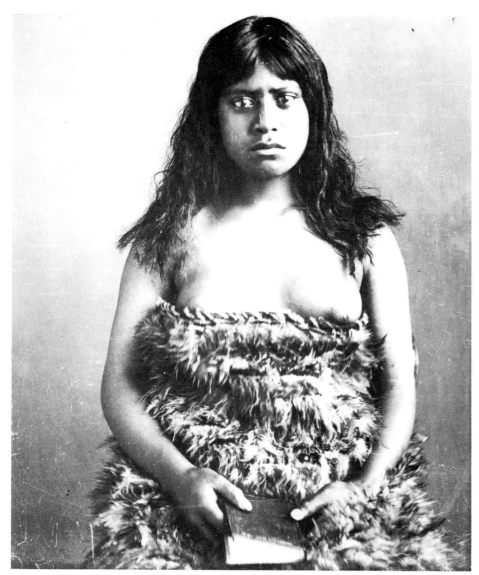

European men had been strongly attracted to Polynesian womanhood from the time they arrived in the country. It was one of the factors that led to a relatively high rate of intermarriage, and to a more widespread acceptance of Maoris by Europeans than that which was experienced by coloured people in other colonised countries. Joseph Banks was the first to record this view when he landed with Cook in 1770. He wrote the Maori women 'were as coquettish as any European could be and the young ones as skittish as unbroken fillies.' Something of this feeling is projected into this photograph taken by a Dutch Mill Hill priest.

The baring of breasts by Maoris had been discouraged by missionaries, and then by a general pervasion of Victorian *mores*. It became something of a quest among some photographers to persuade Maori women to uncover themselves in this manner. While what they were seeking was frequently a sensual effect, the justification given was artistic, or the wish to recreate authentic-looking scenes from pre-European Maori life. This portrait was made in the 1870s in Hawke's Bay. It demonstrates the manner in which Maori women were most likely to have worn cloaks in pre-European times.

The skill of John McGarrigle, believed to be sole photographer for the American Photographic Company studio in Auckland, is evident in this picture. In spite of the number of Maori portraits he took over a relatively short span of time, no two seem exactly alike. Clothing and arrangements of posture give each of them a highly individual quality. The urchin effect here is obtained by the casually opened dress, the hat, and the jaunty angle of the pipe. The position of the hand seems natural and at the same time emphasises the curvature of the breast. The result is a combination of eros and innocence.

Children provided another popular category of postcard photography, again one derived from English Victorian drawing room decor. One Maori writer has dismissed this theme as 'the big-brown-eyes and little-bare-feet touch'. Such photographs were usually exaggeratedly cute, often saccharine in their sentimentality. Like so many others they reflected a European preoccupation with limited aspects of Maori experience and lifestyle. These were taken in Rotorua: one of sisters, possibly twins; the other of two children bathing after a storm has thrown up lake weed.

This study titled 'Trials of Courtship' won second prize for the Northwood brothers in an *Auckland Weekly News* comic competition in 1906. It is totally contrived to suit the photographer's needs. The situation and the use of Maoris to create it is derived from American photography of the same period which lampooned negroes. It is an example of so-called 'coon humour'.

The Northwood brothers in Northland were notable for the large numbers of high-quality photographs they took for pictorial magazines that made Maoris look ridiculous. Most of them were carefully posed and probably used paid models. Patricia Grace has described the category as 'happy-go-lucky, lazy people, mostly not too bright, suitable subjects for much lampoonery and many bad jokes'. The danger was that such photographs, contrived as they were, were the only views that many Europeans had of Maoris. They did much to contribute to stereotypes of Maori ineptness and of European cultural and racial superiority.

Hakas provided photographers with subject-matter that was distinctively Maori, intrinsically dramatic, and often amusing. Such pictures were especially popular for sending overseas. In addition, however, they often verged on the stereotypes of coon humour. This one taken in Northland by the Northwoods is not wholly comical. It is distinguished by superb textures, especially the water running over the boy's feet, and by its indication of the kind of clothing such subjects wore at the time, about 1913.

The so-called 'penny-haka' (a haka performed for money to amuse Pakeha tourists) was the most common example of this category of postcard. It was generally done by children. If they were taken at Whakarewarewa as these ones were, the children were likely to be naked for swimming and diving. This card is titled 'You like haka?' It contributes to an image of Maoris as simpletons.

Maori women were pictured far more often than men in commercial photography. Female subjects could be made to look more exotic and were susceptible to a greater variety of arrangements, clothing and presentation. Another cliche of both portrait and postcard photography was the kuia smoking a pipe. It had a documentary basis — Maori women, unlike Pakeha women, did commonly smoke pipes until the 1950s — and it had the advantage of providing subjects with a ready-made posture and a thoughtful expression. But it was an overdone image, much like the nostalgic 'end-of-an-era' photographs from earlier in the century. This one at least has the merits of being strong and individual. It was taken at Opunake in the 1930s.

Pictures of women with chin tattoos underwent a resurgence of popularity in the 1960s and 1970s when it was realised that few of them survived and that the image might soon be lost irretrievably. A study from 1969 to 1972, for example, located 70 such women. Ten years later only half-a-dozen survived. In an effort to keep the custom alive several younger women asked for moko from Pakeha tattooists in the 1980s. These were not regarded as having the tapu or the authenticity of the traditionally applied tattoos. This subject, Kirikino Epiha of Honikiwi in the King Country, was chisel-tattooed by a Waikato tohunga, Anaru Makiwhara, before World War One. In earlier years she had known Tawhiao, the second Maori King, and had attended his tangi in 1894.

The most common composition for early pictures showing Maoris in their own surroundings was an extended family lined up in front of their sleeping house or meeting house. For the photographer, it related the subjects to their environment and often added an ornate and specifically Maori backdrop. In the eyes of subjects photographed with meeting houses it was only right that they should be seen with their community buildings – such locations were appropriate places for people related to one another to gather, and they were an embodiment of the mana of the family or hapu. If the group had taonga (heirlooms, usually in the form of cloaks, weapons or ornaments) these were likely to be worn for the occasion. This group of Ngati Haua were photographed at Te Wai O Turongo meeting house near Matamata in the 1870s. Their attire is typical of the time, though the cloak and feathers are likely to have been affected for the picture. Deference to their kaumatua Hohua Ahowhenua is indicated by placing him in the centre. Hohua claimed to have seen James Cook near Thames in 1769.

The Burton Brothers — or, more specifically, Alfred Burton — refined this style of photograph. A trip up the Wanganui River through the King Country in 1885 produced a larger and more accomplished set of pictures of Maoris in their own environment than had been seen previously. The area had been virtually closed to Europeans since the early 1860s — an aftermath of the Waikato War and the Hauhau campaign. King Tawhiao came out of internal exile in 1881 and allowed Europeans limited access to the region from that year. The Maoris photographed by Burton in the heart of the King Country, therefore, had had little contact with Europeans for the previous 20 years. Although their clothing and many of their metal implements were European in origin, they were completely Maori in language, values and customs. This group was photographed at Tieke on the upper reaches of the Wanganui River. The woman at right in front, Orini, captivated Burton. But the fact that the blouse she is wearing appears on at least one other Maori model has led to suspicions that the photographer might have been dressing his subjects as he travelled.

Alfred Burton was also responsible for some fine portraits of individuals during the King Country expedition. Ngahino, pictured outside the superbly decorated Waiherehere meeting house at Koriniti on the Wanganui River, was one of them. Burton's eye seemed to be turned more easily by younger women than by men (of any age). This was one source of the subsequent popularity of this collection.

A fine documentary study taken at Waahi Pa near Huntly for the *Auckland Weekly News* in 1907. It shows Maori hosts preparing food for a large hui called to debate legislative and land issues. Waahi was the home of the Maori King Mahuta and he initiated many such meetings during his term of office, 1894 to 1912. It was especially important for the mana of the hosts on such occasions to be able to feed guests lavishly. The picture shows punga communal houses, the hangi area (with smoke and wood), a platform for hanging dried and preserved foods and a bell for calling people to eat, a camp oven, a bucket, billies and tin mugs. A water pump is at right. The mat in the foreground is being laid out for the serving of food. In this instance the men are responsible for the cooking (probably hangi meat and vegetables) and the women for the serving and the drinks.

There seems little doubt that this painting by Walter Wright was inspired by the *Auckland Weekly News* picture preceding it. The composition, while not identical, is very similar (houses in the background, drying platform in the centre middle-distance, women in the foreground, style of clothing and head covering). Titled 'A Native Gathering', it was completed in 1912, five years after the photograph was published. Several well-known artists who did not have easy access to Maori communities painted from photographs during this period.

Real haka, performed for ceremonial occasions, drew documentary photographers as readily as contrived ones appealed to commercial operators. There was something exciting about the coordination of moving bodies, the gestures, the grimaces — another distinctively Maori subject and arrangement. This Ngati Tuwharetoa group was performing at the Waitangi celebrations in 1934. The leap signifies the climax of the dance. The haka was never simply a war dance, although it is frequently described as such. It was a posture dance that served several functions. In earlier years it kept warriors physically and psychologically toned up for battle in much the same way as military drill. But it was and is also a ritual of assertion and defiance. It establishes and flaunts masculinity, and the identity of the group performing it. In the twentieth century it became a common feature of ceremonies to welcome visitors on to marae.

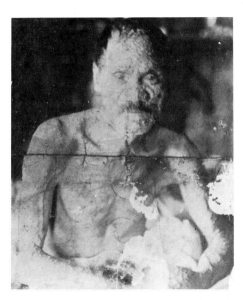

There were aspects of Maori life that the majority of Europeans never saw, either in person or in photographs. One was the catastrophic effect of Pakeha-introduced diseases which helped reduce the Maori population drastically in the latter part of the nineteenth century, and which continued to strike in epidemic proportions in the early years of the twentieth century. The worst toll was taken by influenza, measles and whooping cough. The public health authorities did not begin to take measures to protect the Maori population from these outbreaks until the early 1900s; and the measures were not extensive until the 1930s. This man contracted smallpox near Huntly in 1913. The epidemic infected at least 2000 Maoris throughout the North Island and was responsible for the recorded loss of 55 lives. These figures were by no means complete, however. The Health Department noted that 'since the greater part of the outbreak was among Maoris . . . only about a quarter of the cases were seen by . . . medical men and reported.'

This woman, calloused, crippled and blind, appears to have survived many bouts of illness and disease but at a terrible cost. She was photographed in front of her earth floor whare in Northland in the early 1900s, probably in the Hokianga district. The conditions in which she lived were not untypical of many Maori communities whose inhabitants received no outside assistance to compensate for disease, loss of land, loss of livelihood and very often accompanying loss of morale. Such photographs, which might have jolted Pakeha consciences into securing more adequate public policies towards Maoris, were not published at the time they were taken. It is significant that a visit to a Northland Maori settlement in 1925, the year he became Prime Minister, shocked Gordon Coates into sponsoring legislation to assist Maoris financially and culturally. He described the inhabitants of Te Kao as the 'the poorest people I have seen in my life'.

Although this portrait originated from the
Government Tourist Department, it displays no
attempt to make the subject romantic or
commercial. Taken at the turn of the century it
is an honest antidote to the end-of-an-era
pictures popular at the time. The man's stern
tattooed face suggests he has encountered
suffering and disappointment. But the features
are strong and confident, those of a survivor who
has no intention of lapsing into nostalgia or
oblivion.

Residents of the Maori communities of Mangatawhiri and Waiariki near Mercer pose with their canoe paddles before launching their annual regatta on the Waikato River in August 1901. The strength and vitality they exude contrasts strongly with the squalor apparent in some Maori settlements at the same time, and with the unrealistic photographs that were then popular among urban Pakehas. The alert man at the front is Te Aho Rangi Wharepu, whom Charles Goldie was then depicting in painting as a tired old relic of bygone days. He was in fact still building canoes, reviving rivercraft, tattooing women, and generally bullying and directing the inhabitants of Waiariki pa, of which he was chief.

These young men were known as Iharaira or Israelites. They wear their hair long to indicate that they are followers of the Tuhoe prophet Rua Kenana. They were photographed by George Bourne, who entered the Urewera in 1906 attracted by its inaccessibility and by the uncompromising Maoriness of the inhabitants. The fact that his subjects here do not seem wholly pleased about the picture gives it strength and adds to the arresting quality.

Another strong portrait taken in the Urewera a decade later. The unidentified woman is sitting on the porch of the Te Whai-a-te-Motu meeting house, built for Te Kooti Rikirangi nearly 50 years earlier. She has been tattooed by Te Hokotahi, the last tohunga to perform chisel moko. The black ribbons through her ears are a sign of mourning, worn at tangis or to indicate a family bereavement.

The Goff children – Jack, Puti and Ben – photographed at Kawana on the Wanganui River in 1921. They have prepared for the picture by dressing up in what are probably their best clothes and footwear, by having their hair combed, and (in the case of the girl) by wearing a ribbon. There is no attempt to make them a target of amusement or pity; the camera simply records them as they are. They display confidence and warmth and no self-consciousness as a result of either the incongruity of their dress or of the presence of the photographer. The expedition on which this was taken was an ethnological one that included Elsdon Best and Johannes Andersen. Although not as insulated from European influences as the Urewera, the Wanganui River communities were still regarded as strong repositories of Maori values and custom in the 1920s.

Meeting houses have come to be regarded symbolically as manifestations of tribal genealogies. This is one reason for stylised representations of ancestral figures on the upright pillars inside many houses. By the late nineteenth century this custom was beginning to be complemented by the hanging of photographs of recently deceased members of the hapu on the inside walls, either at the back of the house (as here) or on the side walls between the upright posts. This house was at Mangamaunu, north of Kaikoura.

In the 1890s there was competition among photographers to record tangis, especially those of important chiefs. Some resorted to disguise and duplicity to do so. In other places, however, Maoris allowed such pictures to be taken, even intimate ones of laid-out corpses. There was a strong aversion among Maoris generally to publication of such photographs, however, and they were rarely displayed in Maori homes or meeting houses. In the twentieth century there was markedly more resistance to their being taken because such an act was viewed as a potential commercialising of death and ritual. This one from the Hokianga district dates from the late 1890s.

Photographs began to appear at tangis in the last decade of the nineteenth century. They were used to recall the presence of the deceased person, and of relatives who had died previously. Here Charlie Cowell of Waikato slumps between the coffin and the body of his grandson at a tangi at Waiuku in the early 1890s. The pictures behind are not clear, but he holds one up for the camera to record. This is one of the earliest examples of such ceremonial use of photographs.

Within a decade elaborate display of photographs at tangis was widespread. In this instance near Wanganui the coffin has been covered for the taking of the picture. The portraits visible include several Lindauer paintings, the one at right being of Keepa Te Rangihiwinui or Major Kemp, a kupapa chief who won the New Zealand Cross during the Hauhau campaign. The practice of placing bodies in tents rather than in meeting houses or shelters improvised from traditional materials also spread in some districts from this time.

This rare hahunga ceremony to receive and mourn over exhumed remains was held at Maungapohatu in the Urewera in 1940. The bones are those of Whatu, a son of Rua Kenana, and Miki, leading chief at Maungapohatu at the time of his death. Both had died as a result of accidents and had initially been buried elsewhere. Again, photographs of the deceased and their dead relatives are a prominent part of the proceedings. The flags bear ancestral names indicating the lineage of the deceased and come from different Tuhoe marae.

This photograph from Ans Westra's booklet *Washday at the Pa* caused particular offence in 1964. It was captioned: ' "No good going to bed with cold feet," says Motu. So she climbs up on the lid of the range to warm them near the glowing wood.' A member of the Maori Women's Welfare League complained to the press that this would give the impression that Maori mothers sent their children to bed with dirty feet.

Washday at the Pa depicted a day in the life of a Maori family at Ruatoria. Their house had no hot water, no electric stove and no flush toilet. The publication was withdrawn from schools after protests that the photographs were not typical of Maori living conditions in the 1960s. It was feared that they would make Pakehas less willing to accept Maoris as neighbours and fellow citizens.

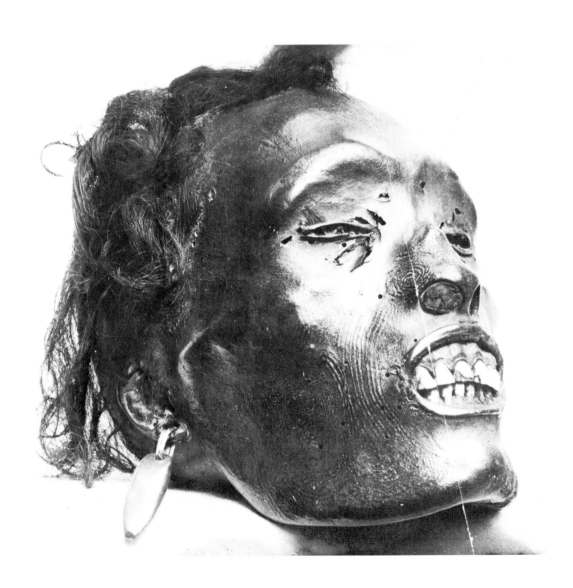

CHAPTER ONE

The Years Before

Maoris have long been amused or offended by the notion that Maori history began with the arrival of Pakeha in New Zealand — as if there was no such thing as history until literate Europeans observed and recorded it. This notion has been strengthened by scholars' use of the expression 'prehistory' to describe the years prior to Maori-Pakeha contact.

It is, of course, nonsense. History does not come into existence with the birth of literature, although literature may well be part of the historical process. History is the story of the human occupation of a place compiled from surviving evidence. The three key features are occupation, evidence and story. New Zealand has had occupation, evidence of it and stories about it for at least 1000 years. The evidence survives in the artifacts and structures of New Zealand Polynesian technology, and the stories in the oral traditions of surviving tribes, many of them committed to paper in the nineteenth and twentieth centuries, many of them still orally transmitted. The resulting combination might not be exhaustive and definitive; but what history is?

The apparently dismissive attitude to the earliest years of New Zealand settlement is reflected in the inadequate attention scholars have given it. In *The Oxford History of New Zealand*, for example, the first millenium gets 24 pages; the last 200 years over 500 pages. And this is a ratio far more favourable to the earlier years than in previous general histories. Part of the explanation lies in •Western concepts of history, especially the insistence on working with contemporary documents; part in an unwillingness or an inability to tap Maori oral sources and documents written in Maori; part in the absence of professional Maori historians; and part in the relatively recent introduction of archaeology and anthropology to New Zealand and the small number of researchers in these disciplines. Consequently, the most pressing need in New Zealand historiography is a work which addresses itself to the earlier period; which locates, collates and analyses all the traditional, linguistic and archaeological evidence relating to the country's initial occupation, and the tribal movements and settlement patterns which followed the occupation and preceded European rediscovery. So-called prehistorians began working towards such a synthesis in the 1950s and 1960s. But since then the relatively few people working in archaeology have tended to turn their attention to more localised considerations. Regrettably, since this book deals primarily with the period since the advent of photography, it can only note this imbalance, not rectify it.

In this context, it is perhaps misleading to speak of 'Maori history'. Paradoxically there were no Maoris in New Zealand before there were Europeans; or, at least, there was no race of people called 'Maori'. New Zealand Polynesians do not appear to have begun to use this expression until the 1840s; and they did not do so on a wide scale until early this century. 'Maori' meant 'normal' or 'usual' — as in 'tangata Maori', an ordinary man. There was no need to distinguish such ordinary people from others until the land was shared by others; a group long separated from other races and cultures had no concepts of race or culture, nor, initially, the vocabulary to express them.

Pre-European New Zealanders identified themselves by hapu (sub-tribe) and by iwi or tribe. They had personal names. But that of the founder of the hapu or iwi to which they belonged by descent, preceded by the prefix 'Ngati' (meaning 'descendants of') determined their identity, as did the place where they lived.

The first question they would be asked by strangers was not *who* they were but where they were from. This was an inquiry about both place of habitation and identity. A person who lived on the banks of the Waikato in the central North Island would announce this fact. He might then recite his genealogy back to Tamaoho, progenitor of his hapu; and then — if he was of senior lineage and well equipped in tribal knowledge — back to Hoturoa, captain of the Tainui canoe. He might then emphasise his wider affiliation to the Waikato confederation of tribes and their association with the river by reciting a whakatauki or tribal saying such as 'Waikato taniwharau, he piko he taniwha'. Waikato, river of a hundred bends, and on every one of them a taniwha. Metaphorically this also referred to Waikato the tribe, and the taniwha to the number of powerful chiefs belonging to the tribe and the number of fortifications along the river. Thus the whakatauki was an assertion of group pride as well as of personal identity.

The pre-tribal origins of the New Zealand Polynesians cannot be established with any precision from traditional sources alone. They had a series of myths and legends to account for the existence of New Zealand, which some called Aotearoa (land of the long white cloud) while most simply used the names given for the North, South and Stewart Islands. They also had a repository of mythology to account for their existence as men and women, and for the origin of the natural elements.

The creation myth was shared in broad outline with Polynesians in several other parts of the Pacific. It revealed that Rangi the Sky Father had been joined in amorous embrace to Papa, the Earth Mother. In this clasp the world was in perpetual darkness, and the nakedness of Papa was covered with vegetation that thrived in dank moisture. The sons of Rangi and Papa constantly lamented the miserable conditions in which they were forced to live between their parents. Eventually they resolved to do something about them. One, Tu-matauenga, god of war, suggested that the parents would have to be killed to be separated. Tane-mahuta, god of the forest and later father of mankind, objected. No, he said. It would be sufficient to prise them apart and let the Sky stand above us and the Earth lie below. Let the Sky become a stranger but the Earth remain our nurturing Mother.

All but one of the sons agreed to this course and they took turns trying to bring about the separation. None succeeded until Tane-mahuta placed his shoulders against the Earth and his feet upon the Sky. Slowly and powerfully he straightened his body and his parents began to give way. The sinews with which they held each other tore and they cried out in pain. But Tane persisted. And in the end he succeeded in fixing the Sky above and the Earth below. As soon as this was done the children of Rangi and Papa knew light for the first time; and the children of Tane — the trees, birds and insects of the forest — were able to breathe, to see and to move.

The one son who had objected to the separation, Tawhiri-matea, was angered by the pain they had suffered and the regard with which Tane-mahuta was now held by other living things. So he followed Rangi to the realm above and there he begot his own offspring: wind, rain and storms. He unleashed these on the children of Tane in retribution. Then he hurled himself down from the skies as a hurricane and uprooted Tane's trees. Eventually, after attacking all his other brothers, Tawhiri-matea returned to the Sky whence he and his children would continue to descend from time to time to plague the Earth and her occupants.

It was Tane-mahuta who then created the first woman out of earth and procreated with her. Their descendants, who also procreated, produced a line of men-like gods and god-like men. One of these, Maui, was credited with fishing up the North Island of New Zealand — an especially appropriate myth in the light of the island's relatively recent volcanic history. Maui was an archetypal hero throughout Polynesia. He was the last-born in his family so that in theory his rank was low. But he compensated for this by being far more resourceful and imaginative than his brothers.

In the fish story (and there are many others) Maui smuggled himself aboard his brothers' canoe in Hawaiiki, the traditional Polynesian homeland. They were annoyed by his trickery and wanted to return to shore. But by this time land was too far away so they continued with their planned fishing expedition. After the brothers had filled the canoe with their catch Maui produced his own hook, the barb of which was made from a fragment of his grandmother's jaw-bone. The brothers refused him bait so Maui struck his own nose and smeared the hook with his blood. He lowered his line and almost immediately hooked a fish of unimaginable magnitude. The only way he could haul it up was by reciting a chant to make heavy weights light.

When the great fish had at last reached the surface Maui left the canoe to find a priest who could make an offering to the gods and perform the appropriate ritual. He warned his brothers not to touch the mighty creature until this was done. The brothers, however, ignored him. They leapt from the canoe and began to scale the fish and to hack bits off it. The fish raised its fins and writhed in agony. The sun rose and made the flesh solid underfoot, its surface rough and mountainous because of the brothers' mutilation. It remained that way, and the name given to it was Te Ika-a-Maui, the fish of Maui.

The name for the South Island was drawn from its jade deposits: Te Wai Pounamu, greenstone water; or Te Waahi Pounamu, place of greenstone. The story of its origin told by the Ngai Tahu people was a variation of the creation myth. According to their account, Rangi the Sky Father had a union with Pohato-te-po before being joined with Papa. One of the children of this first marriage was Aorangi, rendered Aoraki in the southern dialect. Aoraki and his brothers were opposed to the second marriage. In protest they left Hawaiiki by canoe. In the vicinity of the South Island, however, their vessel struck a submerged reef and was wrecked. Aoraki and his brothers climbed to the higher side of the canoe so as not to drown. They waited so long for rescue that they turned to stone and became the Southern Alps. Aoraki or Mt. Cook, the eldest, is the highest of the peaks; the others are the remaining brothers in descending order of seniority according to size. In this version, the Place of Greenstone is actually Te Waka-a-Aoraki, Aoraki's canoe. The Marlborough Sounds at the northern end represent the shattered prow; and Bluff Hill in the far south is the stern. The broken ranges of Southland and Otago are the jumbled remains of the vessel's cargo. Stewart Island (Rakiura) is the anchor stone.

Such mythology served the purpose for which it evolved. It gave meaning and continuity and therefore a measure of security to the lives of the earliest New Zealanders. Recounted, it conveys some of the textures of their collective imaginative life, their 'public dreams'. It offers clues to the manner in which they viewed the world and the puzzle of their existence in it. It is no substitute for what Western scholars understand by history, however, nor should it be confused with history.

The European writers at the turn of the twentieth century who converted Maori myths and legends into a chronological and so-called historical narrative took enormous liberties with the stories they used. They collected a number of migration traditions from different sources, merged them, transferred names from one to another, excised information that did not fit the pattern they created, and came up with an entirely new tradition — a Pakeha account of Maori history. Its basic outline was that New Zealand was first settled by a Melanesian race named Morioris, who were exterminated by the later Polynesian colonists. The country was discovered for the Maori and named Aotearoa by a navigator named Kupe in about 950 A.D. He was followed by Toi and Whatonga in about 1150, and they in turn were followed by a great fleet migration of canoes in about 1350.

Examination of the nineteenth century sources for this account show that there is no justification for believing the resulting story. There was a Kupe, but he was not first and he did not come in 950. Toi and Whatonga might also have lived, but not in the times and circumstances ascribed to them. There might well have been six canoes — and more — with the names assigned to them, but there is no evidence that they sailed together from some point outside New Zealand. Some of their individual stories are now thought to be figurative accounts of tribal migration within New Zealand. Oral traditions of this kind *are* important and they can reveal a great deal about the origins of tribal units, about inter-tribal relationships, about internal migrations, and about the bases for land claims. But they have to be read correctly. The major difficulty about using tribal traditions is that they are rarely simply

accounts of what happened: they are selective attempts to explain and justify to the hapu things that have happened. They are frequently the stories of and the rationalisations of victors. They say little about the vanquished. They cannot and should not be used to provide absolute answers to objective questions such as who were the New Zealand Polynesians, where did they come from and how did they develop the characteristics that distinguish them from other people. Clues to these answers — and still only tentative ones — lie partially in tradition and far more in studies of linguistics, biological anthropology and archaeology.

The avid search among nineteenth century scholars for the origin of the Polynesians is now known to have been an historical irrelevance. The Polynesians themselves never came from anywhere: their characteristics and their culture are now thought to have evolved in the central Pacific some two-and-a-half to three thousand years ago. The ancestors of these people, however, burst from the shores of South-East Asia and the South China Sea between four and five thousand years ago. Some went south-west, ultimately to Madagascar; others south-east along the Malaysian, Indonesian and Philippine chains. This much can be deduced from linguistic and archaeological features, and from the origins of the cultivated plants and domestic animals that these people carried with them into the Pacific.

What made these mighty journeys possible, indeed, what probably led to them, was the introduction of the sail to South-East Asia and the invention of the outrigger to stabilise craft on ocean voyaging. Among the Austronesian languages shared by the people of the Pacific and the South-East Asian archipelagos the words for mast, sail, outrigger float and outrigger boom are among the most widespread and therefore among the oldest.

The Pacific Austronesians who made their way along the Melanesian chain of islands, reaching Fiji by 1200 B.C. and Tonga before 1100 B.C., left behind fragments of pottery with distinctive decorations. It has been called Lapita, and the same name has been given by archaeologists to the people who made it. With their pottery they also carried pigs, dogs, rats, fowls and cultivated plants. All these originated on the South-East Asian mainland with the exception of the kumara, which came from South America.*

A combination of excavation, radio-carbon dating and a study of language and adze forms has led scholars to the conclusion that Polynesian culture was generated by the Lapita people in the central Pacific islands of Tonga, Samoa, Uvea and Futuna. Some have gone further and postulated that the Polynesian language developed in West Polynesia and the distinctive adze types in Samoa in

---

* Proving that at some point Polynesians reached South America (where even the word for sweet potato is the same) and returned to the central Pacific; or that some South Americans travelled west into the Pacific. But the initial theory of Thor Heyerdahl that Polynesians originated in South America runs counter to all other evidence.

particular. It is also deduced that the Polynesian systems of kinship and social structure of aristocrats, commoners and slaves, and pervasive concepts such as mana and tapu, also evolved at this time.

Two further movements of Polynesians appear to have taken place in the last two millenia. Some sailed back to the west and settled the 'outlier' islands in the Melanesian chain, such as the Santa Cruz group, Tikopia and Rennell; others moved to the east again, peopling the Cooks, the Society and the Marquesas Islands. Here Polynesian culture was further differentiated and it was from this region that the eventual migrations to the farthest points of the Polynesian triangle were launched: to Hawaii in the north, Easter Island in the east and New Zealand in the south-west. The characteristics of early Eastern Polynesian culture, the earliest carbon dates and the subsequent rate of growth and spread of population all suggest that the New Zealand landfall was made before 1200 A.D.

The Pacific Ocean covers one-third of the globe. The area traversed by the Polynesians and their immediate ancestors is equal to that of China and the Soviet Union combined. Voyages of this magnitude have led to a debate among scholars as to whether they were deliberate or accidental. Did the Polynesians always set forth blindly into the unknown? Or did they move with some assurance in the direction of tiny land masses and — as they discovered them — move among them with a degree of deliberation and confidence? Traditional accounts speak of voyagers departing from one island or set of islands because of population pressure, or because of political or military defeat. There is little doubt also from traditional evidence that the Polynesians became adept at recognising the signs and locations of distant land in unexplored directions (cloud formations, for example, lagoon reflections, and — for far larger distances — the movements of migratory birds or the appearace of drifting vegetation on ocean currents).

There is no doubt that with their twin-hulled or outrigger canoes and their considerable navigational resources Polynesians were able to make controlled journeys of hundreds and even thousands of kilometres. The navigational techniques included steering by stars, reading currents and swells and understanding how these were affected by contact with unseen land, use of the

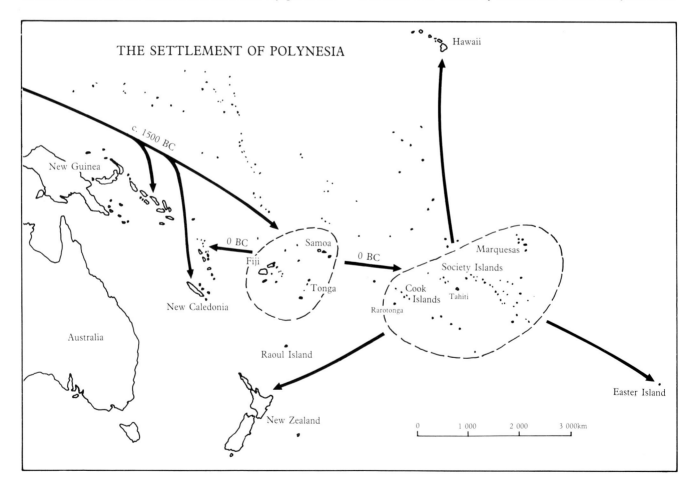

THE SETTLEMENT OF POLYNESIA

c. 1500 BC

New Guinea

0 BC

Samoa

Fiji

0 BC

Marquesas

Society Islands

Cook Islands

Tahiti

Tonga

New Caledonia

Rarotonga

Australia

Raoul Island

Hawaii

Easter Island

New Zealand

0   1 000   2 000   3 000km

'lapa' or underwater luminescence and awareness of the patterns of bird migration. The settlers who reached New Zealand — or at least those whose presence and descendants effectively colonised the country — are unlikely to have been simply blown off course on a voyage to somewhere else. Computer analysis of wind and current movement and the imperatives of sailing techniques suggest that an accidental landfall was far less likely than a voyage of controlled navigation. As mentioned, there would have been signs (bird movements and floating debris) of a large land mass to the south of the central and eastern Polynesian islands. Further, to establish themselves in the manner they did, the colonising canoe or canoes would have had to carry men and women, cultivated vegetables, the Polynesian dog, the rat (although this might have been accidental) and a range of tools and ornaments for practical use and for prototypes for those made subsequently from New Zealand materials.

It is likely that an earlier exploratory discovery of the country was followed by a return journey to eastern Polynesia, and that this led to a planned colonising expedition. Indeed, some of the discovery traditions assert that this is what transpired. Although some scholars have scoffed at the notion, the increasing information that comes to light about Polynesian navigation and recent successful experimental voyages demonstrate its probability. And excavations on Raoul Island — halfway between New Zealand and island Polynesia — uncovered New Zealand obsidian left there between 960 and 1360 A.D. This establishes at least one 'return journey'; and the probability is that it was one of several. Further speculation awaits further evidence, however. And the only incontrovertible evidence of return voyaging would be the discovery of New Zealand materials on the islands of East Polynesia.

The land that the ancestors of the Maoris found their way to more than 800 years ago was unlike anything that Polynesians had encountered elsewhere in the Pacific. It was far larger — more than 1500 km north to south — and more varied than other islands they had colonised previously. It was temperate rather that tropical and sufficiently cold in much of the South Island to prevent the growing of crops. The three major islands had been formed by volcanic activity over 500 million years and much of the interior ruggedness reflected this former turbulence. Great wrinkles in the earth's crust had formed chains of mountains from the centre of the North Island to the Coromandel Peninsula, and from the East Cape down to the Southern Alps.

The land had largely settled by the time the Polynesians arrived, however, with the exception of the North Island plateau and two offshore volcanic islands. Some people have speculated that it was the sight of one of these volcanoes — Whakaari or White Island — that gave the country one of its Maori names, Aotearoa, land of the long white cloud. This would suggest an initial landfall in the Bay of Plenty. The coastal lowlands were covered with broadleaf trees — pohutukawa in the north; karaka, ngaio and nikau; and in the south

the southern rata. Inland, the forest was a mixture of broadleaf, podocarp and beech with a luxuriant bed of fern beneath.

Other than bats, there were no mammals ashore until the Polynesians released their rats (kiore) and dogs (kuri). It is possible that they also brought pigs and fowls with them but that these did not survive. This lack of meat was compensated for to some extent by the proliferation of seafood: fish, shellfish, crayfish, crab, seaweed, sea-egg and the sea mammals, whales, dolphins and seals. The forests contained fern root that provided a staple food when pounded and there were more than 200 species of bird, many of them edible. Inland waterways provided additional resources: waterfowl, eel, fish and more shellfish. To all these Polynesians added the cultivated vegetables they had brought with them, taro, kumara and yam, and the paper mulberry for cloth. For meat, in addition to fish and birds, there were limited supplies of dog and rat. Human flesh, a Maori anthropologist has noted, was eaten 'when procurable'.

The forest also offered larger trees than the first settlers had seen previously. With these they built bigger dugout canoes and evolved a complex tradition of carving. Later too they used wooden beams in the construction of houses. Materials such as raupo and nikau made excellent house walls and roofs. Flax plaited well into cords and baskets and provided fine fibre for garments. And there was an ample sufficiency of suitable stone materials for adzes, chisels and drill points, varieties of bone for fish-hooks, spear-heads and ornaments, and obsidian for flake knifes. Through these artifacts and crafts the New Zealand Polynesians developed one of the world's most sophisticated neolithic cultures. The land contained metals too, but these remained undiscovered.

Perhaps the most spectacular of all the country's resources was the giant flightless bird, the moa, of which there were originally some 12 species. They ranged from the chicken-sized *anomalopteryx* to the 3.7 metre high *dinornis maximus*. They offered a food supply on a scale never before encountered in Polynesia (drumsticks the size of bullocks' legs) other than when whales were cast ashore. And some early groups of New Zealand Polynesians largely based their economy around them in areas where they were relatively plentiful until such intensive exploitation drove the birds to (and perhaps caused) extinction.

The history of the first New Zealand colonists from the time of their arrival until the advent of Europeans is a history of their adaption to the environment just described — the matching of their skills and cultural resources to it, and the evolution of new features and emphases in their culture in response to the conditions that the environment imposed. Ethnologists now recognise at least two distinguishable but related phases of that culture. The first is New Zealand East Polynesian or Archaic, that displayed by the archaeological remains of the earliest settlers and their immediate descendants. The second is Classic Maori, the culture encountered and recorded by the earliest European navigators to reach the country. The process by which the first phase evolved into the second is a complex one and one on which scholars are not yet in agreement or even in possession of sufficient information to establish a basis for consensus. It is complicated by enormous contemporaneous regional variations in culture, and by the fact that in many regions quite different cultural trajectories occurred, resulting in considerable variation by the time of European contact.

What can be said with more confidence is that by the time James Cook and his men observed New Zealand Polynesians they had settled the land from the far north to Foveaux Strait in the south.* The language these inhabitants shared was similar enough for one speaker to be understood anywhere else in the country, although the dialectal differences were pronounced. And while other regional variations were apparent in the details and traditions of the culture, there were aspects of it that appeared to be practised by most of the population. Many of these were inheritances or elaborations of earlier Eastern Polynesian features.

Competitive tribalism, for example, was the basis for what was later to be called Maori life. The family and the hapu (sub-tribe) were the units of society determining who married whom, where people lived, where and when they fought other people and why. Tribal ancestors were venerated along with departmental gods representing the natural elements. The whole of life was bound up in a unified vision in which every aspect of living was related to every other: art, religion, war, food gathering, love-making, death — all were an integrated part of a single fabric. And the universal acceptance of concepts such as tapu (sacredness or prohibition), mana (spiritual power, prestige), mauri (life force), wairua (spirit), hara (faults), utu (satisfaction) and a belief in makutu (sorcery) regulated these aspects of life.

Society was stratified, although not as rigidly as in some other Polynesian cultures such as Tonga and Samoa. People were born into rangatira or chiefly families or they were tutua (commoners); in practice, almost everybody could trace genealogical links to a rangatira line. They became slaves if captured in or as a consequence of battle. Immediate authority was exercised by kaumatua or older heads of families. Whole communities, sharing descent from an identified ancestor, were under the nominal jurisdiction of rangatira families whose authority was in part hereditary and based on the achievements of their forebears. In practice this authority had to be activated and reinforced by talent, performance and regard to the feelings of the kaumatua and followers. Occasionally federations of hapu and tribes would come together under a recognised ariki (paramount chief) for joint ventures such as making war or foraging for resources. The more common relationship among hapu, however, even closely related hapu, was competition mitigated by the cooperation of trading arrangements.

Communities ranging from a handful of households to over 500 lived in kainga or villages with a hapu base. Usually these were close to water and food sources, and to cultivations if the hapu possessed them. Sometimes the settlements were fortified, although fortications were by no means universal. Most were in the North Island and dated later than 1500 A.D. More often they were adjacent to a hilltop pa to which whole communities could retreat under threat. Where such pa existed they were elaborately constructed with an interior stronghold, ditches, banks and palisades. Some proved impregnable to siege; others were taken and lost several times in the course of a lifetime. Such defenses were one of the features of Polynesian life that evolved in a more extensive and more complex manner in New Zealand than elsewhere in the Pacific. Some scholars speculate that the need for hilltop pa originated in the possession of kumara tubers and the need to protect them from marauders. Others see them as a result of increasing rivalry and as a visible statement of status.

Life was mostly organised around food gathering, food growing and (in areas where fighting was common) warfare. Cultivation was carried out communally, and foraging too done in parties on a seasonal basis, to conserve supplies. When certain items were scarce or out of season they often had a rahui or prohibition laid on them by the community tohunga or priest. Warfare evolved as an important competitive element in Maori life in most (although not all) parts of the country. It was sometimes conducted to obtain territory with food or other natural resources (stone for tool making, for example); sometimes to avenge insults, real and imagined; sometimes to obtain satisfaction from hapu whose members had transgressed the social code; and sometimes as a result of disagreements about authority.

Such reasons were often flimsy and could be nurtured from generation to generation. The more important factor, perhaps, was that war or the threat of war kept successful communities and individuals alert, strong and resilient. It also brought about the annihilation of some hapu who did not display these qualities. For the most part, however, warfare was not totally destructive prior to the introduction of the musket. It was carried on more in the nature of competition for status. It often involved only individuals or small raiding parties, and ambush or sporadic attacks of short duration. Even when larger groups met in head-on confrontation or siege the dead rarely amounted to more than a few score. Most fighting occurred in summer months only and, except when an actual migration was under way, fighting away from a hapu's defined tribal territory was not common. For individual males as for tribes, the concept of mana was paramount; it was intensified and enlarged by the status of victor, diminished by that of vanquished. Courage and proficiency in combat were also vital ingredients in initiation and acceptance by male peers, especially in the case of rangatira who expected to exercise authority. And the weapons most favoured were taiaha (long wooden-bladed swords) and short clubs, the latter most commonly called 'patu' or 'mere'.

---

* Although Cook himself, believing Stewart Island to be joined to the South Island, did not actually observe them in Foveaux Strait.

Non-combatants were able to achieve high standing in the arts or in the exercises of esoteric powers as tohunga or chosen specialists ('chosen' it was believed, by the gods). Carving was highly prized and the working of wood, bone and stone in New Zealand reached heights of intricacy and delicacy seldom seen elsewhere. The best of the work in wood was to be seen on door lintels, house gables and canoe prows, and in stone and bone in personal ornaments such as tikis, pendants and necklace units. New Zealand jade or greenstone was especially valued for this latter purpose, and for fashioning into fine carving chisels. Like other Polynesians the New Zealanders had no access to metals.

Personal decoration in the form of moko or tattooing was also a feature of their art. Men were marked primarily on the face and buttocks, women largely on the face and breasts (exclusively chin tattooing on females is thought to have been a post-European development). Only in the Marquesas Islands did such decoration achieve comparable intricacy, with patterns apparent in both positive and negative aspects — a factor strengthening the case for the New Zealand link with East Polynesia. The Maori practice of the art was distinguished by the use of a straight blade in preference to a serrated chisel. This served not only to inject pigment into the skin; it also left a grooved scar which was more like carving in appearance than tattooing in other parts of the world.

In spite of competition, warfare and regional and tribal demarcations among the New Zealand Polynesians, trading was also extensive. South Islanders exported greenstone to other parts of the country for use in patu, adzes, chisels and ornaments. Bay of Plenty settlers distributed a high-quality obsidian from Mayor Island for flake knives. Nelson and Durville Island inhabitants quarried and distributed argillite. Food that was readily available in some districts but not in others, such as titi (mutton birds) from the far south, was also preserved and bartered. People were prepared and able to travel long distances for materials and food. And although ocean-going canoes appear to have disappeared from New Zealand by the eighteenth century — possibly because climatic changes had caused conditions to deteriorate — canoes were still used extensively for river, lake and coastal transport in the course of trade or war. Some of these craft were long and impressively decorated.

The gauze of romance that fictional and some ethnological accounts later threw over New Zealand Polynesian life was misleading. In many of its aspects that life was brutish and short. There was always the danger (for men, women *and* children) of being tortured or killed as a result of warfare. There was ritual cannibalism. There was the possibility of disinheritance and enslavement in defeat. Further, medical examination of pre-European remains reveals that the natural life span was unlikely to exceed 30 years. From the late twenties most people would have been suffering considerably as a consequence of arthritis, and from infected gums and loss of teeth brought about by the staple fern root diet. Many of the healthy-looking 'elderly' men whose condition Cook commended at Queen Charlotte Sound in 1770 may have been, at the most, around 40 years of age.

There were many elements of life that New Zealand Polynesians shared from the Aupouri people in the north to the Ngati Mamoe of the far south: a basic language, religious concepts, competitiveness, conventions of warfare, ways of giving and receiving hospitality. But it has to be stressed that the tribal basis of life and the size of the country had generated innumerable local variations. Settlements varied in size, construction, materials and layout; legends altered from district to district and incorporated local geographical features; dialects had evolved; some areas tattooed extensively, others not at all; clothing varied according to location and climate, as did the patterns of food gathering.

Such were the contours of life that James Cook and other European navigators encountered towards the end of the eighteenth century in the people they called New Zealanders, and who later (from the middle of the nineteenth century) began to call themselves Maori. Their numbers were then around 100 000. They had no concept of culture as such, nationhood or even race. They were tribal beings who were fiercely assertive of the identity that they found in their hapu membership. Their links to other Polynesians to whom they were related were almost as tenuous as those to the Europeans soon to invade their land.

CHAPTER TWO

Contact and Conflict

The first known contact between New Zealand Polynesians and Europeans was not auspicious. Abel Tasman anchored in Golden Bay in December 1642, warned by his principals in the Dutch East India Company that 'barbarian men are nowise to be trusted'. In the thickening dusk his crew exchanged shouts with brown men in canoes, and neither understood the other in the slightest. When the New Zealanders blew pukaea or war trumpets at the Dutchmen, Tasman had two of his own trumpeters play in reply. In effect a Polynesian challenge to fight had been issued and accepted. The outcome was inevitable. The following day four of Tasman's company were killed by the New Zealanders when they attempted to row from one of their vessels to the other. Ignorant of how this had come about the navigator condemned an 'outrageous and detestable crime', named the region Murderers' Bay and then departed without setting foot on New Zealand soil.

Nearly 130 years later the English explorer James Cook displayed a more comprehending regard for New Zealand's inhabitants. His instructions about native populations differed from those given Tasman. The Earl of Morton, president of the Royal Society, had written that such people were 'human creatures, the work of the same omnipotent Author, equally under his care with the most polished European... No European Nation has the right to occupy any part of their country, or settle among them without their voluntary consent'.

Cook too was attacked. But he did not use such incidents as a ground for either departure or excessive retaliation. After only a fortnight on the New Zealand coast he noted shrewdly that a canoe-load of aggressors had dropped astern after the

Englishmen had fired over their heads. 'Not I believe at all frightened...but content with having showed their courage by twice insulting us. We now begin to know these people and are much less afraid...' Cook recognised the bravado that was an inherent element in the New Zealanders' competitiveness and capacity for survival — the propensity for taking the offensive in uncertain situations so as to encourage themselves, discourage a potential adversary, and hence to make their own survival more likely. It was a long-established code of behaviour. After such exchanges, assured both of their own courage and their safety, the New Zealanders were often willing to barter and to offer friendship.

These early encounters contained the seeds for future patterns of race relations in New Zealand. In most respects other than in technological development and knowledge of the wider world, New Zealand Polynesians were more than a match for Europeans. They were lively, curious, adaptable, potentially strong allies. But they were also (in subsequent European eyes) inconsistent, unreliable and even treacherous. This was largely because their vivacity and versatility were matched to a vastly different set of preconceptions and values than those held by Europeans. Maoris would take up many of the gifts offered by the evangelists of Western culture such as literacy, Christianity and agricultural and pastoral techniques. They would experiment with them and turn them to Maori purposes, determined by Polynesian concepts of relevance. If these tools did not then meet Maori expectations, they were likely to be discarded; if they did, they would be used in distinctively Maori ways. Maoris were to take up with gusto the business of selling land, for example; only to find in many instances that their understanding of what had taken place in land transactions was very different from that of the Europeans involved.

It was the inability of most Europeans to distinguish between Maori and European expectations in this process — or to even admit the existence or the validity of Maori expectations — that led to most of the difficulties between the races in the nineteenth century.

In the course of three visits between 1769 and 1777 Cook's relations with the New Zealanders were as cordial and mutually respectful as he could make them. There were misunderstandings, there were shootings in the course of attacks, kidnapping and thefts, and in 1773 ten of his men were killed and eaten on Arapawa Island. But the English navigator acted at most times with restraint and common sense.* The presence of Tahitians on two of his voyages permitted the collection of a considerable body of material about the New Zealand Polynesians including information on language and on the nature of their culture, much of it volunteered by the New Zealanders themselves.

Cook was followed closely in 1769 by the Frenchman Jean de Surville who sighted the country only two months later and passed within 50 miles of the Englishman during a storm off the northern coast. A second Frenchman, Marion du Fresne, visited the Bay of Islands in 1772 and was killed by New Zealanders as an apparent result of some inadvertent transgression against custom there. His second-in-command, Julien Crozet, levelled the village concerned and massacred some 250 inhabitants in retaliation.

New Zealand was now — literally and figuratively — on the map. Consequently it was increasingly on the routes of European and North American vessels. But from the 1790s those vessels brought sealers, whalers and traders rather than explorers. The whalers began calling in 1791, the sealers the following year. Initially it was the latter who were more important. They concentrated their activities in the south, from the Otago coast around to Dusky Sound. Gangs were left by ships at camps for months at a time to slaughter the sea mammals in their thousands. Then the sealers would be collected with their cargo and moved on to other locations or returned to New South Wales. The period of most intensive sealing was the decade up to 1810. From that year the focus of activity shifted to the sub-Antarctic islands.

Whaling affected New Zealand and New Zealanders over a far longer period. Deep-sea whaling ships called regularly into Kororareka in the Bay of Islands for supplies, alcohol and women from the early 1790s. A number of Maoris joined crews

and spent some years at sea travelling to Australia, other parts of the Pacific and even to North America. Shore-based whaling took over from the 1820s. Stations were established in Cook Strait, Banks Peninsula and Otago. Shortly after others were set up on the Taranaki and Hawke's Bay coasts. Almost all these stations were close to Maori communities and relied heavily on them for food and other supplies. Because whaling was seasonal, most stations organised subsistence agricultural activities to support whalers at other times of the year. Inevitably they began to marry Maori women and Maoris of both sexes worked in the settlements that grew up around the stations.

While sealers did encounter Maoris (especially in Foveaux Strait), bartered with them and occasionally fought with them, it was the whalers who had the first significant effect on the lives of Polynesian New Zealanders. In the Bay of Islands crops were grown specifically for trade with European ships, additional slaves were acquired by local chiefs for labour and prostitution, and alcohol became readily available. In addition Maoris there began to acquire metal tools and European clothing (and, slowly, muskets).

Europeans at shore whaling stations, especially those who had taken Maori wives and begun to raise families, became part of local tribal life. They too introduced tools, utensils and European garments to their districts. But the *mores* that dominated such communities remained Maori rather than European. The country still belonged to Maoris, Maoris were numerically dominant, and the European presence, in spite of the potential force of arms, depended on Maori goodwill. Away from these places, especially inland, Europeans had little effect on Maori life at this time other than being indirectly responsible for the gradual spread of muskets and diseases.

Other vessels touched on the New Zealand coast for timber and flax and a trade grew up in both from the 1820s. Until the 1830s the influences of such trade on Maoris tended to be apparent only in those places where Maoris were involved or providing supplies for those who were: in the Bay of Islands, Hokianga, Whangaroa, Mahurangi, Thames, Mercury Bay, Maketu. Such contacts gave Maoris access to European goods, tools and clothing, and added grain and vegetables to traditional Maori crops — barley, oats, peas, maize, wheat, potatoes, pumpkin; and fruit. By the 1830s, usually with the assistance of missionaries, Maoris were exporting many of these to New South Wales (and later still to California). As in the case of the whalers, European influences were strongest where traders settled and married Maoris; but again, the *mores* of such settlements (that of Philip Tapsell at Maketu, for example) were Maori rather than European.

Inevitably, missionaries followed. Samuel Marsden of the Anglican Church Missionary Society was the first to visit in 1814. He was followed by the Wesleyans in 1822 and the Catholics (from France) in 1838. Proselytising did not begin in

---

* Which he did not do in Hawaii in 1779 in the circumstances that led to his death.

earnest until the 1820s. Like Europeans before them missionaries tended to settle in or close to existing Maori communities. Unlike their predecessors they wanted to change Maori life (by 'civilising' the New Zealanders) and they did not normally take Maori wives or lovers. Their influence at first was minimal. When it did become apparent it was more in the creation of a Maori interest in literacy and the growth of Maori expertise in agriculture than in conversion to a Christian church.

These effects were at first felt in the far north of the country where all denominations began their missions. As Ngapuhi Maoris gradually came under Christian influences and began to release their considerable number of slaves in the 1830s, it was Maori evangelists so freed who began to carry news of the gospel to most southern parts of the country. These men had advantages over European missionaries, of course; they knew the country they were moving through, they spoke the language fluently, and they were known in their own tribal and hapu districts. When missionaries themselves eventually reached other parts of the country in the 1830s and 1840s, they frequently found their potential congregations familiar with the Christian message (although the Old Testament often appealed more than the New). And in some cases such groups already had Maori Bibles and prayerbooks, printed in the Bay of Islands from 1827, and many of them held services on the Sabbath as a matter of course.

The missionaries themselves began to record conversions and baptisms in the north from the late 1820s. Frequently these proved to be impermanent. Maoris would often take from Christianity what seemed to fit their own needs and value structure and discard the rest. The Papahurihia movement which began in the north in the early 1830s, for example, was the first of many such 'Maori' religions. In these the adherents identified strongly with the Israelites of the Old Testament as a disinherited but chosen people promised deliverance and fulfilment by God. Such movements blended Biblical ingredients with Maori. They represented an acceptance by Maoris of belief in Te Atua, the God of the Bible. But they were very much a Maori path to that God and a rejection of missionary insistence on Westernisation along with conversion.

The most dramatic early effect of the European presence in New Zealand, however, was the introduction and eventual widespread use of the musket. The acquisition of these weapons by the New Zealanders began in the 1790s as a consequence of the demand for timber and flax. In the Bay of Islands in particular traders were only too willing to barter guns for these commodities. Maoris in turn were only too willing to acquire them — they revolutionised the shooting of birds — and it was only a matter of time before their value in battle became apparent.

The first recorded use of muskets in tribal warfare was at Moremonui near Manganui in 1807, when an armed raiding party of Hokianga Ngapuhi were intercepted by Ngati Whatua. In this instance both the use of guns by Ngapuhi and the outcome were indecisive. Over the next seven years muskets continued to be used in skirmishes among Ngapuhi and between Ngapuhi and Ngati Whatua of Kaipara, but they were present in limited numbers and tended to be used in hand-to-hand fashion, in the manner of traditional weapons, and so were not the cause of carnage.

The situation changed in 1814, however. Ngapuhi began a series of raids to the south — to the Coromandel Peninsula, Bay of Plenty, East Coast, Taranaki and the central North Island. They set out to avenge old scores, to acquire slaves, and ultimately to obtain flax, cloaks and smoked heads to trade for additional weapons. By now they were relatively heavily armed, some 30 or 40 muskets among about 400 men, and they used them with devastating effect. Musketless defenders sent out their best fighters to protect their pa from the first onslaughts only to see them incapacitated or killed by gunfire. The invaders would then finish off the survivors with hand-to-hand fighting. The scale of attacks from the north increased after the chief Hongi Hika visited England and Australia in 1820 and 1821. He returned with over 1000 muskets and set off south again with more than 2000 men. At Mokoia and Mauinaina Pa on the Auckland isthmus he built towers and fired at the defenders over their fortifications. Ngapuhi took both pa, slaughtered over 1000 people and took many more back as slaves to work their flax cultivations.

The pattern changed as other tribes acquired muskets for defence, and then for aggressive expeditions of their own. Between 1810 and 1839 there were in all some 40 major armed raids touching all parts of the North Island except the King Country, and involving the northern half of the South Island. Of these, 30 were conducted by Ngapuhi, and the remainder by Waikato, Ngati Toa, Ngati Raukawa, Taranaki, Ngati Whatua, Ngati Tuwharetoa and Tuhoe. The Ngati Toa attacks on the Ngai Tahu and those of Taranaki on the Chatham Island Morioris were especially devastating. Survivors also acquired muskets, however, and a new type of fortified pa evolved specifically designed for musket defence (flying buttresses allowed crossfire and there were shallow trenches for shooting out under palisades). A balance of weaponry if not of actual power was established, but at a terrible cost in human life. This was the major factor that brought such raids to an end in the late 1830s.

It did not mean the finish of inter-tribal fighting, however. Skirmishes involving loss of life continued into the 1850s and 1860s. And tribal fighting was a major feature of the later New Zealand Wars as some groups joined up with the Imperial forces to carry on vendettas with traditional enemies, this time under the righteous banner of the British Crown.

Organised colonisation of New Zealand by Europeans began in earnest in the late 1830s. The Wakefield family's New Zealand Company took steps to establish settlements at Wellington, Nelson and New Plymouth. A French colony was set up at Akaroa on Banks Peninsula. Partly as a consequence of these private initiatives, and partly because of reports of appalling behaviour on the part of riff-raff Europeans in the Bay of Islands, the British Government decided to take steps to annex New Zealand. It hoped to do this with the consent of the native inhabitants. Indeed, protection of the New Zealand Polynesians from the alleged excesses of European behaviour and from the consequences of musket warfare was one of the primary reasons for the goverment acting when it did. Captain William Hobson was dispatched to the Bay of Islands from New South Wales in 1840 as Lieutenant Governor, and he drew up a treaty by which the New Zealanders themselves would cede sovereignty of their country to the British Crown.

The Treaty of Waitangi has been a source of contention and confusion among Maori and Pakeha New Zealanders from the late nineteenth century. Much of the confusion results from there being separate (and differing) English and Maori-language versions, and from differing versions even in English. It seems to have been drafted hastily shortly before the first signing ceremony. The men responsible were neither diplomats nor lawyers, and Hobson himself was severely ill at the time (he died two years later). The missionary Henry Williams equally hastily translated it into Maori, but in so doing he virtually rewrote it, apparently so as to make it more acceptable to the Maoris who would debate its merits.

The English version said that the Maoris would cede sovereignty to Queen Victoria; the Maori version coined the work 'kawanatanga' or governorship. The second article in English guaranteed the chiefs and tribes 'full exclusive and undisturbed possession of their Lands and Estates Forests Fisheries and other properties'; the Maori version referred to 'rangatiratanga' — 'the entire chieftainship of their lands, their villages and all their property'. The English text gives the Crown 'the exclusive right of Pre-emption' (that is, the exclusive right to buy Maori land); the Maori version is open to the interpretation that the Crown should have first offer only. A confused debate over the terms of the treaty took place among 45 chiefs and the European sponsors of the document in front of British Resident James Busby's house in February 1840, and the chiefs all subsequently signed it on 6 February. Later it was carried to other parts of the country, although the version in Maori offered for signature to chiefs at Waikato Heads was different again from both the Waitangi ones. In spite of obvious misunderstandings, reservations and the refusal of some chiefs to sign the document, and the fact that other important chiefs were not consulted at all, Hobson proclaimed British sovereignty over the whole of New

Zealand on 21 May 1840 and set up his capital at Kororareka. The following year it was shifted to Auckland.

Most Maoris had welcomed European settlers when they had first encountered them. Because of the persistence of tribal competitiveness, chiefs saw Pakeha as a source of protection and a means of consolidating local power; they would be a source of muskets, trade goods and useful advice and a factor to enlarge the mana of the sponsoring chief and his hapu and kainga. Large-scale immigration in the 1840s brought a change in perspective, however. In 1830 there were just over 300 Europeans living in the whole of New Zealand. By 1840 there were about 2000. And the Wakefield settlements (and the later ones in Canterbury and Otago) brought thousands more. The Ati Awa chief Wharepouri told Edward Jerningham Wakefield at Port Nicholson (later Wellington) that he had expected about 10 Pakeha to settle there, one for each pa; when he saw the 1000 who stepped off the first New Zealand Company ship at Petone, he panicked. It was beyond anything he had imagined; it seemed like an alien invasion.

Previously European settlement had taken place on Maori terms, with Maoris in control of the process. Slowly Maoris close to European coastal communities in the 1840s began to realise the extent to which their identity and customs could be swallowed by this mighty influx of foreigners. The Maori oratory of these years began to employ proverbs about the power of saltwater to contaminate freshwater (a nice metaphor this, because European flesh was reputed to taste markedly more salty than Maori); and the propensity of the kahawai for devouring the mullet.

Further, there was growing dissatisfaction over the manner in which land purchases were being carried out — by private buyers such as the Wakefields, and by government officers. Sometimes only one faction of owners, whose claims might have been doubtful, were dealt with; others less malleable were ignored. Sometimes the goods or cash passed over in transaction were subsequently seen to be inadequate. And promises to set aside Native Reserves, even schools and hospitals in some areas, were not kept. Perhaps the most fertile seed for conflict in all this was mutual misunderstanding over what constituted land ownership. For European buyers it was a signed deed. For Maoris it was a variety of factors including inherited rights, rights of conquest and rights of occupation and use. They sometimes refused to recognise the validity of sales that had been conducted with unauthorised persons, that were the result of trickery, or that had not resulted in subsequent occupation and settlement.

It was an instance of trickery that led to the first major clash of the New Zealand Wars, at Wairau in 1843. The Ngati Toa refused to recognise a fraudulent deed to land there held by Captain Arthur Wakefield for the New Zealand Company.

When Nelson settlers including Wakefield attempted to clear the Maoris off the land, fighting broke out. Twenty-two Europeans were killed, together with half-a-dozen Maoris.

The Governor of the day, Robert FitzRoy*, held that the greater blame for the 'massacre' (as it was termed) lay with the Nelson colonists. The anger of Wellington settlers at this verdict turned to fear as the Ngati Toa leaders at Wairau, Te Rauparaha and his nephew Te Rangihaeata, settled back on the northern side of Cook Strait, at Plimmerton and Pauatahanui. Over the next three years these chiefs became drawn into land disputes in the adjacent Hutt Valley. The tribes who had sold land around Wellington Harbour to the New Zealand Company, mainly Te Ati Awa, had settled the district under the patronage of the principal conquerors and owners, Ngati Toa. And yet Te Ati Awa had not consulted Ngati Toa over the sales, and hence Ngati Toa did not recognise the validity of the transactions and participated in armed resistance to them. There were clashes at Taita, Boulcott's Farm, Pauatahanui and the Horokiri Valley. They ended with Governor George Grey's arrest of Te Rauparaha, and Te Rangihaeata's withdrawal to Horowhenua. As an aftermath of this campaign there were further skirmishes in Wanganui in 1847 involving chiefs who had fought with Ngati Toa. But there were no further engagements in the lower part of the North Island.

While tensions had been mounting in Wellington even more extensive conflict had broken out in the far north. On 8 July 1844, the Bay of Islands Ngapuhi chief Hone Heke (or Ngapuhis acting for him) chopped down a flagstaff at Kororareka. Although he had signed the Treaty of Waitangi, Heke had become disenchanted with the effects of European colonisation. He believed the flying of the British flag deprived chiefs of their mana and Maoris of their land. He announced his determination to remove this symbol of Maori subjugation and called on the Governor to raise a Maori flag in its place.

At first FitzRoy took no action other than to visit the area two months later, when most local chiefs expressed loyalty to him. On 10 January the following year, however, Heke cut down the new flagstaff. FitzRoy offered a reward for his capture and sent for more Imperial troops. Heke meanwhile gained the support of Kawiti, another powerful Ngapuhi leader, and together they attacked Kororareka on 10 March 1845. After one day's fighting (600 Maoris against 250 armed defenders) they withdrew, leaving 13 Europeans dead and having lost somewhat more of their own fighters. In their wake a powder magazine exploded accidentally and set fire to much of the town. Maoris and Pakehas joined in subsequent looting.

* Commander of the *Beagle* on its epic scientific voyages from 1831-35.

Two wars were waged in the months that followed, sometimes simultaneously, sometimes separately. Tamati Waka Nene and most of the Hokianga chiefs attacked Heke and his allies in a revival of earlier tribal conflict; and then these kupapa or 'friendly' Maoris (meaning friendly to the British Crown) joined the Imperial forces for joint actions on Heke's and Kawiti's defended positions. The end came 10 months later when Lieutenant Colonel Henry Despard's troops breached Kawiti's pa at Ruapekapeka on a Sunday, after it had been deserted by the defenders.

James Belich, in his major revisionist analysis of the New Zealand Wars, argues that — in every sense that mattered — Heke and Kawiti won the northern war. They were never defeated in any of its set-piece battles. They lost few men killed (about 60 to the Imperial forces 300). And they succeeded in tying up the British forces in exactly the way they had sought to. 'By building new pa in isolated locations, the Maoris were able to channel military operations into economically unimportant areas. A British force attacking a new pa could not simultaneously attack Maori base areas. The resources used in such an expedition could not be used against other targets . . .'

The war had several important consequences. It was followed by 13 years of peace nationally, apart from small-scale tribal skirmishes. Imperial troops developed a high regard for Maori skills in warfare. In particular, great admiration was expressed for the ingenuity of the fortified pa at Ohaewai and Ruapekapeka. In the space of about 30 years Maoris had developed their strongholds from simple pa, to musket pa, to cannon pa, to virtual trench warfare. This evolution was noted by the Imperial Forces. Major General Mould of the Royal Engineers made detailed reports on the construction of Maori rifle pits and trenches. The effect of these reports was to be seen in the use of trench warfare for the first time in Europe in the Crimea in 1853; and even more so in World War One when the use of the machine-gun made underground defences a necessity. Thus the inventiveness of Maori strategists contributed directly to the planning and conduct of international conflicts on the other side of the world.

The decade that followed was, on the surface, one of peaceful interaction between Maoris and Europeans. The modes of interaction differed in different parts of the country. Some Maoris, of course, such as Tuhoe and Ngati Maniapoto, still saw virtually no Europeans other than itinerant missionaries. Others, such as the Waikato tribes, were expanding their crop production and supplying virtually the whole of Auckland's flour and vegetable requirements. Some hapu sold land willingly to the still-growing numbers of immigrants, often simply to assert the validity of their claims over those of competitors. Others declined to do so and went so far as to form Land Leagues committed to no further sales. These latter were experiencing many of the misgivings about Maori survival first expressed in the 1840s. By 1860 the European population in New Zealand surpassed that of the Maori for the first time, and it seemed to some chiefs that tribal culture and the mana of traditional Maori society would be entirely erased if steps were not taken to preserve them. And for some, a prerequisite for conservation was a ban on further land sales.

A series of meetings in the North Island in the 1850s canvassed the idea that Maoris should unite under a king. This movement, inspired by Te Rauparaha's son Tamihana, arose in part from the fact that the presence of Europeans had created a sense of 'Maoriness' (and it was in this decade that the word Maori came to be used for the first time by the New Zealand Polynesians to describe themselves). It also arose from a belief that the key to apparent European superiority lay in their unity under the British Crown. If Maoris could achieve a similar unity under their own monarch, it was argued, they would be able to match European confidence and cohesion, retain their lands and preserve customary law and traditional authority.

With these objectives in view the elderly and ailing Waikato chief Te Wherowhero was selected first Maori King in 1856 at a representative gathering of tribes at Pukawa near Taupo. He was installed in 1858 at his capital at Ngaruawahia and took the name Potatau. In the eyes of most European colonists this was an act of disloyalty to the British Crown, as was an expression of allegiance to a Maori monarch; in the eyes of Kingitanga supporters, the mana of the two monarchs would be complimentary and serve different functions. Wiremu Tamihana of Ngati Haua, remembered as the Kingmaker, voiced this view at Potatau's raising-up ceremony: 'The Maori King and the Queen of England to be joined in accord; God to be over them both.'

The movement was also viewed by Europeans as a blatant attempt to prevent land sales at a time when the towns of Auckland and New Plymouth were spilling over with colonists. Many settlers began to voice the opinion that only war could erase Maori disloyalty and open up land for further settlement. In this atmosphere war did indeed break out. Fighting began in Taranaki where government officers had bought land from a minor Ati Awa chief not entitled to sell it. The owners occupied the block and resisted forceful attempts to remove them. Governor George Grey used Ngati Maniapoto participation in this conflict and an alleged threat to attack Auckland as an excuse to order the invasion of Waikato and the subjugation of the King Movement. Imperial and volunteer troops led by Lieutenant General Duncan Cameron crossed the Mangatawhiri Stream in July 1863 and the Waikato War had begun.

It ended with the fall of Orakau nine months later, and two further battles at Tauranga. Six major engagements and dozens of skirmishes had caused over 1000 Maori and 700 European casualties. It was followed by massive confiscations (1.3 million hectares) which further crippled and embittered the vanquished tribes. This latter action also secured for the New Zealand Government the land they had been seeking to reward their troops and to settle new colonists. The land taken was selected more for its fertility and strategic importance than for the owners' part in the so-called rebellion: some tribes who had remained loyal to the Government lost land along with those who had not; and the most bellicose group, Ngati Maniapoto, lost nothing.*

The New Zealand Wars were still not over, however. As the fighting in Waikato was winding down, a messianic movement that would generate further combat was gaining popularity in Taranaki. Pai Marire (known to Europeans as Hauhau) promised its followers deliverance from European domination. Its founder, Te Ua Haumene, identified closely with the Psalms of David and wove Biblical and Maori elements into a ritual that included incantation and dancing round a niu pole, a gigantic version of the traditional Maori divining stick. The movement also revived warrior traditions and the pre-European practice of ritually eating the hearts and eyes of slain victims. In the minds of its followers it was an emphatic rejection of the European ways advocated by missionaries; in the minds of Europeans it was barbaric and the choice of name utterly inappropriate (Pai Marire means 'good and peaceful').

From 1864 to 1868 government and Hauhau supporters fought sporadic skirmishes in Taranaki, the Bay of Plenty, the East Coast, Rotorua and Wanganui. The campaign also spawned a further one. After fighting at Waerenga-a-Hika near Gisborne in November 1865, a Maori on the government side who came to be known as Te Kooti Rikirangi or Te Turuki was wrongfully arrested and deported to the penal settlement in the Chatham Islands. He broke out of prison there, commandeered a ship and returned to New Zealand to wage the most effective guerrilla campaign seen in the country. He was chased by kupapa and European troops through the East Coast, Urewera and central North Island for four years, and he finally withdrew to sanctuary in the King Country in 1872. Traditionally the last shots of the New Zealand Wars are regarded as those fired by Gilbert Mair's Flying Arawa Column at Te Kooti's retreating forces on 14 February 1872.

If the wars themselves were over by 1872, the threat of them was not. Pakehas were still forbidden to cross the Aukati Line into the King Country where the Maori King Tawhiao lived with his followers. Three Europeans who did so were slain. This chapter too came to an end when Tawhiao emerged from his exile in 1881 and laid down his arms before Major William Gilbert Mair, Resident Magistrate at Alexandra. This might have signalled the end of armed conflict; but it was not the end of tension.

* The New Zealand Government showed little interest in the precipitous limestone hills and valleys of the King Country until it wanted to push the Main Trunk Railway through there in the 1880s.

Maoris continued to be confused about the status of land supposedly Pakeha owned — as a result of sale or confiscation — but not occupied or used. In 1877 the prophet Te Maiharoa led a heke (migration) of Ngai Tahu from Temuka to the Upper Waitaki Valley, to reoccupy old tribal grazing land. Two years later the community he had established there was forcibly evicted by police. And in 1881 the Native Minister John Bryce led 1300 troops into Parihaka Pa in Taranaki to destroy it and arrest dozens of the male inhabitants. This was in retaliation for a passive resistance campaign against the surveying of the Waimate Plains, uninhabited confiscated land which the Government intended to sell.

One further incident threatened the uneasy peace. In 1898 the Hokianga Country Council imposed a ten shilling tax on all dogs in its territory. This was regarded as unfair by local Maoris; they resented taxation of any kind when they did not receive amenities in return, they did not have a great deal of cash, and they owned on average far more dogs than Europeans. A group of dissenters from the Te Mahurehure tribe gathered in the village of Waima and sent a message to the county office that they would shoot anyone who forced them to pay. The Government over-reacted and sent five ships to the area loaded with armed police and troops. A potentially explosive situation was averted by the Member of Parliament for Northern Maori, Hone Heke (grand-nephew of the 'axe-man') who dashed to the area on horseback from Whangarei and persuaded the rebels to lay down their arms.

Thus ended the so-called Dog-tax War without a shot being fired. And so did the era and the climate that had produced the violence of the New Zealand Wars. From the late nineteenth century *Pax Britannica* was in effect over the whole country. When Maoris took up arms in the future it was not in defence of tribal or even Maori interests; it was abroad on behalf of the whole country as members of national Expeditionary Forces.

Early views

This Wanganui River community in the 1860s is in disrepair, but is apparently not deserted (a person sits in a blur at left, and a blanket and a mat hang on the cross-bar). The state of the dwellings suggests the settlement could be suffering from depopulation, possibly caused by European-introduced diseases which took their highest toll during the 1840s and 1850s. The house to the right is wooden walled, that on the left made from raupo. The roofs are largely bark strips, common in that part of the country. A raised pataka or storehouse stands at the middle right, and behind it a largish building which could have been a chief's house.

One of the earliest surviving photographs of a Maori settlement. It is the village of Te Wairoa near Mt Tarawera, taken by Bruno Hamel in 1859. The whares are built largely from raupo, though several appear to have nikau roofs. They are grouped about a larger wharepuni or meeting house, where community discussion and rituals would take place. All materials visible, including the fences (to contain stock) are those that had been used traditionally, although one hut at left has a European-style chimney. Because of its proximity to the Pink and White Terraces, this village later became the focal point for tourist traffic to the North Island thermal region. Nearly three decades after the photograph was taken the village was buried in the massive eruption of Mt Tarawera in 1886.

Moriori or Chatham Island Maoris, pictured in the early 1870s. The man second from right, Te Teira, displays traditional Moriori garments: a flax rain cape, a kura or forehead ornament and tufts of albatross down in his beard. He brandishes a staff of a kind commonly carried by Moriori men. Pumipi on the right wears a woven flax garment, as does Ropiha on the left, with the addition of a European woollen shawl. The woman in the blanket is Uauroa, Ropiha's wife.

Hamel travelled with the Austrian geologist Ferdinand Hochstetter on the latter's survey of the Auckland province in 1859. In March the photographer recorded this village on the bank of the Waikato River, probably Kupakupa close to the site of the present township of Huntly. Here too huts are built from tightly bound raupo. The inhabitants group at right in largely European clothes, the norm by this time in communities that had regular contact and commerce with Europeans. Hochstetter wrote of this part of the journey that the waters of the Waikato 'roll through the most fertile and most beautiful fields, populated by numerous and most powerful tribes... Never up to the time of my journey had a boat of European construction been known to float upon the proud Native stream.'

A display of traditional Maori costume in England in 1863. The group was taken there by a former Wesleyan lay-preacher, William Jenkins, with the object of raising money by exhibiting the members as curiosities. Here they pose for the camera in a park. Their dress includes korowai cloaks (all but one of the figures at left), an ornamental cloak with taniko decoration (women at centre), dogskin cloaks (men at centre right, standing and sitting), and rain capes (men at right). By the 1860s such clothing was reserved largely for ceremonial or photographic occasions, including the ornamental headbands and feathers. The man and woman sitting in the centre are Hare and Harata Pomare, whose son was made a godchild of Queen Victoria in the course of the visit.

These Ngati Tuwharetoa have been swimming in hot springs near Waipahihi on Lake Taupo. Their clothing is a mixture of traditional (rain and dogskin capes), transitional (blankets worn as kilts, skirts, shawls and even toga-like garments) and European (skirts and blouses). The women appear not to be self-conscious about partial nakedness. The fashion of wearing bandoliers and blankets as kilts dated from the wars of the 1860s, in which some of these men were involved. The bearded man in the centre is the chief Te Rangitahau, who escaped from the Chatham Islands with Te Kooti and was well-known for killing prisoners with his patu. The dogs visible are of European rather than Polynesian origin, and the blurring of some of the children emphasises that it was necessary for subjects to remain motionless to allow the photographer time for an adequate exposure. The paddles and the vessel at top right suggest the party had travelled to the site by canoe.

Te Rangitahau's house was at Opepe and was probably photographed the same day as the preceding picture was taken. It is a standard whare with raupo walls and roof, typical of this period (early 1870s) and of earlier years. The reeds that make up the walls are packed finely between upright poles and held with horizontal ties. The roof thatching is less compressed. There is an open window for light and ventilation and a small porch. Brushwood and earth give additional protection to the outer walls. There is a tantalising glimpse of the interior showing a metal pot of the billy variety and bedding against the wall. The woman in front is one of Rangitahau's wives.

Wairarapa Maoris at Mangakuta Pa near the present town of Masterton in the early 1870s. They wear predominantly traditional clothing, probably affected for the photograph (the children are in kilts and the woman in the centre has a skirt under her taniko cloak). The house has a bark thatch, held in place by manuka poles. The ground has been dug away at right to drain the living area. Painted decorations on the bargeboards were replacing carving in some areas at this time. This one is a representation of Maui fishing up the North Island. Plaited food baskets, still in common use, lie in the foreground.

This studio group is identified simply as 'Maoris from Wellington, 1860s'. If this is correct they are probably Ati Awa from one of the three pa established around the New Zealand Company settlement. These people had not been involved in the sale of the area to the company, and they continued to resent the unsought proximity of Europeans for many years. The korowai cloak and the position of the man sitting suggests they are regarded as people of importance, possibly leaders of a rangatira family.

Pataka or raised storehouses were used to protect a family or hapu's food, and sometimes its valuable ornaments or relics. The largest and most ornamentally carved were prestigious additions to a settlement. Smooth supports were designed to prevent rats climbing into them (later, when European rats became more numerous and showed themselves to be more cunning than the native kiore, metal collars had to be fitted to the uprights). This pataka was built for the Ngati Tuwharetoa paramount chief

Te Heuheu in 1855 and stood initially at Pukawa, the village on the shore of Lake Taupo where the Waikato Chief Te Wherowhero was chosen as Maori King. Subsequently it was moved to nearby Waihi village, where it was photographed in 1869. Storage gourds can be seen at left and in the doorway. The blankets worn as kilts were typical of the time. The rifles and bandoliers suggest the men were taking part in the Te Kooti campaign, which continued for a further three years after this picture was taken.

Although this picture is considerably later than the preceding photographs it is relevant as an early view of Maori life because it appears to contain nothing of European manufacture, other than a rope at top right. Taken in the early 1900s, it shows Pai Kanohi of Tuhoe on a storehouse porch at Ruatahuna. He is wearing a flax rain cape, and has been potting pigeons in gourds protected by woven flax. A carved funnel helps to compress the boned birds through the holes and to pour in pork fat to preserve them. Tuhoe people retained traditional artifacts and customs later than other Maoris because of the relative inaccessibility of the Urewera. This made them a favourite target for ethnologists and photographers.

Early associations

There are no photographs of first meetings between Maoris and Europeans, but this encounter on the bank of the Waipa River in March 1859 was not unlike earlier ones. Again, it is Hochstetter's expedition, the first to be photographically documented in New Zealand. Here Hochstetter (centre in white hat) and Julius Haast (right) are received by the Waikato chiefs Tarahawaiki and Takerei (in light blanket) at Te Kowhai pa. The geologist recorded: 'We...seated ourselves next to the two chiefs upon the unrolled mats...[Takerei] sat cowering, a dirty woollen blanket around him, smoking his pipe and casting gloomy glances about him. At the same time he gave natives, who were passing to and fro, short, quick orders. There was something extremely imposing in the proud, austere mien of the man...but at the same time also something exceedingly savage...At length, potatoes, eels and milk were placed before us....'

The Ngapuhi chief Eruera Maihi Patuone was one who claimed to have seen James Cook in 1769, at Te Puna near Cape Brett in the Bay of Islands. 'I looked upon the faces of these strange people,' he said in old age, 'and I wondered greatly.' As an adult Patuone joined Hongi Hika to fight tribal musket wars the length of the North Island. In later years he befriended Europeans and lived out his last days in Auckland, where this photograph was taken as he approached his century. The artist Richard Laishley completed a pencil portrait of the chief from this picture in 1882.

The Treaty of Waitangi in 1840 resulted in the proclamation of British sovereignty over New Zealand. This ceremony too predated the use of the camera in the country, but participants lived on to be photographed in later years. Patuone signed, and the woman on the right, a Ngapuhi chieftainess named Pare Ngahako, danced with Lieutenant-Governor Hobson at the celebratory ball the night the treaty was signed in the Bay of Islands.

This man, baptised Aperahama (Abraham) was Christianised while he was a slave among the Ngapuhi. Released after the conversion of the northern tribes, he made his way back to his Wanganui people, bringing with him the message of the Bible. Such evangelists were sometimes more successful than European clergy. Their Maoriness, their blood relationships with various hapu and their complete fluency in their own language often gave them political and persuasive advantages over their mentors.

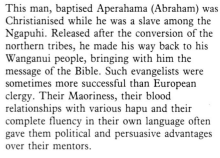

Christian missions among the Maoris had been established some 30 years by the time photographers began to record their work. In addition to winning souls, their major goal was to educate Maoris in Christian ways, including literacy. Those who were able to read could further their own education, especially their religious education, and carry the gospel to their kinsmen in parts of the country as yet unreached by European evangelists. Hence most mission stations had native schools. This one was at Tarawera on the shore of Lake Tarawera and was run by the Spencer family. Here pupils and teachers turn out with their Maori prayerbooks in their Sunday best for Hamel's camera in 1859.

These South Island Maori converts were photographed by Dr A. C. Barker outside St Stephen's Church, Tuahiwi, in 1867. This Ngai Tahu settlement grew up around the church after the demise of Kaiapohia Pa. The European woman standing is the wife of the resident missionary, James Stack. The bearded man third from left is believed to be the tattooed chief Hakopa Te Ata-O-Tu. As a young man he had been captured by Te Rauparaha at Kaiapohia and held on the Kapiti coast until Ngati Toa embraced Christianity and released their slaves in the 1840s. The waistcoated man second from right is believed to be Pita Te Hori, an assessor for the Native Land Court.

One of the most indefatigable missionaries to the Maori was Mother Mary Aubert (right). Born into a French aristocratic family, she arrived in New Zealand with Bishop Pompallier in 1860. She is shown here in Auckland in 1868 with pupils at the Nazareth Institution, a boarding school for Maori girls. At left is Sister Peata, from the Bay of Islands, the first Maori nun. After a disagreement with Pompallier's successor Mother Aubert left Auckland and worked with Maoris from Meeanee in Hawke's Bay. She established a children's home and reopened a school at Jerusalem on the Wanganui River in 1883, and founded her own religious order there. She wrote a textbook on the Maori language and became an expert on Maori herbal remedies. She was 91 years old when she died at her Home of Compassion in Wellington in 1926.

In areas where converts had been won, the missionary's next task was to build churches. This one photographed at a bush settlement at Opanaki (Kaihu) in Northland in the 1880s is typical of early places of worship. It was raised under the supervision of the Catholic priest James McDonald (centre with beard), who ministered to northern Maoris from 1880 until his death in 1890. The use of Maori materials and large wooden crosses was characteristic of McDonald's churches. His visits to each settlement were necessarily infrequent, however. In his absence, Maori catechists would lead the community in prayer, maintain religious instruction, and generally keep the Faithful faithful until the return of their priest.

One role open to mission-trained Maoris was to work as servants in European households. Large numbers of men and women held such jobs in service especially in Anglican homes in Auckland up to the outbreak of the Waikato War in 1863. Maori women were especially in demand as maids. One of them, Mary (right), worked for the Spencers at the mission house at Tarawera. She is pictured with the Spencer's daughter, Emily Way, and Emily's two sons Holroyd and Cecil.

Another offshoot of missionary instruction was an expansion of Maori horticulture. Pre-European Maoris in many districts cultivated crops, especially kumara, taro, yam and gourd. Missionary instruction extended that expertise. By the late 1850s and early 1860s Maori growers were supplying practically all of Auckland's grain, fruit and vegetable needs. Most of these crops were grown in the Waikato and on the Coromandel Peninsula. Supplies diminished in the late 1850s as a result of economic depression, and virtually dried up altogether as a consequence of the Waikato War and subsequent confiscation of Maori land. Here Maori vendors in north Waikato offer melons and peaches to members of the Imperial Forces in 1863.

The first Europeans most coastal Maoris saw were whalers, especially in the Bay of Islands, Cook Strait, Banks Peninsula and Otago. From the time that shore stations were being established in the late 1820s, Maoris became actively involved in the industry. Most European whalers took Maori wives and a significant number of prominent Maori families trace their descent from such unions. These photographs were taken early in the twentieth century at the shore station at Te Kaha in the Bay of Plenty, run entirely by Maoris of the Whanau-a-Apanui tribe. Lookouts on an adjacent hilltop would ring a bell as they sighted whales moving up the coast, and teams of station workers would give chase in whaleboats. After harpooning the whale and waiting for it to die, they towed the carcass back and processed it on the beach. Photographs show (above) a line of men tearing off blubber and (below) flensing or slicing off whale meat. This carcass contained about 11 tonnes of oil. The Te Kaha station closed in the 1930s. These pictures are unusual in that they were taken by a Maori Photographer, the Rev. Hakaraia Pahewa, minister at Te Kaha.

The business that most often brought Maori and Pakeha together, temporarily, was the sale of land. There are of course no photographs of the earliest transactions. From 1865 they were preceded by sittings of the Native Land Court, to determine ownership and title. Such sittings often encouraged Maoris to sell, as they represented a way of establishing final precedence over other claimants. In this instance the Ngati Kahungunu tribe of Hawke's Bay have gathered at Papawai to sign over ownership of Lake Wairarapa to the Crown in January 1896 for £2 000 and 'ample reserves for the benefit of the Native owners'. Judge Butler of the Native Land Court sits at the centre of the table. The Government representative, Liberal Member of Parliament and Ngati Kahungunu tribesman James Carroll, sits on the judge's right. The Papawai chief and Kotahitanga leader Tamahau Mahupuku sits on the ground to the left of the table.

The most intimate of associations, racial intermarriage, occurred with increasing frequency as the nineteenth century drew to a close. In the 1891 census 219 European men were recorded as married to Maori women; many more lived in *de facto* relationships. Such unions occurred more often in rural than in urban districts, more frequently in Maori than in Pakeha communities, and usually with a Maori wife marrying a European husband. It was not unknown for Maori men to marry European women, but this was decidedly less acceptable, especially in European circles. This South Island couple, Murari Pihawa and her unidentified husband, were photographed at Hokitika. His coiled stock whip suggests he is a drover. Such intermarriage was proportionately more common in South Island communities than in the north.

Conflict

Tawhiao the second Maori King with Poihere, one of his four wives. Unlike his father Te Wherowhero, Tawhiao did not want to be a warrior. He was a prophet, a poet, and a man of peace. But from the time he inherited the kingship in June 1860 his kingdom was under threat. Government and settlers wanted access to the fertile but Maori-owned Waikato and Waipa Valleys, and they chose to regard a separate Maori monarchy as treasonable and as a danger to the order of the whole country. Steadily the Waikato and Maniapoto tribes — who were largely responsible for maintaining the kingship — became isolated from other Maoris, once the latter sensed serious conflict. Open war broke out in 1863 with the Governor's decision to invade Waikato. Tawhiao fought with his troops for the first and only time at the Battle of Rangiriri in November of that year, in defence of his territory. He was defeated. A year later his territory was confiscated and he retired to the fastness of the King Country for two decades of exile.

Wiremu Tamihana Tarapipipi Te Waharoa, chief of Ngati Haua. Tamihana was known as the Kingmaker because of his role in persuading Te Wherowhero to become the first Maori King with the name Potatau in 1858. From that time Tamihana's descendants inherited the title and anointed successive Maori Kings. After his rejection of tribal warfare in the 1830s he was a determined peacemaker who did everything possible to avert the Waikato conflict. Government Magistrate John Gorst noted that he was 'a pleasant man to argue with. He heard patiently all you had to say, took the greatest pains to find out exactly what you meant, and replied calmly and always to the point. I have met many statesmen in my long life but none more superior in intellect and character to this Maori chief whom many would call savage.' Tamihana died in 1866 shortly after this photograph was taken, heartbroken at the failure of his plans and his dreams.

The New Zealand Wars were difficult to photograph. The earlier tribal skirmishes and first organised fighting between Maori and European forces in the 1840s predated the camera. Cameras *were* present during the wars of the 1860s. But their primitive nature — the length of time required for exposures and the laborious nature of plate preparation — ruled out action photography. Further difficulties were created by the guerilla character of much of the fighting from the mid-1860s. It was however possible to take portraits of combatants, to photograph battle sites and to arrange some of the groups involved. This Ngati Whatua war party posed for Daniel Manders Beere near Kaipara Harbour in 1863. The clubs and cloaks would have had ceremonial rather than functional uses by this time. The muskets and tomahawks were real and dangerous enough, however, and Maori fighters had become adept at using both. The garments too — largely blankets worn as rapaki or kilts — are a fair representation of what most 'rebel' Maoris would have worn in combat.

63

Cartes de visite of Maori fighters were extremely popular during the wars. They were especially in demand to send overseas, to show friends and relatives what the exotic adversaries looked like. This one shows a Waikato 'Kingite', Tutewana from Piako, posed as if for battle. He wears a korowai cloak as a kilt, probably at the suggestion of the photographer. His firearm is a double-barrelled muzzle-louding percussion shotgun. This was a civilian weapon owned by most frontier settlers and farmers at the time; it was not manufactured for military use. Few Maoris had access to proper military weapons. Although the huia feathers seem excessively ceremonial for combat, they were regarded as protective for somebody of rangatira rank.

This small community, believed to be on the Waipa River, was photographed in the course of the 1863 war. Most Waikato Maoris sought to live close to the river because it allowed transport by canoe, because of the presence of fish, eel and waterfowl, and because they regarded the water as a repository for the spirits of their dead and the mana of their tribe. Hapu settlements such as this one would have been quickly overrun by the invading Imperial forces and, if they remained loyal to Tawhiao, its members would have had to go into exile with him. A substantial European dwelling is visible at left.

Kumate, another Maori King supporter, was taken prisoner at the Battle of Rangiriri in November 1863. His photograph was circulated widely in *carte* albums as one of the first 'rebels' to have been captured and imprisoned. He does not appear vanquished in this study, taken soon after the fighting, although his future at the time must have seemed bleak. One New Zealand photo-historian has suggested that such pictures helped to mitigate European antagonism towards Maoris and eventually to swing some settler sympathies behind Maori causes. Kumate's moko, which runs down his cheeks from his nose, has been partially hidden by a beard, which suggests that he had embraced Christianity in the years prior to the war.

A coup for the Imperial forces under Lieutenant General Duncan Cameron. After the victory at Rangiriri they pushed straight up the Waikato River to Tawhiao's capital at Ngaruawahia. Most of the inhabitants had already retreated up the Waipa, taking with them the paraphernalia of their administration (including a printing press, which they abandoned at Te Kopua). Here British troops guard the King's whare, and the prisoners who had remained there to plead for its preservation.

Fraternising with the so-called enemy in the course of the wars was not uncommon. This photograph was taken by Assistant-Surgeon William Temple. The subjects are identified as (from left) Lieutenant Bates, 65th Regiment, Lieutenant Urqhardt, Annie, and Temple himself. There is no indication of where it was taken but Temple participated in the Waikato War and was awarded a Victoria Cross for bravery at Rangiriri. The shelter is probably a temporary one used by troops in the north Waikato, and Bates' tomahawk suggests it could have been built by the soldiers.

Te Ua Haumene of Ngati Ruanui in Taranaki inaugurated another phase of the New Zealand Wars. Mission educated, he announced that he had been visited by the Angel Gabriel and told that the Maori were now God's chosen people. With this message he founded a religion which Maoris knew as Pai Marire (good and peaceful) and which Europeans called Hauhau, after one of its chants. This movement was one of the first that seemed to offer Maoris a Maori path to the God of the Bible, without requiring the Europeanisation of beliefs and behaviour that missionaries insisted upon. Pai Marire spread rapidly through the western, central, East Coast and Bay of Plenty regions of the North Island, and also influenced South Island Maoris. It preached Maori unity, self-reliance, and a form of nationalism. It also revived old combat rituals such as smoking heads and eating parts of adversaries' bodies. From 1864 to 1868 it was the focus of Maori discontent with the European occupation of New Zealand, and it sowed the seeds for the Te Kooti Rikirangi's rebellion and the later Ringatu religion.

Re-enactments of battle scenes were also popular with *carte* collectors during the campaigns against Pai Marire followers. Here kupapa or 'loyal' Maoris recreate a scene of hand-to-hand fighting in a Maori village. A heavily laden loyalist has been knocked to the ground, a Hauhau is about to remove his head with a tomahawk, but another kupapa comes to the rescue to shoot the villain through the chest. The caps, tartan kilts, rifles, bandoliers and boots were standard issue to Maori troops fighting for the Government. The background of raupo huts is real enough and it is likely that this photograph was taken by Daniel Mundy at Kaiteriria in 1870.

So great was the influx of prisoners from the Hauhau campaigns (800 after the siege of Waerenga-a-Hika alone) and so strong the insistence of European settlers on adequate punishment for rebellion, that existing jails in the 1860s were unable to cope with the numbers. Ships were pressed into service as prison hulks, including this one in Wellington Harbour. The captives had been rounded up in 1866 after an assault by government troops on Wereroa Pa, 20 miles north of Wanganui. Conditions on such ships were so confined and unhealthy that in summer months prisoners were paroled and allowed to go swimming and fishing.

European opinion in New Zealand was shocked by the killing of the Rev. Carl Volkner in Opotiki in 1865. Volkner, a former Lutheran, had transferred to the Anglican ministry and been appointed to Opotiki in 1861. In 1864 and 1865 he reported to Governor George Grey on the movements of Hauhaus within his region. Many local Maoris regarded this as spying and he was eventually hanged outside his church. Here a group of Maoris congregate in front of the whare where Volkner's fate was debated, alongside the tree from which he was hanged. The photograph was taken for evidence, shortly after the killing. A camp oven is in the foreground.

Throughout the Hauhau and Te Kooti campaigns the Arawa tribes of the Rotorua and Bay of Plenty supported the Government steadfastly. One of the most vigorous units to take part in the fighting was the Flying Arawa Column, led by Captain Gilbert Mair. Here Mair (at left, with spade) and his men listen to the reading of a proclamation at their camp at Kaiterima. They have just prevented an attack on Rotorua by Te Kooti's forces in February 1870. The flag at right was captured from Te Kooti's men at an earlier engagement at Te Porere, in September 1868.

Despite the fierce mien that made many Europeans afraid of him, Renata Kawepo fought with the Government against Te Kooti. The Ngati Kahungunu chief was mutilated in circumstances that were characteristic of Maori fighting, in which utu or repayment was almost always a factor. After Renata had killed one of Te Kooti's followers at Te Porere near Taupo, the wife of his victim attacked him and gouged out his right eye. In a sequel that was also characteristically Maori, Renata protected the woman from punishment and then married her. This photograph was taken shortly before his death in 1888.

In the years following the New Zealand Wars peace was by no means assured. Whole sections of the North Island, such as the King Country and the Urewera, were closed to Europeans and sheltered armed Maoris who could have burst out and overwhelmed outlying farms and settlements, had they so wished. Voluntary militia groups were formed throughout the island to defend such areas against possible attack. Some kupapa Maoris acted as scouts with the Armed Constabulary, others actually joined up. Wirope Hoterini Taipari of Ngati Maru formed and led the Thames Native Volunteers. He was a great favourite with Europeans in the Thames and Coromandel districts, and he was appointed an assessor of the Native Land Court. His uniform and those of his contingent were provided by the Government under its Defence Act of 1886.

69

A warriors' reunion. These Ngati Maniapoto chiefs, all of whom had fought for Tawhiao in the 1860s, assembled at Haerehuku in the King Country to be photographed by Alfred Burton in 1885. Rewi Maniapoto (back left) was the leader who reputedly called out to Major William Gilbert Mair at the battle of Orakau in 1864: 'E hoa ka whawhai tonu ahau kia koe ake, ake, ake. Friend, I shall go on fighting you for ever and for ever.' In later years he became a friend of Pakeha officialdom and he was given a government house in Kihikihi, and a government memorial when he died there in 1894. Wetere Te Rerenga (back right) had been accused of murdering the Wesleyan missionary John Whiteley on the Taranaki coast in 1869, but charges were never pressed. After the deaths of Rewi and Wahanui Huatare, Taonui (back, second from right) became the acknowledged paramount chief of Ngati Maniapoto and Ngati Raukawa.

Veterans of government forces also held
reunions, though in circumstances that were
decidedly victorious. Here Major Ropata
Wahawaha, who led Ngati Porou troops against
Pai Marire and Te Kooti followers, is given a
place of honour at Oamaru in 1886. Although
middle-aged when he took up arms, Ropata
matched Te Kooti in determination and ferocity,
and he was ruthless about killing prisoners. On
one occasion alone, at Ngatapa, he had 100 men
stripped, shot and pushed over a cliff. Later he
caught Kereopa, alleged killer of Carl Volkner.
Ropata was awarded the New Zealand Cross and
a sword of honour from Queen Victoria. He was
appointed a life member of Parliament's
Legislative Council, and died in 1897.

CHAPTER THREE

Maori Life

The Maori population declined sharply in the nineteenth century as a result of contact with Europeans. Polynesian genes had been separated from the continent of Asia for some 5000 years, and therefore from continental diseases. Their bearers had no natural resistance to influenza, measles and whooping cough, and venereal disease and tuberculosis were previously unknown to them. Changes in living conditions also led to typhoid and dysentery in epidemic proportions. The precise extent to which such diseases coupled with the casualties of the musket wars reduced Maori numbers in the first half of the century is unclear because of uncertainties about the reliability of Maori statistics. Current demographic calculations suggest that the population at the time of Cook's visits was in the order of 100 000. In 1843 Ernst Dieffenbach travelled the country extensively, spoke to those who had travelled further, and estimated the native population to be nearly 115 000. That one or both early figures is incorrect seems likely; or the Maori population remained relatively stable from the 1770s to the 1840s.

What is far more certain is that numbers did decline dramatically from the 1840s to the 1890s. Epidemics of influenza, measles and whooping cough were reported with some frequency in the 1840s and 1850s, as far more Maoris had contact — directly or indirectly — with Europeans; there were also dysenteric outbreaks of massive proportions over the same period. The fertility rate declined markedly as women suffered from general ill-health and from the effects of syphilis, gonorrhoea and tuberculosis. In parts of Waikato in the late 1850s over one-third of married Maori women were found to be barren. Communities visibly shrank in the face of these onslaughts: some Ngati Ruanui villages in Taranaki, for example, lost one-third of their population as a result of death from illness between 1846 and 1852. Nationally the Maori population dropped from Dieffenbach's estimated 114 800 in 1843 to 56 049 in 1857-58, to 42 113 in the 1896 census. As such figures became known they contributed to a widespread belief that the Maori people were headed towards extinction. Wellington Provincial Superintendant, Dr Isaac Featherston, echoed liberal European sentiment in the late nineteenth century when he spoke of the responsibility to 'smooth the pillow of a dying race'.

Conditions in Maori settlements varied enormously, however, from district to district — so much so that it is difficult to generalise about Maori life in the latter half of the nineteenth century. One reason, of course, is that the basis of this life remained hapu and tribe. Maoris generally still did not view themselves as 'Maori' (that is, as a single race and culture) even after the word Maori had come into use in the 1840s. Consequently there was as yet little incentive for them to behave in a homogeneous way, other than to continue — in characteristically tribal manner — to disparage and to compete with Maoris from other hapu and other places. The very persistence of tribal feeling had prevented the continuation of 'nationalist' experiments such as the Kingitanga.* It had

---

* Although the Maori King Movement survived the Waikato War, it did so as the almost exclusive preserve of the tribes of the Tainui waka federation: Waikato, Ngati Maniapoto, Ngati Haua, Hauraki. It had in effect ceased to be multi-tribal in the second half of the nineteenth century, although it was subsequently to become so again.

prevented Maoris from acting as a pressure group commensurate with their numbers. Even though four Maori seats were created in the national Parliament in 1867, tribalism and regionalism at first prevented its members from acting in concert from common Maori aims (as did the fact that some of the early members were not proficient in English, and few European members spoke Maori).

In spite of such diversity and divisiveness, most Europeans rarely distinguished one Maori from another or one tribe from another — a fact especially evident in cartoons of the Maori in the late nineteenth century. Maoris were all simply 'Native' in the language of official usage; those of part-Maori descent were almost always identified exclusively with that side if their features or colouring were even slightly Polynesian in character. A European visiting a Maori settlement was very much aware that he was in a world different from his own. The dispositions of such communities, the provision of communal meeting, cooking and eating facilities, the style of houses, the materials from which they were built, the nature of the activities that went on in and around them, the language that was spoken, the kind of food that was eaten and the manner in which it was prepared, the general broadcasting of excreta — all these features suggested to Europeans a distinctively Maori lifestyle, and one that seemed indistinguishable from place to place.

Traditional Maori clothing had gone out of general use by the 1850s (and much earlier in communities involved in whaling and trading and those close to European settlements). As the settler population had swollen in the previous decade, so European clothing had become widely available, new and second-hand, along with blankets. Clothing and blankets were sold by travelling merchants and storekeepers who reaped excessive rewards in some areas, exploiting the market for both commodities. There was a simultaneous Maori demand from the same entrepreneurs for pipes, tobacco, axes, spades, cooking utensils (especially billies, camp ovens, kettles, buckets and knives), and for metal to make other tools.

Traditional garments made from flax, flax-type plants and dog skins had been time-consuming to prepare and had not provided satisfactory protection and warmth. Blankets were welcomed as a means of keeping warm at night without having to rely entirely on fires inside houses without chimneys, which had detrimental effects on eyesight and lungs. Blankets were also adopted widely as garments: typically one around the waist would serve as a skirt or kilt, one around the shoulders as a shawl; people also took to wearing them toga fashion, in imitation of traditional cloaks. As the century wore on traditional clothing — cloaks, waist mats, flax skirts and so on — came to be used exclusively as ceremonial costume. They would often be worn as part of haka and action-song performances; or, in the case of cloaks, placed over European dress to emphasise the person's Maori identity or rank within the Maori community.

Generally in the nineteenth century Maori settlements continued to be built around hapu membership and they ranged in size from half-a-dozen households to several hundred. Each community was likely to have five kinds of building: whare mehana or sleeping houses, kauta or communal cook houses, pataka or storehouses, whata or shelters for storing wood, and — with increasing frequency as the century drew near its close — wharepuni or community meeting houses. A whare mehana might shelter an immediate family (husband, wife and children) or an extended one. It would be used for sleeping and for the storage of personal possessions, rarely for cooking and eating, which would more commonly take place in community facilities. The size and style of these and other Maori constructions gradually changed with the availability of European tools, garments, utensils and other materials.

In the earlier years of the nineteenth century whare mehana were typically small (about 4.6 metres by 3.7), low (1.8 metres) with low doors and poor ventilation. Wooden houses often had earth heaped against the walls for further insulation; raupo ones, which became more common in the mid-nineteenth century, were free-standing. Usually they were warmed by small charcoal fires or embers spread on the floor, and lit with lamps made by floating wicks or charcoal in containers of fat. As European clothing spread and blankets became generally available, the houses became larger and better ventilated and were built above the ground. Chimneys and European-type fireplaces were being added in many districts from the 1870s.

Wharepuni or community sleeping houses increased greatly in size to the kinds of dimensions (18 to 24 metres long, 8 metres wide) that were to become common in the twentieth century.* The incentive for constructing larger community buildings was greatest where tribes had regular inter-hapu or inter-tribal meetings to sustain — such as Waikato with its Kingitanga huis (poukai) and Tuhoe with its Ringatu gatherings (tekaumarua). In general, observers noted in the 1870s and 1880s that large and lavishly catered meetings were becoming an increasingly common feature of Maori life since fighting was no longer available to provide excitement or a focus for community effort. The larger and more lavish the hui, the more mana accrued to the host community — prestige in Polynesian terms being measured by what was given away rather than by what was accumulated. Such gatherings required adequate accomodation and were a factor in the enlargement of meeting houses. Another factor was the availability of pit-sawn timber and European tools; the latter aided large-scale construction and the evolution of

---

* There were no large permanent meeting houses in pre-European years, although temporary shelters of considerable length were not uncommon; the permanent meeting house became possible and desirable with the advent of European garments and tools, and with the increase in inter-tribal huis after the New Zealand Wars.

increasingly elaborate styles of carving, especially in Arawa territory. A knowledge of European architecture also modified the styles of smaller buildings in some areas, even where traditional materials were still in use; some dwellings, such as those in Tawhiao's settlement at Whatiwhatihoe, had doors at the side covered with verandahs.

In most districts traditional building materials — raupo, muka, punga, earth sods, bark, nikau — continued to be used into the 1880s. Houses were likely to have wooden frames, usually of manuka, and wall material of reed or wood packed against them. Sod walls remained in favour in some South Island communities at this time — partly because wood was not always available and partly because they gave more adequate insulation from the colder climate. Roofs were thatched with reed, nikau or tussock, or they were covered with bark. Such structures were still visible in the early years of the twentieth century, although by then such use was in noticeable decline.

Generally, as pit-sawn timber and corrugated iron became available in the last two decades of the nineteenth century, Maoris were quick to make use of them where they could afford them. House styles changed in the process. Important and wealthy people increasingly came to live in European-type houses, often indistinguishable externally from a rural Pakeha homestead. Other Maoris tended to opt for simple rectangular huts and cottages with fireplaces and chimneys. Some leading subsistence lives combined European *and* Maori building materials. Te Puea Herangi of Waikato, for example, used punga walls for conventional cottages into the 1930s and 1940s. While people engaged in seasonal work or foraging activities — flax cutting, gum digging, mutton birding, for example — continued to build traditional-type shelters and camp sites, these latter should not be confused with so-called substandard permanent housing.

In the nineteenth century most families slept in their whare mehana, worked with other families in communal cooking areas or kitchen shelters and stored food in common storehouses. With the advance of the twentieth century there was a tendency for individual family dwellings to be extended and to include cooking and eventually full kitchen facilities for day-to-day living. Cooking on a large scale for huis, however, would still be done communally, as would washing clothes (in rivers or portable tubs), harvesting communal crops and foraging for seafood and for wild vegetables such as puha and watercress.

In European eyes most Maori accommodation in the nineteenth and early twentieth century was decidedly substandard. Indeed, an absence of toilet facilities of any kind, a lack of running water, overcrowding in sleeping quarters, a lack of ventilation and generally unhygienic conditions for the preparation of food — all these features were to be characteristic of Maori communities and individual dwellings until the 1940s. 'Maori housing' in European usage was synonomous with poor

housing. These features were the first to be criticised and then combatted by Maori health authorities when they were appointed for the first time in the early 1900s. They were not obviously inimical to Maori lifestyles, however, and therefore there was little immediate incentive for communities to change them. Latrines tended to be built under the supervision of a visiting health officer and then abandoned when he left. But such conditions did contribute to the spread of tuberculosis, typhoid fever, dysentery, and diarrhoeal and respiratory diseases, and generally made outbreaks of any contagious illnesses more likely to affect whole communities. Inasmuch as sickness debilitated people or shortened their lives, then such conditions were inimical to the survival of Maori people and hence of Maori culture. And once Maori leaders had made such a cause-and-effect connection, they fought hard to change them, locally and nationally.

Some communities attempted to anaesthetise themselves from health problems and from grief from resulting deaths with excessive use of alcohol — with the result that their members became even more susceptible to ill-health and less capable of coping with the crises that illness brought. In this way whole villages and hapu in some areas were prone to sink into sloughs of despondency from which it was difficult to emerge. Te Uira Te Heuheu, a Tuwharetoa woman who married into such a community in Waikato in 1913, was shocked. 'There seemed to be no sense of direction,' she wrote later. 'Life just drifted by.' (Her shock, it should be noted, arose from the fact that such conditions were by no means universal; some Maori communities, especially those with a sound economic base on the East Coast of the North Island, in Hawke's Bay and in parts of the South Island, were coping with their vicissitudes with determination and considerable success.)

For a long time the official attitude to problems of Maori health and welfare was to ignore them. There were, in effect, two New Zealands: Pakeha New Zealand, served and serviced by comprehensive systems of national and local government administration; and Maori New Zealand, largely ignored by both except when those systems wanted to appropriate resources such as land, income or manpower. Maoris were unable to obtain housing finance until the 1930s. Few doctors saw Maori patients, hospitals rarely took them and most did not want to. The Auckland Health Officer — in whose district lived the bulk of the country's Maori population — stated in 1911 that Maori health should be of concern to Europeans; but only because the unchecked spread of Maori diseases could lead eventually to Europeans contracting them. 'As matters stand,' he wrote, 'the Native race is a menace to the well-being of the European.'

In spite of these fears of contamination, the Maori population was well insulated from the non-Maori throughout the nineteenth century and for the first half of the twentieth. In 1900 more than 95 percent lived in rural communities that were so scattered as to cause not only geographic separation of Maori from Pakeha, but also separation of Maori from Maori. The major concentrations were north of Whangarei, in South Auckland, Waikato, the King Country, the Bay of Plenty, the East Coast, Rangitikei, Wanganui and Taranaki. Families continued to live for the most part in kainga with a hapu base; or, in more isolated districts, in individual family homes outside kainga. The South Island Maori population, which numbered only 1400 in 1901 out of a national total of 45000, lived in half-a-dozen major kaika or 'kaiks'* close to but separate from European settlements in Canterbury, Otago and Westland.

Life for people in such settlements tended to be family, community and hapu-oriented. On occasions this orientation would extend to wider tribal units, especially when land matters were discussed or disputed; or to a waka federation such as Tainui or Mataatua. This latter was especially likely where wider organisations such as the Kingitanga and the Hahi Ringatu activated more extensive relationships and obligations on a regular basis. Effective leaders were the kaumatua or family heads, while whole hapu would be spoken for at wider hui by rangatira who usually had a whakapapa claim to leadership, but whose tenure also depended on retaining the confidence of their kaumatua.

Major decision-making on community matters was centred on consensus-forming discussion among family heads on local marae. In the South Island, kaikas had established runanga in which whole communities were likely to be involved, and which would be chaired and spoken for by upoko runanga or community heads. In rare cases, such as Waikato-Maniapoto and Ngati Tuwharetoa, ariki or paramount chiefs would speak for federations of tribes; more often, as in the case of the Ngai Tahu/Ngati Mamoe land claim in the South Island, tribal spokesmen would be rangatira dominant at a particular time or nominated by the rest of the tribe to represent them for a particular project. Within these defined but flexible structures communities organised their rounds of huis, tangis and church functions, arranged marriages to strengthen useful alliances among families and hapu, planned, constructed and maintained community facilities such as meeting houses and dining halls, dealt with local conflict and often resolved it, and discussed the perennial issues raised by prospects of land sales or public works in the vicinity of the kainga.

A few Maori communities were for a time spectacularly and successfully self-reliant, sustaining their inhabitants and protecting them from the effects of disease, alcohol and demoralisation. Te Whiti O Rongomai's pa at Parihaka, with its Taranaki tribal base, was one such successful experiment. From the late 1880s it had its own slaughterhouse, bakery, bank and prison, and it generated its own electricity for lighting. A similiar experiment in Maori independence which made use of European technology was launched by the prophet Rua Kenana in the Urewera in the early 1900s. Other pa, such as Whatwhatihoe in the King Country and (a decade later in the 1890s) Waahi near Huntly were not as well equipped in Pakeha technology as Parihaka and Maungapohatu, but they were able to nourish their inhabitants and to provide lavish accomodation and hospitality for visitors, Maori and Pakeha. Some, like those in the South Island, close to European centres of population and mingling with Pakeha in work and sport, were by the beginning of the twentieth century almost indistinguishable in external appearance from a Pakeha village. Others such as the smaller Tuhoe settlements in the Urewera had changed very little in appearance since the wars of the 1860s.** In these as in other respects, Maori life was characterised by diversity.

Most of these communities made a precarious living from mixed subsistence farming. The scale of Maori horticulture had diminished greatly from the days of the 1840s and 1850s when the Waikato, Hauraki, Arawa and Bay of Plenty tribes had been the country's major crop producers and exporters. Later in the century, most of their good land bought or taken from them, denied access to the government assistance given Pakeha farmers for land development, Maoris in most parts of the country could barely produce sufficient meat, grain, vegetables and fruit to feed themselves. In some places — the Urewera, for example — communities lived close to starvation. In other areas, such as Maketu in the Bay of Plenty, Maori labour and produce were plentiful.

Where families and communites were unable to be self-sufficient — and this was the case in the majority of Maori settlements — Maori labourers came to rely increasingly for income on seasonal work created by the expanding European rural economy. It was common for Maori gangs in rural districts to take up fencing, drain laying, shearing, crop harvesting, flax cutting and processing, scrub cutting, felling timber and gum digging; or road and railway public works. Often whole families or hapu would specialise in specific jobs. In many areas such work was available from Pakeha farmers or local bodies adjacent to hapu settlements. Where individuals left their own kainga in search of such work they tended to settle in other rural Maori communities, adopting the identity and kawa of their hosts, or of the family and hapu into which they married. This served to mitigate the appearance and effects of de-tribalisation which — while it was under way from the early years of the twentieth century — did not become dramatically apparent for another

---

* Renditions of 'kainga' in South Island dialect.

** The Urewera was the last Maori district to be 'penetrated' by Europeans, and for this reason it became a popular target for ethnologists from the early 1900s. These men, most interested in manifestations of the 'old-time' Maori, tended to ignore or condemn the experiment in acculturation being conducted by Rua Kenana.

generation as a result of migration for work and the demise of small communities through depopulation.

The commitment to Maori values remained strong, in spite of the fact that most Maoris had been nominally converted to Christianity (the largest number to the Church of England; the rest to Roman Catholicism, Methodism, Mormonism and Presbyterianism in that order). Mana and tapu were still decisive factors, determining who led communities, who deserved respect, and what was or was not done. It was still widely believed that hara or 'faults' in a Maori sense created chinks in an individual's personal tapu, and that this in turn left the individual vulnerable to makutu, sickness, madness or death; most instances of actual sickness or death were explained in these terms. Tohunga continued to perform Maori karakia or religious rites and to practise folk medicine, sometimes with disastrous results when dealing with 'Pakeha' illnesses such as measles or influenza (immersion in water was a common feature of Maori ritual).

In some areas Maoris were 'Christian' in some contexts — a wedding or church service, for example; and 'Maori' in others, such as combatting makutu or performing ritual prior to planting crops or felling trees. Some people practised Christian and Maori religions simultaneously: most Waikato Maoris under the Kingitanga, for example, were both followers of Pai Marire and baptised Methodists. This was not seen as contradictory. Maoris increasingly came to view life in terms of taha Maori and taha Pakeha — the Maori and the Pakeha sides of themselves and of the world in general.

Increasingly, the focal point of Maori life was the hui. People who could no longer fight one another came together to compete in other ways: to surpass the hospitality of their previous hosts and put them back in debt; to issue oratorical challenges and display astonishing feats of memory in the recitation of genealogy and tradition; to debate other people's versions of genealogy and tradition; to display prowess in haka, action song, wielding the taiaha and handling canoes.

The hui was an established Maori institution throughout the country. The Ngai Tahu of the South Island restored their tribal identity by meeting regularly and debating how to act in concert to prosecute their land claim. The people of the Wanganui and King Country met to debate Native Land Court questions, where the Main Trunk Railway should be allowed to go, where roads could be laid, and the extent to which Maori communities should be relocated to take advantage of these new arteries of communication. Ngati Kahungunu hapu met to discuss the Repudiation Movement which challenged Pakeha land purchases in Hawke's Bay. Tuhoe met to debate whether they should allow surveying and gold prospecting in the Urewera. Waikato tribes came together interminably to discuss new proposals for Maori political representation, the mana of the Kingitanga and the sale and leasing of land.

But in a sense these were simply excuses for, not causes of, hui. Essentially hui were occasions on which hapu could come together in wider tribal units, to renew old relationships, to sing, to dance, to tell stories, to argue in and listen to lengthy whaikorero. More and more in the latter years of the nineteenth century these huis were becoming inter-tribal ventures as leaders and followers felt impelled to debate the great questions of the day. By the 1890s a feeling was growing among some leaders that a form of 'Maori' rather than specifically tribal political activity should be attempted to promote common Maori causes, particularly in dealings with the national Parliament.

All such meetings were conducted according to Maori kawa, though the details of such etiquette varied slightly from tribe to tribe and from district to district. In some the hosts spoke first, in others the visitors; in some hosts and visitors alternated speakers, in others they followed one another until each group finished separately; most tribes forbade women speaking on the marae, some tolerated it, a few encouraged it; all these things had evolved and become fixed in the years that tribes were separated from one another. The general structure was similar throughout the country, however. Successive waves of visitors would be called on to the host marae, they would pause to tangi for the dead of both sides, they would be greeted by speeches and waiata that asserted the identity of the hosts and they would reply in kind with their own speeches and songs, they would hongi with the hosts to indicate that the tapu of visitor status had been removed through the ritual of welcome, and then they would be fed.

The hui ritual that remained strongest, and which some called the heartbeat of Maori culture, was the tangihanga or ceremony of mourning for the dead. This practice was modified slightly over the years to incorporate some Christian elements and to meet public health requirements. But basically its sequence and effect did not change from the nineteenth to the twentieth centuries. When a person died the body was laid out on the marae of the family or hapu. It was exposed to view (at first on mats and blankets, later in open coffins) for days while mourners came to pay respects and to comfort the bereaved. The tupapaku (corpse) was addressed in oratory and lament, as were the spirits of his relatives who had predeceased him. Fine mats, cloaks and tribal heirlooms were also on display, to demonstrate the mana of the hapu and to symbolically warm and protect the deceased. From the 1890s photographs were incorporated into the ritual to recall the presence of the dead. At about the same time portraits also began to be placed on meeting house walls, an extension of the concept which regarded such houses as representations of the genealogy of the hapu.

The duration of tangis varied. Until the end of the nineteenth century they could go on for weeks, even months if the deceased was sufficiently important (the last one of considerable length was that for King Tawhiao in 1894, which lasted nearly two months). Public health legislation early in the twentieth century restricted the mourning time and it became customary to hold ceremonies within the space of one week; improving systems of transport and communication also reduced the need to display the body for longer periods. The ceremonies ended with a Christian funeral service, usually conducted by a Maori minister, and a European-type burial in which many of the deceased's personal possessions were likely to be interred with the body. A year or more later another ceremony would be held to 'unveil' the headstone, and this fulfilled some of the functions of the pre-European hahunga or exhumation rite, which ended the period of mourning. Late in the nineteenth century Maori women began to wear black clothes for tangis and the practice continued in many areas, long after Europeans in New Zealand had stopped wearing mourning garments.

Although the proceedings of the country's Parliament were remote from the daily lives of most Maoris, some legislation had intimately affected them. Since European settlers had been granted so-called Responsible Government by the British Parliament in the 1850s and 1860s, one of the greatest difficulties had been devising ways to ascertain ownership of Maori communal land and hence who to deal with in sales transactions. The problem increased as the European population in New Zealand increased. Inevitably too, Pakeha buyers wanted the best agricultural and pastoral land available.

In an attempt to accelerate such transactions the Native Land Court was established in 1865, its functions superceding many of those of the earlier Native Land Purchase Department. This later institution held sittings presided over by a judge to investigate claims to land, to rule on the validity of such claims, and to record the names of successful claimants as owners. Although the court was undoubtedly intended to facilitate the transfer of Maori land to Pakeha ownership, Maoris themselves showed a considerable willingness to bring land to the court and often to offer such land for sale. The reasons for this were complex. In some cases owners simply wanted money with which to purchase other commodities; in some instances the land concerned was not wanted; but in many cases court sittings and sales seem to have been initiated by Maoris simply to prove the validity of their claims over those of rival Maoris. The sittings became, in other words, another forum for the inter-hapu and tribal rivalries that had always characterised Maori life. In many instances spurious claimants launched proceedings simply to annoy an opponent, or to take utu (satisfaction) for some wrong previously inflicted on them. In this manner court sittings became an extension of — or at least a sequel to — tribal confrontation.

The Native Land Court also became a major institution in Maori life in the late nineteenth and early twentieth centuries. Some old people, repositories of tribal tradition, became almost professional court-goers as claim clashed with counterclaim. More important, perhaps, the court minutes carefully recorded all the evidence and thus became the country's first and only archive of Maori oral history on a large scale. Families often accompanied elders to sittings in the towns nearest the tribal land under discussion and camped close to the court. Thus the hearings became occasions for reunions and huis.

The national Parliament also instituted four Maori seats, in 1867. One of the factors which made this acceptable to European Members of Parliament was that it gave the North Island a more favourable balance of seats in relation to the South, which had by far the larger population. The early members were kupapa Maoris and tended at first to be the nominees and proteges of the Government's Native Minister. They had little contact with the grass roots of Maori communities where national politics (other than the disposal of Maori land) were not at issue. But by the close of the nineteenth century these members were surprising and then annoying successive governments by opposing Maori legislation of the day as not being in the interest of the Maori people. They were not at all effective in changing the course of such legislation in the nineteenth century; but their seats did serve as a Trojan horse to introduce Maori considerations into Parliament and eventually into legislation in the twentieth century, when they were held by more able and more sophisticated members.

By the close of the nineteenth century the prognosis for Maori culture and for the Maori population did not seem favourable. Numbers were falling rapidly, as was the Maori percentage of the population as a whole. From constituting 50 percent of the nation's citizens in 1860, Maoris made up only 10 percent by 1891. Their remaining lands constituted only 17 percent of the whole country and a great deal of this was marginal and in effect useless. No money was available for Maori agricultural and pastoral development. While some communities were thriving healthily on their own holdings — most notably those on the East Coast and parts of the Bay of Plenty — others were demoralised and handicapped by malnutrition, alcohol and disease. It was an awareness of these factors in 1907 that led Archdeacon Walsh to write of the 'The Passing of the Maori' in the *Transactions and proceedings of the New Zealand Institute*. He summarised: 'The Maori has lost heart and abandoned hope. As it has already been observed in the case of the individual, when once the vital force has fallen below a certain point he died from the sheer want of an effort to live; so it is with the race. It is sick unto death, and is already potentially dead.' It was in an attempt to rectify these same conditions that a number of Maori leaders decided to experiment with new forms of political and social activity.

Dwellings and domestic activities

This photograph of a chief's house and the fenced marae area in front of it was taken on Mayor Island in the Bay of Plenty in the 1880s. It shows part of a kainga. It was from houses of this sort that larger meeting houses had begun to evolve in areas where larger huis were taking place to discuss major issues of the day, such as Native Land Court transactions and the progress of the Main Trunk Railway. At this time, however, no such issues or needs disturbed the lives of Ngai Te Rangi Maoris on Mayor Island, which they called Tuhua. Gables and tekoteko (the carved face or figure at the apex) were characteristic of houses such as this and provided the basis for the larger carved house facade that became popular in the late nineteenth century in areas that had the expertise and the resources to construct them.

These houses built from traditional materials, raupo walls and roofs, stood at Karaka Bay on Wellington Harbour in the 1870s. European materials were also starting to appear on dwellings in areas such as this close to Pakeha settlements, however. The house in the foreground has a corrugated iron ridge held in place against Wellington winds by wires weighed down with logs, a hinged door and a netting fence. The garden around the house is fenced off to protect vegetables from wandering stock. In most communities at this time it was more common to locate gardens away from the immediate living area.

The layout of this village of Ranana on the lower Wanganui River in 1885 is typical of most Maori settlements of this period. The large shingle-roofed meeting house and marae lie in the centre of the community and face the track that leads into it. Around it are whare mehana (sleeping houses), kauta (kitchen shelters) and raised pataka (food storehouses). A niu pole, a feature of Hauhau ceremonial, stands at the centre of the marae, indicating that the inhabitants have retained the Pai Marire religion. Alfred Burton who took the photograph was told that huis were becoming larger and more frequent in this area as a substitute for the tribal fighting of earlier years.

A group phtographed by Burton at Pipiriki. The combination of blankets and European garments was typical of the Wanganui and King Country districts at this time. Two bark-roofed pataka stand at left and a meeting house at rear. To the left a traditionally made rain cape hangs with two European-style jackets.

Te Kumi, near the present town of Te Kuiti, was another settlement visited by Burton in 1885. Two years earlier a railway surveyor named Charles Hursthouse had been captured and held here by the prophet Te Mahuki, who regarded himself as the Te Whiti O Rongomai's representative in the King Country. Typically, the village is close to a stream (a source of water, food and transport by canoe). The house in the foreground has largely punga walls and that to the right ones of horizontal logs. Both would have needed interior linings of material such as raupo or cabbage tree leaves to retain warmth and prevent draughts. Roofs are of thatched raupo, held down by logs.

A Ngati Kahungunu group at Waiohiki Pa in Hawke's Bay in the 1860s. Dress is characteristic of the time, although the man at rear wears a flax rain cape. Two other males wear army caps, a reminder that the New Zealand Wars were still in progress. The patterned structure at right is a raised wooden tomb. This pa was declared tapu, possibly because of the presence of human remains, and was no longer occupied at this time.

Another of Burton's pictures, taken at Taumarunui. The woman at right, Rane, is weaving a flax cloak and wearing one of the blouses that Burton carried around for his Maori models. The house has ponga outer walls, raupo lining and a bark roof. A window has been blocked off and a pheasant hangs above it.

A family group outside its whare mehana at Taumarunui, also caught by Burton. Three of the women smoke clay pipes, which became immensely popular among Maoris from the time of the earliest contact with whalers and traders. The woman at right has a wooden one. Most Maori communities grew tobacco among their cultivations at this time. Ornamentation worn by the men includes a greenstone tiki (probably affected for the photograph) and a watch on a fob chain.

Domestic animals were another popular European contribution to Maori life in the nineteenth century. Although the ancestors of the Maori had brought dogs with them from East Polynesia, these seem never to have been numerous (possibly because they were one of the few sources of meat). European dogs and cats were acquired rapidly as they became available and had reached Maori communities throughout the country by the 1870s. This woman in Wairarapa in the 1880s cherishes her cat and its kittens. The Maori name for cats, Ngeru, is derived from the word for sleek, and is an indication of the extent to which such animals were stroked and cared for.

A superbly built house made of tightly bound raupo walls and a muka (flax fibre) roof. The photograph, another by Burton in 1885, is of King Tawhiao's residence in Whatiwhatihoe, the Maori settlement near Pirongia that was the headquarters of the Maori King Movement in the 1880s. The man at left is Whitiora, a Kawhia chief who was one of the Tawhiao's most influential advisors. Three years earlier he had helped the Austrian collector Andreas Reischek to enter the King Country, ostensibly to study birds. Reischek reciprocated by stealing Maori corpses from burial caves adjacent to Hauturu, Whitiora's home village.

Another chief's house, this one belonging to the Wanganui kupapa Mete Kingi Terangi Paetahi. Photographed at Putiki in the 1860s, the building includes Maori and European features. It has raupo walls and a bark roof. But the entrance and verandah extending from the side wall is an innovation brought about by an acquaintance with European houses. Formerly the door would have been under one of the end gables. The carving of the verandah lintel is also an innovation but one based on the Maori custom of decorating the smaller lintels above doors.

A log-walled kauta at Pitoritori on the Puniu River, 1885, another of Burton's pictures. The Puniu was the northern boundary of the King Country and it was close to Alexandra (Pirongia) and Te Awamutu. People who lived on its banks enjoyed contact and commerce with European settlers. Results of such contact can be seen in the saddle and chain at right and the bridle hanging at left. Firewood is piled at the front of the house and along one wall. Because it was built for food preparation and cooking only, there was no need for the walls to be sealed tightly. The men pictured, Tukorehu and Kohika, had fought against the Imperial troops in the Waikato War.

Another cook-house and kitchen, at Parihaka in the 1880s. The women in front are scraping potatoes with shells and the one at right fetches cooking water in buckets, which were in widespread use in Taranaki by this time. Three women have pigment daubed on their cheeks, a feature of Parihaka action song costume (they are also holding pois). The boy at left grasps what is described as 'a feather windmill', which could have had ceremonial significance at Parihaka because of Te Whiti's choice of white feathers to symbolise his teachings. The walls of the kauta are made from horizontal logs between upright supports. Some of the wood so laid (such as that at left) would also be used for firewood. There is a ventilation hole at the apex of the front wall.

A further view of Parihaka, in October 1885, showing a wealth of detail. This was one of the first Maori communities to have gas and electric lighting, and a street lamp can be seen at left, above the roofs. The houses at this time, with the exception of Te Whiti's, were largely of Maori style and materials. But they showed European influences, such as the verandah at centre right. There is a hinaki for catching eels visible in the foreground, a boy wearing two hats, two others showing off on a post and on horseback, and three men in the centre with their legs crossed in precisely the same manner.

A late nineteenth century photograph of women cooking over a fire outside a kauta, probably at a Wanganui River settlement. The three major utensils of such work — a kettle, a large billy and a camp oven — can be seen in the foreground.

A group alongside a cooking fire in the Wairarapa in the 1880s. The kettle and teapot are held over the open fire on a raised and portable metal frame. The buildings at rear, made from pit-sawn timber and shingles, may indicate a European settlement (especially the shed at left, which is similar to the kind that housed traction engines at this time).

Like most other Maori activities, washing clothes tended to be done communally. Most settlements were located close to suitable rivers or ponds where women could go to wash, scrub and rinse garments. Planks around the edge of the water were used for scrubbing-boards. This group is at work in the King Country in about 1905.

Views of interiors of houses and meeting houses are rare. This meeting house porch was photographed in Hawke's Bay in the 1870s and reveals considerable detail: a raupo ceiling, kowhaiwhai rafter patterns (extending, unusually, to the upright pillars), tukutuku wall panel decoration and a flax mat covering the earth floor. The carved outside post and a paepae (porch wall) large enough to sit on are also clearly visible. The models would have adopted Maori costume for the photograph only; the boy on the fence outside wears conventional clothes.

Tokanganui-A-Noho was one of the most magnificent meeting houses built in the nineteenth century. It was a gift from Te Kooti Rikirangi to the Ngati Maniapoto people, in return for the refuge he was given in the King Country in the 1870s. The carvings and other decorations were largely the work of Te Kooti's East Coast followers who were sharing his exile, which is why many of them are painted, a style that was not indigenous to the area. In addition to traditional features the house has an oil lamp hanging from the ridge pole. Bracken and flax mat bedding is piled against the far wall. The building was opened in about 1872 and was later moved from its original site to be close to the railway in the present township of Te Kuiti.

This group is believed to have photographed near Auckland in the 1880s. Although the house is built largely from traditional materials, it shows European influences which were to become pervasive through Maori communities. It is higher than earlier Maori houses, allowing ample room for passing through the entrance and standing upright inside. It has a hinged door, a glassed window at head height and a brick chimney, which allowed indoor fires without smoking up the interior, and which eventually led to cooking inside what had previously been sleeping houses only. This style of whare was to become a standard one in many Maori settlements by the turn of the century.

Some chiefs, especially those whom the Government wished to cultivate, were given large houses virtually indistinguishable from the homes of wealthy Europeans. One such was the Ngati Maniapoto leader Wahanui Huatare, pictured here in 1885 with his family on the verandah of his home at Alexandra. The house was built by the Government in return for Wahanui's eventual cooperation in securing the opening of the King Country for the Main Trunk Railway.

A juxtaposition of traditional Maori and conventional European housing was for a long time a feature of Whakarewarewa, the Maori village on the site of what became the city of Rotorua. This view looking towards Lake Rotorua and Mokoia Island was probably taken in the late nineteenth century.

The major reason that the Tuhourangi hapu of Te Arawa settled at Whakarewarewa was to make use of the natural steam and boiling water for cooking and bathing. These women are heating a variety of kettles and billies and the one at left has lowered a flax basket of meat or vegetables into the boiling pool. Such sights helped to attract tourists to the area from the 1870s.

Arawa women were also highly skilled at making finely woven and decorated flax mats for floor coverings in houses and meeting houses. These women pose with samples of their craft made for the meeting house Rauru.

This family group was photographed at a Wanganui River settlement in the early years of the twentieth century. The house is of traditional design and materials. Cooking utensils stand in the foreground, in front of the fire, and the woman in the centre stands behind drying tobacco leaves. Housing styles in this district and in the Urewera adapted more slowly to European influences than elsewhere, because of difficulties of access and consequent isolation.

Utapu Pa, also on the Wanganui River, at the turn of the century. A European style building (possibly a church) stands in the middle of the settlement, behind the house at centre. The ruggedness of much of the interior of the North Island meant that horses such as those shown here were welcomed by Maoris as an alternative to travelling on foot or by canoe.

Elderly Maoris tended to resist changes to their lifestyle, a fact many Europeans mistook for poverty and degeneration. Mata Kukae was over 100 when this photograph was taken at her home at Taumutu in the South Island in 1898. She was a member of the Ngati Moki hapu of Ngai Tahu. Her house was made from loosely bound reeds and she had a sacking door. Her clothes here appear to have been made from sacking and canvas. Like many women of her time she enjoyed smoking a pipe. She was one of the last survivors of Te Rauparaha's siege of Kaiapohia in 1832, and she died eight months after this picture was taken.

A well-made raupo house at Maketu in the early 1900s with the by now popular entrance and verandah extending from a side wall. The photograph illustrates much of the clutter of family and domestic life including a nursing baby, a dog, a cat, two buckets and a large tub.

The availability of pit-sawn timber and corrugated iron were changing the appearance and improving the durability of Maori buildings in many places from the late nineteenth century. This meeting house, Tauwhare at Galatea, incorporates both. The extended family here may have assembled for a tekaumarua (twelfth of the month, the Ringatu Church holy day when adherents gathered for 24 hours of prayer and fasting). The bell under the right gable was used to summon worshippers to services. The man third from right has a flax floor mat wrapped around him in rather ungainly fashion, an attempt to signify his chieftainship for the photograph. It is also noteworthy that there are eight dogs in the picture, a further indication of the popularity of domestic animals.

Two other groups of early pit-sawn Maori
dwellings, the first in the King Country, the
second in Hawke's Bay.

These girls collecting wild bamboo were
photographed somewhere south of Auckland at
the turn of the century.

Foraging for food was followed by communal distribution back at the kainga. Here Te Pokiha of Koriniti divides an eel catch among the families of the Wanganui River settlement.

An unidentified view of the preparation of hangi food, taken about 1905.

A Ngai Tahu family with Pakeha visitors outside their thatched cob cottage near the mouth of the Waitaki River in 1900.

A slab whare with chimney and a bark roof, King Country, early 1900s.

This cottage near Wellington in the 1890s combined Maori and European materials: verandah, raupo walls, corrugated iron roof, brick chimney.

Whakarewarewa in the 1890s.

The hot pools at Whakarewarewa were a source
of cleanliness and of unending recreation for the
inhabitants of the village. They were also a
continuing source of interest to photographers.
This group in the 1890s includes Guide Sophia,
the woman at left with a pipe.

Other styles of bathing: conspicuously modest costumes used for swimming in Lake Rotorua around 1910; and a group on the Wairarapa coast identified as Willy Nepe and family of Waipawa, a Ngati Kahungunu community.

A paling house with a a thatched muka roof, a kind common in the Hokianga district in the early 1900s.

Men making rope from flax, location not identified, early 1900s.

A Tuhoe family cooking in the Urewera, 1920s. Many such homes were isolated in heavy bush and had undergone few changes since the late nineteenth century. Most were self-reliant for meat and vegetables, growing what they needed. Commodities such as tea, flour and sugar had to be packed in by horse. The house is punga walled and thatched with nikau.

Another Tuhoe woman, photographed at about the same time, weaving a cloak. The incidence of skills such as this declined sharply throughout the twentieth century as traditional teaching systems broke down and incentives for wearing traditional costume diminished. From the mid-nineteenth century the use of cloaks had been primarily ceremonial — to indicate rank on public occasions and to place over the coffins of rangatira at tangis.

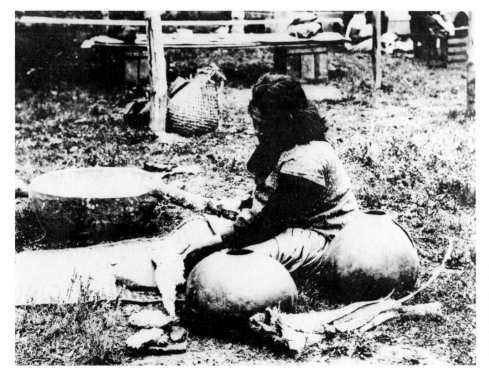

This photograph taken at Koriniti on the Wanganui River in 1921 reveals the survival of some earlier Maori technology. The woman is pounding bark for eventual use in basket making. The containers at right are gourds, which could be used for carrying liquid and storing food, such as pigeons preserved in fat. The large bowl is made of wood.

The same woman plaits a large patterned flax mat outside the meeting house at Koriniti.

A whare near Mangatangi in Waikato in the 1920s. Dwellings such as this were not isolated from European influences and technology the way that Wanganui and Urewera settlements had been, nor were they the outcome of a conscious choice to retain a Maori lifestyle. They illustrated the poverty and hopelessness in which many landless Maoris lived up until the election of the first Labour Government in 1935.

A Hawke's Bay family group, 1929. During the Depression of the late 1920s and early 1930s unemployment benefits were initially not given to Maori workers in circumstances such as these because, it was alleged, they could live 'off the land' in a manner that the Pakeha unemployed could not. It was also at about this time that the Health Department began to face up to the fact that poor Maori health was related to crowded and insanitary living conditions. From the mid-1930s the department made concerted efforts to eliminate dwellings such as this one.

Preparation of a hangi at Te Whaiti in the Urewera.

Cooking in camp ovens near Rotorua.

People living near thermal areas, such as these Whakarewarewa women in 1928, made use of naturally heated water for washing clothes.

For the majority of Maoris the production of hot water for washing clothes or bathing was a laborious process. This Ngati Tuwharetoa woman near Lake Taupo boils it on an open fire in kerosene tins and then carries it to a large tub.

These Northland women sort and grade burnt fern roots from peat swamps, for use as charcoal in cooking and heating.

To save limited public funds during the Depression, Te Puea Herangi of Waikato mixed traditional materials with European ones when she built houses for workers on Maori land development schemes in the early 1930s. She is pictured outside one such house in 1934, at Tikitere near Rotorua, with a visiting Australian newspaper proprietor and his wife. This house and all the others in the schemes under Te Puea's supervision were built by Maori workers.

An 'average Maori home' in the 1930s, according to the New Zealand Labour Party, which used this unidentified print as evidence in the formation of its Maori policies. This cottage housed a husband and wife and five small children. It was typical of many rural districts, such as Northland. There was no running water, no heating and no toilet facilities of any kind. Labour, recognising the extent to which such conditions contributed to ill-health, and especially to highly contagious diseases such as tuberculosis and typhoid, instituted a crash programme in Maori housing and had brought about some noticeable improvements by the late 1940s.

There were also districts in which Maoris had no housing difficulties and lived in residences outwardly identical to those of Pakehas (although decoration — especially the range of living room photographs and Maori ornaments — and the enactment of Maori rituals such as mihis means that the interiors of such homes could be distinctively Maori). Here the Hadfield family pose outside their home in Tuahiwi near Kaiapoi in the early 1920s.

Another South Island couple whose home, furnishings and clothing were little different from those of their Pakeha neighbours: Tini Te Uki and her husband Pai Te Uki, photographed at Kaiapoi. The book she holds is *The Young Carthaginian* by George Alfred Henty (1832-1902), a writer of popular historical novels, including one about New Zealand called *Maori and Settler: a Story of the New Zealand War*.

Transport

Prior to the introduction of the horse by Europeans in the nineteenth century, canoes provided the major means of transport throughout New Zealand. Connecting rivers and lakes were used in a system not unlike the later network of roads. Coastal transport too was made possible by these vessels. In some areas, such as on the Wanganui and Waikato Rivers and the Rotorua lakes, canoe transport remained commonplace into the early 1900s. This view shows the craft and crew which carried Alfred Burton up the Wanganui in 1885. They were lent by the kupapa chief Major Kemp. Burton wrote: 'The pair of oars we had were only used in the lower part of the river before the rapids were reached. Each man has his paddle and also his pole. These latter are made of manuka, shod with metal, and are from 10ft to 12ft long.' The photograph was taken near Ranana.

Taheretikitiki was built and carved for Paora Tuhaere, the Ngati Whatua chief at Orakei who died in 1892. After his death the tribe gave the vessel to King Mahuta, and it was used frequently in the late 1890s and early 1900s to ferry visitors from Huntly Railway Station on the east bank of the Waikato River to Waahi Pa on the west. Waahi was then the headquarters of the King Movement. It was also used ceremonially with the crew peforming manoeuvres and saluting with paddles, to demonstrate Waikato's unsurpassed prowess in rivercraft. The pulley system in the background was a means of ferrying goods across the river to the Waahi landing.

These canoes pictured on Mokoia Island on Lake Rotorua in about 1905 were probably the last in New Zealand to rely on traditional-type sails. They were used for transport to and from Ohinemutu, and from other Arawa settlements around the lake.

More canoes photographed at about the same time on the shore of Lake Taupo.

protected. 12. 8. 02.

South Island Maoris had an additional form of river and lake transport, and one they had evolved for themselves: mokihi or canoes made from reeds. The additional bouyancy and flexibility of these craft made them especially suitable for running or fording the fast boulder-strewn Canterbury rivers. Similar craft had been used by the Chatham Islands Moriori. This one went on display at Temuka in 1902, as Maoris from the Arowhenua Pa mounted a float to celebrate the coronation of King Edward VII.

Coastal tribes were involved heavily in sea transport, especially on the East Coast of the North Island where some Ngati Porou hapu operated their own trading vessels between Gisborne and Auckland. An absence of roads in this part of the country also meant that the sea was the major means of bringing in supplies and shipping out agricultural produce, especially wool. This photograph was taken at Waipiro Bay in about 1910. The group in the foreground has been fishing, while further out a larger boat brings in stores from the schooner at anchor.

Many of the landing places on the East Coast were little more than jetties attached to indentations caused by river mouths. The ruggedness of such coastlines, and their potential danger in bad weather, can be seen from this photograph of a boat which has just put off from Port Awanui during World War One.

Passengers on a Port Awanui schooner, probably travelling to Gisborne in about 1917.

Taare Bradshaw of Bluff was one of the best-known Maori sea captains in the South Island. He was a trader, fisherman and oysterman for over 50 years. He is seen here (left) at the helm of *Brittania*, a vessel from which he fished commercially in Foveaux Strait and Fiordland. He is ferrying a Dr Moorhouse of the National Acclimatisation Society to Fiordland in about 1922, to assess the condition of the Wapiti herd there.

Maoris took to horse riding with relish and skill once the animals became generally available in the mid-nineteenth century. They were in demand as a means of transport, to haul heavy loads, and as a source of recreation. From the late nineteenth century Maori race meetings were a feature of rural community life and were especially well attended in Waikato, the Manawatu and the Chatham Islands. These girls line up for the start of a race at Reporoa in about 1905.

The extent of Maori reliance on horse-drawn transport by the late nineteenth century is apparent from the large number of buggies drawn up for this hui at Pakirikiri near Gisborne in 1894. Waikato Maoris travelled in convoys of such vehicles for their round of poukais.

Collecting firewood was a major daily chore for households dependent on wood fuel for cooking and heating. This couple use a horse and cart for the job at Waikanae Beach near Gisborne in 1897.

One of the earliest attempts at action photography in New Zealand, this picture shows a Ngati Tuwharetoa party setting off for a wedding from Tokaanu on the shore of Lake Taupo in 1909. The cart carrying passengers has just swerved to one side of the road, causing them to grimace and clutch one another.

Motorbikes, especially the large and powerful American varieties, also found favour among Maoris using rural roads, from the early 1920s. This group used their machine to reach work at a mill near Matawaia in Northland in the late 1920s.

Maoris generally could not afford cars prior to World War Two. But leaders such as Te Puea Herangi and Apirana Ngata were able to fulfil an enormous number of engagements and supervise a wide range of activities because of the increased speed and mobility the motor car brought them. In this sense it was a factor in consolidating their claims to regional and national leadership. Te Puea, for example, was able to organise four land development schemes in Waikato and Rotorua, and to continue extending facilities and activities at Turangawaewae marae in Ngaruawahia. She had little difficulty doing these things simultaneously because her car enabled her to reach all these places in the 1930s without difficulty. She is seen here in 1929 at the wheel of her first car with (from left) Papi Pokaia, one of her adopted children, her husband Tumokai Katipa, and her niece Tungia Te Ao.

Huis

In this early picture of a Maori gathering, a family assembles on the marae area in front of their wharepuni or meeting house to receive visitors. Such guests will be welcomed formally on the marae, fed from the separate kauta at left, and later possibly bedded down in the meeting house. This photograph was taken at Maketu in the 1880s and is of special interest because it shows but one section of a much larger pa, and emphasises the fact that each whanau or extended family there had its own marae.

Visitors going on to another marae at about the same period, possibly at one of the Wanganui River communities. Here hosts and guests pause with bowed heads to tangi for the dead on both sides, a ceremony that always precedes mihis (speeches of welcome). The fact that the host women have greenery in their hair makes it likely that the gathering is a tangi. The tangata whenua stand to the right-hand side of their meeting house. Such positioning could vary according to the kawa or etiquette of particular tribal areas.

Tangata whenua at Waahi Pa near Huntly in the mid-1890s stand to welcome visitors in front of King Mahuta's meeting house. Two hold greenstone patu as an expression of the mana and antiquity of tribal associations. This would have been the kind of view that greeted visitors walking on to a marae at this time.

An unidentified kaumatua addresses a hui in the course of mihis at another nineteenth century hui. The tokotoko (stick) on which he leans would have served not only to support him but also to emphasise words and gestures as he spoke. An accomplished speaker on such an occasion moved about and gesticulated a great deal. As is customary, the rest of the visitors sit while a speaker is on his feet.

Among the experiments in inter-tribal cooperation in the late nineteenth century were a series of well attended huis at a Maori 'Parliament' at Pakirikiri near Gisborne. Such meetings required catering on a vast scale, including the construction of large and well-ventilated kauta, such as this one built in 1894. Firewood is piled up at right in preparation for cooking and hangi stones have been heaped up at left.

It was customary for visitors to late nineteenth and early twentieth century huis to bring food as part of their koha or gift to the host tribe. The more guests brought, in fact, the more mana they acquired. This gave a competitive quality to the presentation, and such contributions would be piled high on the marae for all to see. These gifts at a hui in about 1900 include sacks of potatoes, biscuits and pigs.

Action songs were a popular part of the entertainment generated at huis. These women poi dancers perform at Puniho in Taranaki in the 1880s, their white feathers identifying them as followers of Te Whiti O Rongomai. Both Te Whiti and Tohu Kakahi of Parihaka made extensive use of poi song words and actions to illustrate and spread their spiritual teachings.

The male contribution to action song would be the haka. In the days of tribal warfare it had helped to condition warriors physically and psychologically for fighting. In later years it became a ritual means of personal and tribal assertion of identity. It was done frequently as a part of hui welcoming ceremonies, especially by hosts. This group performs at the opening of a church in the late nineteenth century, somewhere near Gisborne.

These women, more Ati Awa followers of Te Whiti, perform poi at a hui near Wellington in the mid-1890s.

Preparations for a major hui at Waahi Pa in 1909. Here food is being organised on a large scale. The pile of wood at left will be used for hangi and surface cooking fires. At centre left is a huge pile of potatoes and a group of women peeling them. The cooking area itself is at right, with pits ready for the hangi and (behind them) pots cooking on fires.

Food being distributed outside Uenuku meeting house, Maketu, at a hui in the early 1900s.

Members of a food line at another hui at about the same time perform for the camera. The use of enamel plates and mugs is widespread by this time, the former replacing the kono or plaited food container in many districts.

Another photograph from the Maketu gathering, early 1900s. The group wears 'hui clothes' characteristic at the time for Maoris who had access to cash incomes. The large number of dogs in evidence was also a feature of such meetings.

Large-scale huis required accomodation for large numbers of people. Major marae had therefore to be well equipped with sleeping facilities, especially bedding to keep visitors warm at night in meeting houses. Here women of Putiki marae on the Wanganui River air blankets, cloaks and quilts in preparation for a gathering in the early 1900s.

European technology was harnessed in a variety of ways to meet specifically Maori needs, and hence to strengthen Maori practices and institutions. Here a traction engine heats water for cooking and washing at a hui at Manutuke in 1913.

Gisborne Maoris, with luggage for a lengthy stay, arrive at Waiomatatini marae on the East Coast in 1917 for a hui to raise funds for Maori troops enlisted in World War One. Proportionately, the Ngati Porou people of the coast made the largest manpower contribution to the Pioneer Battalion.

Tupaea, a Tuhoe chief, leads his women out of the Porourangi meeting house and on to the marae at the same hui.

Most maraes, including Waiomatatini in 1917, did not have permanent dining rooms large enough to cater for guests at huis. So they erected marquees and laid tables elaborately underneath them.

Fresh and locally grown fruit and vegetables ranked as hui delicacies. Here children eat maize and women melon at the Waiomatatini hui. The latter include Arihia Ngata (later Lady Ngata), Mrs Reweti Kohere and Mrs W. Pitt.

Food preparation was the other major task that fell largely to women (although men were likely to do much of the actual cooking, especially managing the hangi). These women peel thousands of potatoes at Turangawaewae marae in 1938 prior to the hui at which Turongo House was opened and Princess Te Puea Herangi presented with a CBE for services to the Waikato people.

Laying down a hangi at Otaki for the re-opening of Raukawa meeting house in March 1936. Potatoes, eels and fish heads have been placed in a flax mat over hot stones and will then be sealed off with a further flax mat and sacking and covered with earth to allow the food to steam cook.

Ngati Raukawa women at the same hui weave kono containers for food in preparation for the hakari or feast that will follow the opening of the house. Although most marae had ample supplies of crockery by this time, kono were often used to hold food for unusually large gatherings.

Visitors to a smaller hui near Stratford in Taranaki help themselves to food from a table. The tent and the placement of the table suggest that this marae did not have a permanent dining room.

Food laid out for guests at the same Stratford hui, next to airing bedding. It includes sandwiches, cakes, bananas and soft drinks. With the widespread availability of preserved items such as tinned fruit and soft drinks, specifically Maori food became a less dominant feature of huis in the twentieth century (especially at tangis, where catering often had to be done at short notice). But food such as rewena (Maori bread), kai moana and native pigeon remained the delicacies at hui meals.

Another group sitting down to eat outside at a hui in the early 1900s. By the 1920s most major marae were equipped with large dining rooms, and leaders such as Apirana Ngata encouraged the building of permanent kitchens and dining halls alongside meeting houses as standard marae facilities.

A rare photograph of a meeting house interior set up for a Christmas hakari. It was taken at Tane-Nui-A-Rangi house at Maungapohatu in the Urewera in 1927. Normally such eating would be done in dining rooms, tents or outdoors. Most tribes regarded the presence of cooked food in meeting houses as a serious breach of tapu.

Ngai Tahu Maoris gathered for a hui at
Rapaki Pa on Banks Peninsula, just prior
to World War One. While most of the group
are members of the Ngati Wheke hapu from
Rapaki itself, including four daughters of the
upoko runanga Teone Taare Tikao, others are
visitors from other South Island kaikas. It
was customary for a group photograph to be
taken to commemorate such occasions, and for
members of the group to adopt some Maori
costume if it was available. The girls with poi
had probably been performing.

A range of faces, expressions and clothing at a North Island church hui.

The Donnellys were one of the most important Hawke's Bay Maori families. George Donnelly, an Irishman, had in 1877 married Airini, daughter of the Ngati Kahungunu chief Karauria Pupu. They lived at the Otatara Homestead in Taradale. This picture showing the excitement of Maori welcoming rituals was taken as Ngati Kahungunu hosts receive visitors for the marriage of the Donnelly's daughter Maude in the early 1900s. The woman at front pukanas (rolls her eyes) and waves greenery, in this context a signal for visitors to come forward and be welcomed.

A panoramic view of a large and highly
organised Maori gathering. This was the
Turongo Hui, held at Turangawaewae marae in
Ngaruawahia in March 1938 for the opening of
Turongo House (at right). The photograph
shows Mahinarangi meeting house (left of
Turongo), the open marae for the performance
of ceremonials, a tent that extended the sleeping
accomodation and (at left) Kimikimi Hall, used
as a kitchen and dining room. The number of
visitors on this occasion was over 5 000, making
it one of the largest inter-tribal huis held up to
that time.

One of the most appealing features of huis for the participants was the opportunity to meet relatives and old friends, to make new friendships, to swap news and to perform and watch others perform (and in Maori situations 'performance' could range from whaikorero, to waiata, to action song and to animated conversation). These kuia moko (tattooed women) are taking part in a hui at Turangawaewae in the 1940s. The black dresses were customary for women of their age to wear on most North Island marae.

In addition to tangis, weddings were a common justification for large Maori gatherings from the late 1890s. Most rangatira families organised church weddings with all the Pakeha trappings of ceremonial in addition to the specifically Maori ones. This photograph was taken at Waikawa near Picton in the 1890s. It shows the wedding of Matiu Love, member of a leading Ati Awa family and descendant of the early Taranaki whaler John Love.

This Ngai Tahu wedding took place at Tuahiwi near Kaiapoi in the 1920s. The bride and groom are not identified. But Henare Uru, Member of Parliament for Southern Maori, stands at left.

A Ngati Rangitane wedding in the 1930s. Here Helen Kuiti marries Wi Edwards at Mata-pounamu near Ohau in the Manawatu.

Tangihanga

Death was a far more frequent feature of Maori life than it was of Pakeha life in the nineteenth and early twentieth centuries. This was largely because Polynesians had been isolated from the continent of Asia for some 6 000 years. They had no immunity from continental diseases such as influenza, whooping cough, measles and smallpox. As a consequence such diseases spread in epidemic proportions when they reached New Zealand through European contact, and decimated the populations of some Maori communities. The institution of the tangihanga, which continued very little changed from the nineteenth to the twentieth centuries, ensured that the dead were usually displayed for public and private mourning to a far greater extent than Western culture allowed. This man laid out at Waahi Pa, Huntly, is a victim of the 1913 smallpox epidemic. According to official statistics this outbreak affected 2 000 Maoris and caused the deaths of 55. But the Auckland District Health Officer believed the reported figures represented only about one quarter of the total cases.

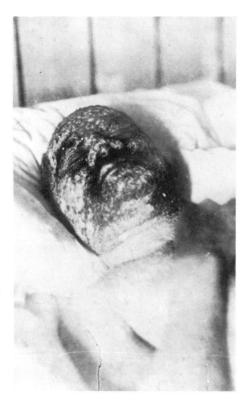

Typhoid was another killer in Maori communities, and was spread through poor sanitation and frequent contamination of food at huis and tangis. This camp isolates victims of a 1924 epidemic in the Urewera and is set up alongside the Presbyterian mission station at Maungapohatu. In the nineteenth century public health authorities had virtually ignored such outbreaks. More effort was made to mitigate their effects in the twentieth century, though nursing facilities in the early years were most often provided by Maori community leaders such as Te Puea, or by missionaries such as the Rev. John Laughton (whose father is at left here). Three children died in this outbreak.

Epidemics meant that Maori communities frequently mourned the deaths of several of their members at a time. During the influenza epidemic in November 1918, for example, 50 out of a total of 200 inhabitants died at Mangatawhiri Pa in Waikato. They were farewelled and buried at the rate of half-a-dozen a day. The bodies of these women — apparently a mother and daughter — are laid out together on a Hokianga marae in the 1890s. It is customary for the northern tribes to place their dead inside meeting houses and halls for the duration of mourning rather than outside, as is the case with other tribes.

One of the earliest tangi photographs taken, near Opotiki in the 1880s. The manuka and raupo shelter has been especially built for the tupapaku (corpse) and the immediate mourners, a custom some tribes retained in the belief that it would avoid spiritual contamination of homes and meeting houses. The body lies on an improvised bed, with flax mats beneath. The head is adorned with plumes, which in this case are peacock feathers (not traditional decoration, but one that found enormous favour in some areas in the late nineteenth century because of their size and bright colours). The woman at right has green leaves in her hair, an indication of mourning that spread throughout the country in the nineteenth century and was retained in the twentieth.

135

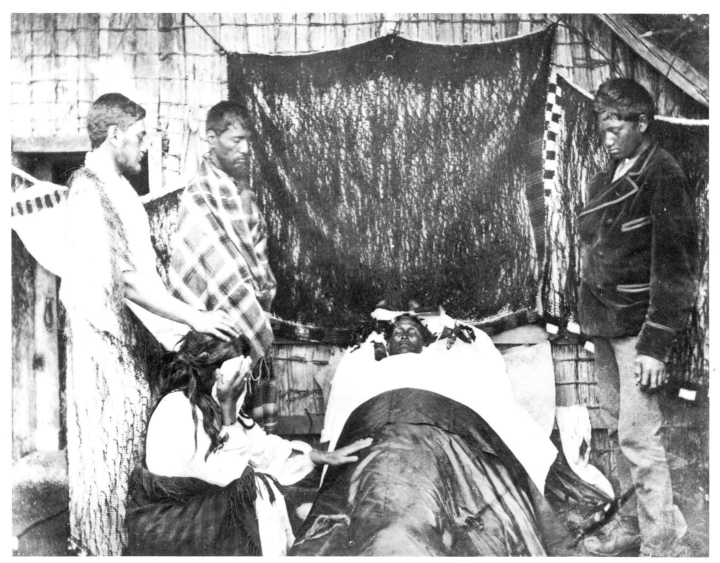

A slightly later tangi, held on a meeting house porch. By this time reasonably formal European attire (at right) is accepted as appropriate for Maori functions, though this is complemented (at left) by the ceremonial wearing of a korowai cloak. Family or tribal cloaks are hung behind the coffin, as is a patu (right of the doorway). The display of such taonga or treasures was regarded as an indication of the mana of the family or hapu, and a visible demonstration of their connection with the past.

Children were sometimes given tangis every bit as elaborate as those for adults, especially children of rangatira families (though the number of non-hapu members attending was likely to be fewer than at those for adults who had led accomplished public lives). This one is at Hokianga in the late 1890s. A watch and fob chain are placed on the coffin in the manner of more traditional heirlooms, such as mere and tikis. For this photograph the coffin has been carried outside the meeting house.

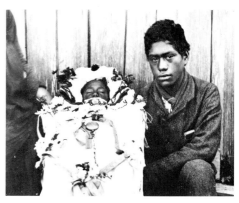

Photographs begin to appear at tangis in the 1890s, to recall the presence of the tupapaku and of relatives who have died previously. This one was held at Hotunui meeting house at Parawai, close to Thames. The hosts are members of the Ngati Maru tribe and are grouped to the right of the house. Manuhiri or visitors (most of them Pakeha in this instance) stand to the left. Fine mats are displayed on the meeting house porch along with the photographs, and the coffin lies to the right, the traditional position for it according to the protocol of most tribes. The female mourners have leaves woven around their hats as well as in their hair. Hotunui was carved at Whakatane between 1875 and 1878, and presented to Ngati Maru in May 1878 to commemorate an inter-tribal marriage. The house was given to Auckland Museum in 1929.

Visitors from Taranaki advance on to Arawa Park in Rotorua in June 1901, preceded by their own marae flag. At this time in this area men and women moved forward in one group. In later years the custom was to place women at the front. Both sexes have adopted formal European attire but many of the men wear cloaks to emphasise their importance or chiefly status. The sticks are for ceremonial use in oratory rather than for walking. The white feathers in hats indicate that the wearers are followers of the prophet Te Whiti, who was still alive at this time.

The funeral of Keke Mata Cowell at Awhitu, Manukau Heads, in October 1896. She was a Ngati Apakura who had lived at Rangiaowhia in central Waikato until it was sacked by Imperial troops in 1864. Following the government confiscation of her tribal land that year she took refuge with relatives at the southern head of Manukau Harbour. Here the coffin has been closed and sealed immediately prior to burial, a signal that the tangi has come to an end. All but one of the women present wear black dresses, a mourning custom that Maoris adopted from Europeans in the late nineteenth century and retained. The children are at ease close to the body, an indication of the informal manner in which they were allowed to be part of the proceedings.

A double funeral in the early 1900s at the Arahura marae between Greymouth and Hokitika. The Arahura Pa was the traditional headquarters of the Poutini Ngai Tahu people of the South Island. In earlier years they had been responsible for gathering and trading greenstone from the Arahura River, seen here. The deceased couple named Williams being carried to the hearse had died on the same day: the wife first and then the husband, who said he wanted to join her and simply lay down beside her and did so. Horse-drawn vehicles mingle here with early cars, and large numbers of mourners have left bicycles at the roadside.

A Ngati Mutunga burial at Big Bush in the Chatham Islands in about 1917. The death was that of a child of Ngatiki Te Aho Piripi. The Chathams Maoris at this time were a combination of Taranaki Maoris who had migrated there and slaughtered many of the Moriori inhabitants in the 1830s, and South Island and East Coast Maoris who had intermarried there. Ngatiki wears a black arm band.

Tribal relics and gifts on display at a South Island tangi, believed to be near Blenheim, in about 1910. These consist largely of korowai and feather cloaks, and mere and patu, the latter made mainly from greenstone and whalebone. Until the 1920s tahuaroa ceremonies frequently followed the burials of important chiefs. At these gifts would be displayed and ritually offered from one visiting tribe to the next, until actual distribution took place among leading figures of the visitors and hosts. Te Rangi Hiroa wrote of such a ceremony in 1921: '...the tahuaroa consisted entirely of cloaks of various kinds...The feather and tag cloaks...were hung over a line stretched between short stakes on the marae. They made a goodly show and both custom and material linked the changing present with the receding past.' The custom of burying relics with important chiefs also continued but with diminished frequency as supplies of tribal treasures likewise diminished.

Ngai Tahu women at a tangi at Moeraki pose with heirlooms brought for ceremonial display — again, mainly patu and cloaks. The clothing is varied. Some wear full mourning costume with black dresses and greenery in hair. Others are simply dressed formally. The wearing of black clothes at tangis was not as universally observed in the South Island as it was in most areas in the north.

Raukawa meeting house in Otaki at the time of Hema Te Ao's tangi in April 1932. The carved bargeboards at the front have been removed because the house was undergoing renovation. The Pakeha woman appears to have been placed by the photographer so as to conceal the coffin and the body, possibly at the request of relatives. The porch is well stacked with hanging mats, paintings and photographs, including one of King Tawhiao to whom the Ngati Raukawa chief was related through his Tainui genealogy. It was believed at the time that the building or restoration of a meeting house was always paid for with the loss of human life, and that Hema's death was the price for this one. The completed house was re-opened by King Koroki in 1936.

Hema Te Ao's funeral procession passes down the main street of Otaki. It was common for most mourners to follow the coffin from the scene of the tangi to the graveyard for the burial service, after which a hakari or feast would complete the ceremonies. Hema, son of an early Maori Member of Parliament, had an interesting connection with the Waikato Kahui Ariki or royal family. His son Tungia had married Hera Herangi, elder sister of Princess Te Puea. When Tungia died, Hema in turn married Hera, his own daughter-in-law. They separated when he became a follower of the prophet Ratana in the 1920s.

If a group of visiting mourners did not include suitably accomplished women, it was customary for men to call to the dead as they entered a marae. Here Wharepouri Te Poi performs this role at a tangi in Parihaka in about 1930. He was descended from a great Ati Awa fighting chief and was recognised as one of the leading rangatira in Taranaki. Parihaka at this time was losing its permanent residents and beginning to acquire an air of dereliction. But families associated with the pa returned regularly for huis and tangis.

A Maori funeral in North Auckland in 1931. The deceased was Penetana Te Tai, a Hokianga chief from Waihou. In the picture the body is laid at Waipuna marae at Panguru for part of the tangi, before being buried at Waihou. It was common in districts that contained a number of marae to take the body from one to another, allowing each hapu to pay its respects on its own ground. In this area, almost all Maoris were Catholics.

Preceded by a band, mourners follow a coffin to the cemetery at a funeral in Stratford. Brass bands became a prominent feature of Maori ceremonial in some areas, particularly Waikato and Taranaki, from the 1890s. They were especially in demand to play hymns at funeral services and march tunes for processions. In the main they played European band tunes and hymns, and occasionally modern Maori songs. The Ratana Church used brass bands from the 1920s as part of its political activities.

The tangi of Te Puea Herangi of Waikato in
October 1952 was the largest seen anywhere in
the country up to that time. More than 10 000
people attended over seven days before the body
was buried on Taupiri Mountain. For the
Waikato tribes this was an occasion for lavish
ceremonial displays. Her cloak-draped coffin is
surrounded by mourners, members of the Maori
Women's League at left and clergymen at right.
It was believed that such coverings not only
indicated the high rank of the deceased but also
kept her metaphorically warm with the mana of
the items. The porch of Mahinarangi meeting
house, built by Te Puea 23 years earlier, is also
draped with cloaks. Many of the women wear
greenery and floral tributes have been laid out in
front of the coffin.

Agriculture

The New Zealand Polynesians were experienced and sophisticated horticulturists before the arrival of Europeans in the country. Their major crop in the North Island was the kumara, a smaller variety than the far more popular Hawaiian type that was introduced in the nineteenth century. Others included taro, yam, gourd and paper mulberry. These pictures were contrived by early ethnologists to demonstrate pre-European methods of cultivation. The first shows Tuhoe Maoris at Ruatahuna in 1898 using the ko or digging stick. Like most other Maori activities affecting the survival of the hapu, digging, planting and harvesting were carried out communally. Only the man in the foreground, Paitini Tapeka, is wielding a genuine ko; the others use sticks. In the second a woman from the Wanganui district uses an adze-like hoe.

Much of the Maori labour force in the early 1900s was made up of sharecroppers available for hire by Pakeha farmers, many of whom were leasing Maori land. This group with plough, spade and dray is about to prepare the ground for planting. The picture is believed to have been taken on Mokoia Island in about 1910.

Harvesting for the hapu and kainga was still carried out communally in the twentieth century. These diggers work to a set rhythm called by the man with the raised stick at left (in much the same manner that a fugleman would direct canoe paddlers). The kumaras are being collected in kits, and the man at right brings a drink for the workers. The group is an Arawa hapu, photographed at Maketu in the early 1900s.

The common procedure was for men to do the heavy manual work such as digging, lifting and carrying, and for women to plant, weed and pick up crops. This group collects potatoes on a dug-over plantation in the King Country in the early 1900s. The woman at the back nurses her baby as she works.

Another early photograph from Maketu. The two men in the centre work a maize-shelling machine powered by the motion of the two horses at right. The cobs are brought over by cart, the bagged grain stands at right in sacks. The large structure behind was probably a whata kanga, a shed for drying the maize cobs.

A team of collared horses pulling a double furrow plough to harvest potatoes at Morven in the South Island in 1910. The horses' flanks have been shaved to reduce sweating.

Another view of potato harvesting at Morven after the crop has been collected and bagged. The workers, largely members of the Ngati Huirapa hapu of Ngai Tahu, appear to be posing with the property's owner or leaseholder. These people too would have been sharecroppers.

Unidentified Maoris workers prepare a hangi for sharecroppers during a pause in harvesting in the early 1900s. A traction engine stands in the background. These machines were commonly used for haulage, and as a power source for threshing.

Kumaras and potatoes were stored in dry underground shelters to prevent their deterioration. Here Mokena Pahoe of Waipiro Bay poses in about 1905 with a type of storage pit that became common throughout the North Island in the nineteenth century. Earlier rua or pits had been dug deeper in the ground, making the crops less accessible.

Maoris became heavily involved in shearing wool from the 1880s — initially in Hawke's Bay and on the East Coast of the North Island, and subsequently in rural districts throughout the country. This was yet another activity that could be carried on by family or hapu-based gangs. They also belonged to the Amalgamated Shearers Union of Australasia, which had copies of its rules printed in Maori in 1886. This was the first Maori association with organised trade unionism. The Maori gang shown here was photographed shearing at Rangatira in Poverty Bay in 1893. The tents were the shearers' quarters.

Another gang shearing in the Bay of Islands in about 1900.

East Coast Maoris also owned and raised large flocks of sheep from the late 1900s. These pictures were taken at a Ngati Porou saleyard near the present township of Ruatoria in the early 1900s.

Tobacco was another favourite Maori crop from the late nineteenth century. Maoris took up the custom of smoking with enthusiasm, initially with clay pipes introduced by the earliest whalers and traders and later with cigarettes. This girl stands in a field of tobacco at Jerusalem on the Wanganui River in 1921. Harvested leaves can be seen drying at back right. In some other areas, such as the Hokianga, Maoris attempted to grow tobacco for export at about this time, but such experiments were not successful.

In addition to pastoral and horticultural farming, Maoris became increasingly interested in dairying from the early 1900s, often as sharemilkers. From the late 1920s legislation introduced by Sir Apirana Ngata allowed more Maori owners to develop and farm their own land, and they were encouraged by Ngata to run cows. In addition to the cash income that such herds would provide, the availability of fresh milk was regarded as an important factor in improving the health of Maori children. This group helped on a Northland farm about 1910.

Foraging

Flax gathering remained a major source of
income and cultural activity for Maoris in the
early 1900s. Mills throughout the country still
bought the plant for processing into a variety of
products. And although they no longer made
clothes or thatched roofs from flax fibre, it was
still in demand for mats, baskets, piupius and
ceremonial cloaks. This family group is working
on the bank of the Whakatane River.

Drying flax at a seasonal camp on the Wanganui
River in 1921. It was common practice for
families to set up shelters for part of the year to
harvest and process wild crops, or to gather
food. These men have brought a live pig (bottom
left, next to its own shelter) for eventual use as
food.

Whitebaiting remained a favourite seasonal Maori pastime on North and South Island rivers. It was both an immediate source of food, and of cash income when sold to Pakeha commercial buyers. This photograph is believed to have been taken in the Bay of Plenty in the late nineteenth century. Corrugated iron adds to the effectiveness of a manuka windbreak. The whitebait trap is made from traditional woven material; by the early 1900s Pakeha-manufactured fine seine nets were in use. The kettle, billies and tin mugs indicate that meals were taken on the site.

South Island Maoris had a rich source of food for their own use and for exporting to other parts of the country. This was the muttonbird islands of the south-east coast and off Stewart Island. The birds, young petrels, were gathered from nesting burrows. Ngai Tahu families held hereditary rights to such harvesting and exercised them in April and May of each year. This woman cleans the oily birds, which have already had their down removed.

Sharks were regarded as prize catches in pre-European times. They contained an enormous quantity of food, some of which would be eaten fresh and the rest dried and stored for future use, especially for huis and tangis. Shark fat was made into an oil for rubbing on the body and for use in lamps. Shark catches were hardly less popular in later years, and dried shark remained a hui delicacy. This white pointer was caught in Bluff Harbour in the 1890s by the Ngai Tahu fisherman Taare Bradshaw (centre in cloth cap). Other Maoris in the picture include Rose Rendell (woman at left), Rose Bradshaw (centre) and Cissie Wheeler (right).

Eels were another constant and favourite source of food for Maoris, and one not restricted by season or geography. These members of the Tauwhare and Tainui families belonged to the Poutini Ngai Tahu tribe on the West Coast of the South Island. The eels have been taken from the Kokatahi River near Hokitika.

Of traditional Maori kai moana (seafood), shellfish was the most popular and the easiest to collect in some districts. Here (above) Manawatu Maoris gather pipi at the outlet of the Manawatu River near Foxton. In the second picture, taken at Waikawa Beach near the mouths of the Otaki and Ohau Rivers, collectors prepare tohimanga shellfish to send to Rotorua. The photographer, Leslie Adkin, noted: 'After removal of the shell, the fish is boiled, the intestinal part cut off and then placed in a flax kete ready to be dried. This food is exchanged for [piupiu] made by their Rotorua friends.'

For Maoris living inland, rivers and lakes which had been stocked with trout from the 1890s provided another source of fish, and one which had not been available in pre-European times. These children were responsible for this catch in the early 1900s, probably from the shore of Lake Taupo. In 1926, the Ngati Tuwharetoa people of this district conceded their rights to the bed of the lake and the streams running into it in return for annual payments from the Government. These payments financed the activities of the Tuwharetoa Trust Board, whose funds were used primarily to help with the education of members of the tribe.

These pictures of South Island Maoris catching
and preserving eels were taken at Little River on
Banks Peninsula, on the shore of Lake Forsyth,
in 1948. They show (top) gaffing the eels from a
baited inlet, (left) cleaning and boning the catch,
and (above) boning outside and drying the catch
on racks, a process known as pawhera. The man
and woman primarily involved are Hira Nutira
and Tiemi Whaitiri of the Ngati Irakehu hapu of
Ngai Tahu.

CHAPTER FOUR

Leadership

At the very time that prospects for Maori survival seemed bleakest, the seeds for racial and cultural recovery were already sown. By the 1890s the population decline had run its course. Maoris generally were acquiring immunity from the diseases that had earlier taken such shocking tolls, as a consequence of previous exposure and of marriage with Europeans. Fertility was improving; the birth rate was climbing; and although infant mortality rates remained high, more people were being born and more were surviving. The census of 1901 would show the first documented increase in the Maori population: from 42000 five years before to 45000.

Further, political consciousness was fermenting on marae all over the country in the last decade of the nineteenth century. There was talk of claims for land unjustly taken; of seeking redress under the Treaty of Waitangi; of petitioning the Crown to alleviate Maori grievances (two deputations had gone to Britain for this purpose in the 1880s, both unsuccessfully); and of experimenting with new political structures. Inter-tribal huis were being held on a wide scale to debate these and other issues. In the national Parliament a Maori member, James Carroll, was acquiring considerable influence within the ruling Liberal Party. And a group of young Maoris, sophisticated in things Maori and Pakeha, were completing their education and laying foundations for a new style of Maori leadership.

At the same time traditional modes of leadership persisted. In areas where hapu had not been broken up by mortality or alienation of land, hereditary rangatira families remained in effect community spokesmen. Families with ariki claims — the

Te Heuheus of Ngati Tuwharetoa, the Kahui Ariki in Waikato, the Taiaroas in the South Island — still threw up leaders who acted for federations of tribes. But patterns of leadership were changing. Increasingly the way was opening for men with acquired vocational or organisational skills, quick wits and eloquence to make bids for community and tribal leadership against or alongside those whose claim was purely hereditary. This was especially so in the case of the small number of Maori pupils who received primary and secondary education, or who trained for a church ministry.

Some among this breed of leaders were prepared to go further than mere lamentation of Maori grievances on Maori marae. They determined to use the system of government to obtain redress and to secure better living and working conditions for their people. In the South Island, such members of the Ngai Tahu tribe used adversity and a sense of injustice to regenerate tribal identity and spirit. Conditions on which they had sold much of their land — that reserves be put aside, hospitals and schools built and landmark boundaries be observed — had in many instances been ignored. Ngai Tahus with education and some familiarity with the European world exerted pressure on their rangatira and on tribal runanga (committees) to obtain compensation from the Government for these grievances. They formed (or re-formed) committees in South Island kaika, they sent organisers around these settlements (which, being scattered over the whole of the South Island, comprised one of the largest tribal territories in the world), they formed a parliamentary-type body to represent the entire tribe, and they besieged the national

159

Parliament with letters, petitions, deputations and other representations. They elected a succession of Members of Parliament for the specific purpose of promoting their claims.*

In Waikato, after failing to persuade the Government to set up a national Maori Parliament, the Maori King Tawhiao set up his own Kauhanganui at Mangakawa near Matamata in 1892. It too debated land claims, especially the question of compensation for the 360 000 Waikato hectares confiscated by the Government in the 1860s. A Kotahitanga or Maori unity movement originating in Northland picked up membership throughout the country, mainly from among traditional rangatira such as Te Heuheu Tukino, and held its own 'Maori Parliament' meetings from 1892 to 1902, latterly at Papawai marae in the Wairarapa under the leadership of Tamahau Mahupuku. All this was novel, in concept and in scale. It looked for a time as though tribalism was being submerged and a feeling resembling Maori nationalism stirring throughout the country. It did not persist, however. The Kingitanga Kauhanganui became increasingly a forum for the Ngati Haua tribe and was deserted by others, including the remainder of Waikato; and the Kotahitanga movement was defused by another which came to be called the Young Maori Party.

The Young Maori Party was not, strictly speaking, a party (some would go further and argue that it was neither young nor, in its origin and orientation, Maori). It was an association of professional men that grew out of the education most of them had received at Te Aute Anglican College in Hawke's Bay. In particular it was a product of the activities of pupils in the 1880s and of a Te Aute Old Boys Association in the 1890s. The group was initially known by the cumbersome and pretentious title of the Association For the Amelioration of the Condition of the Maori Race; later it came to be called the Te Aute Association; and later still the Young Maori Party. Its members had come under the commanding influence of the school's headmaster, the Rev. John Thornton, who believed that 'when a weaker nation lives side by side with a stronger one, the weaker, poorer and more ignorant one will die out if it does not emulate the stronger.' This was the ideal he inculcated into his Maori pupils: if the Maori people were to survive they would have to adopt the features of Western nations that had made the latter strong and pre-eminent throughout the world.

The more able and ambitious of Thornton's pupils left Te Aute in the 1880s and 1890s determined to improve the health, literacy and technological progress of the Maori people. They tried to do this at first by holding consciousness-raising meetings among themselves, at which they discussed papers with titles such as 'the decline of the Maori race: its causes and remedies'.

These were full of Christian fervour and read like sermons. The pupils themselves have been described as advocating the wholesale adoption of Pakeha culture and the scrapping of surviving elements of their own. 'To them Maori society was degraded, demoralised, irreligious, beset with antiquated, depressing and pernicious customs. Their task...was to reconstruct this society to make the race clean, industrious, sober and virtuous.'

While they were being educated they went out into Maori communities to preach their message of survival through social and religious reform. Some of them devoted school and university vacations to walking tours that took them to rural villages and marae. On one such trip in June 1889, Maui Pomare, Reweti Kohere and Timutimu Tawhai visited a dozen Hawke's Bay settlements over a month, led prayers, and lectured their elders on how to improve their spiritual welfare and material circumstances. All were still pupils at Te Aute at the time.

The most prominent members of the group were Apirana Turupa Ngata of Ngati Porou, Te Rangi Hiroa (Peter Buck) of Taranaki, Pomare of Te Ati Awa, Kohere and Tutere Wi Repa of Ngati Porou, Edward Pohua Ellison of Ngai Tahu and Frederick Bennett of Te Arawa, although Bennett did not attend Te Aute. Ngata was born in 1874 near Te Araroa on the East Coast of the North Island. He was brought up by an aunt, the wife of the kupapa chief Major Ropata Wahawaha. He was sent to Te Aute at the age of 10 and subsequently won a bursary that allowed him to study at Canterbury University College. In 1893 he became the first Maori to obtain a degree when he graduated B.A. He then moved to Auckland where he worked for a law firm and studied for an LL.B., which he gained in 1897. Committed by this time to a crusade to save the Maori people, Ngata became the full-time travelling secretary of the Young Maori Party. In particular he encouraged and supervised the setting up of Maori tribal committes under the Maori Councils Act of 1900, and he lobbied sympathetic Maori Members of Parliament, especially James Carroll. In 1905 he himself entered Parliament as Member for Eastern Maori, a seat he was to hold for the next 38 years.

The year of Peter Buck's birth is uncertain. It is thought to be 1877. He was the son of an Irish-born settler and a Taranaki Maori mother. Buck spent his early years at his birthplace, Urenui, and attended Te Aute from 1896 to 1898. From there he went on a scholarship to Otago University College and graduated M.B. and Ch.B. in 1904. He was a Native Health Officer from 1905 to 1909, and in 1909 was elected Member of Parliament for Northern Maori after the death of the former Kotahitanga proponent Hone Heke. The selection and support of a candidate from a tribe outside the electorate was an unprecedented gesture, an act of gratitude to the southern tribes for bringing Heke's body north from Wellington, and an acknowledgement of Buck's outstanding ability.

---

* The first instance of widespread Maori agitation resulting in the election of Members of Parliament for a particular purpose.

Buck sat in Cabinet as Minister Representing the Native Race in 1912. In 1914 he contested the Bay of Islands seat unsuccessfully and then enlisted in the Army. After distinguished war service he was appointed Director of Maori Hygiene in 1919. His interests from this time turned increasingly towards ethnology and anthropology, however, and in 1927 he resigned his Health Department post to work for the Bishop Museum in Hawaii. He later became director of the museum and held a chair in anthropology at Yale University. He made only two subsequent visits to New Zealand, and he was knighted in 1946.

Maui Pomare was also from Taranaki, being born north of New Plymouth in 1876 into a rangatira family. He attended Te Aute from 1889 to 1892. In 1893, influenced by a kitchen staff member at the college, he travelled to Michigan in the United States to attend a Seventh-day Adventist College, from which he graduated M.D. in 1899, becoming the first Maori doctor. He was appointed a Native Health Officer in 1901, under the Maori Councils Act, and held that position until he entered Parliament as Member for Western Maori in 1911. He served continuously as a Cabinet Minister from 1912 until the Reform Government went out of office in 1928, being responsible successively for the Cook Islands, Health and Internal Affairs. He died in the course of a visit to Los Angeles in 1930.

The initial spearheads for Young Maori Party policies were Buck and Pomare, particularly through their work as Native Health Officers. Both believed strongly that the Pakeha and Western culture were to be permanent features of New Zealand life, and that the most promising future for the Maori lay in progressive adoption of Western practices, institutions and technology. In particular they advocated health and hygiene measures to halt the population decline; literacy; and the extension of agricultural assistance to Maori land. They also called for a strong degree of individualism in Maori life and the adoption of the Protestant work ethic; and the abolition of what Pomare referred to as the 'pernicious' customs of tohungaism, the tangi and the hui.

Buck wrote in his annual report for 1906: 'The [Maori] communism of the past meant industry, training in arms, good physique, the keeping of the law, the sharing of the tribal burden, and the preservation of life. It was a factor in the evolution of the race. The communism of today means indolence, sloth, decay of racial vigour, the crushing of individual effort, the spreading of introduced infectious diseases, and the many evils that are petrifying the Maori and preventing his advance.' Pomare added: 'The Maori having been an active race and having always been kept in a state of excitement by wars and the rumour of wars, can now only find vent for his feelings on the racecourse, gambling and billiard-playing, with an occasional bout in the Land Court.'

Pomare and Buck also believe that Maoris had to introduce individual competition, amongst themselves and between themselves and Europeans. 'As long as [the Maori] can depend on his communist brother for a meal,' Pomare wrote, 'so long you will have him lazy.' Pomare's and Buck's own careers were to reflect this highly competitive, devil-take-the-hindmost view of life. It contrasted strongly with that of hapu and community cooperation held by traditionally oriented Maori leaders. Both began to feel that they were making insufficient progress in their work as medical officers, however; their clear, well-argued annual reports spoke of the same difficulties year after year. Both felt they were not supported by the Health Department and by Parliament as strongly as they should be, and both concluded they were more likely to bring about policy changes and a commitment of more public funds to Maori health from Parliament itself. Thus they accepted candidacies to join Ngata in the House of Representatives.

The approach of the Young Maori Party to Maori-Pakeha relations, and the approach of its members to Parliamentary tactics, had been pioneered a decade earlier by their mentor James Carroll. Carroll had been born in Wairoa in 1858, son of a Pakeha settler and a Ngati Kahungunu mother. He was sent to primary school in Napier, where he did not show particular aptitude. From the age of 12 he worked on his father's sheep station, then later joined the office of Native Affairs in Wellington, becoming a Native Land Court interpreter. From there he transferred to the job of interpreter in the House of Representatives, which gave him an intimate knowledge of parliamentary procedure and an enormous confidence in speaking publicly in both languages.

Carroll first stood for Parliament in 1883, but was defeated for the Eastern Maori seat by Wi Pere. He took the seat in 1887, however, and held it until 1894 when he transferred to the European electorate of Waiapu (later Gisborne). He thus became the first Maori to hold a European parliamentary seat. He was a member of the Liberal Cabinet from 1892 and Minister of Native Affairs from 1897. On several occasions he served as acting-Prime Minister, and he was knighted in 1911.

Carroll believed strongly that the most rewarding strategy for Maori parliamentarians was to compete with Pakehas on their own terms and, where possible, to beat them. This was the advice he gave to Young Maori Party members, especially Ngata, Pomare and Buck. He was popular in Pakeha circles: he never used his Maoriness to reproach his colleagues as some of his predecessors had done. He joined in social occasions with gusto, was a considerable drinker, delivered superb stories and impromptu speeches, and followed horse racing with an impressive knowledge of form and pedigree. His only handicap in the eyes of his colleagues were a propensity for falling asleep without warning and an alleged reluctance to exert himself.

Carroll frequently subordinated Maori considerations to the

policies of the Liberal Party to which he belonged, especially to the party's determination to acquire arable Maori land for European farming and to assimilate the Maori race and culture. He did this because he believed there was no future for Maoris separate from that of the Pakeha. When he drew attention to Maori needs it was usually by way of pointing them out as obstacles to be tactically circumvented. Although his tai hoa policy for a time delayed further large-scale acquisition of Maori land, and although he was genuinely sensitive to the difficulties of Maori landowners, he agreed fundamentally with the policies of Prime Minister Seddon and Lands Minister John McKenzie. He believed that the progressive opening up of Maori land for Pakeha leasehold would work to the advantage of Maori owners and Pakeha lessees.

In pursuit of these ends Carroll adopted the role of Maori troubleshooter for the Liberals. He was frequently sent to huis to contain and mollify Maori opinion; he was used to woo the Maori King Mahuta to accept seats on the Legislative and Executive Councils; he was also often assigned the task of humouring the Maori Members of Parliament. He was rewarded for these things by the trust of his Pakeha colleagues, with the portfolios of Native Affairs and acting-Prime Minister, and with his knighthood, the first given to a Maori. His famous injunction to Maoris to hold on to their Maori culture ('kia mau ki to koutou Maoritanga') came late in his career, after World War One, and in his eyes was more a celebration of the role of pageantry in Maori life than a serious proposal for the conservation of Maori values and institutions.

The Young Maori Party leaders emerged initially in the Carroll mould, and he was fond of referring to them as his 'young colts'. They admired his commanding presence, his oratory and his capacity for manipulation within the political party system. He encouraged them to follow careers similar to his own. Like him, they had to become national figures at a time when Maori stocks were low in Pakeha eyes and overt racism often rampant. In order to win acceptance for themselves as Maoris, they had to first win acceptance as men — and this in effect meant acceptance as Pakeha. Pomare stated this most baldly in 1906: 'There is no alternative but to become a pakeha.' They rejected many features of Maori life that were frowned upon by Europeans; they showed themselves not only as capable as Europeans in competitive situations but often more so. This was the impulse that drove them initially, and the parliamentarians succeeded both in their own and in Pakeha eyes.

Young Maori Party views were voiced at Maori meetings around the country from the 1890s, especially by Ngata in his role as travelling secretary. Its members also lobbied Members of Parliament. They convinced Carroll that unless some of the measures demanded by the Kotahitanga movement were adopted, then sitting Maori members would steadily lose support because of the apparent inability of the existing political system to deliver policies that met Maori needs. The major result of this and related submissions on Maori health and welfare was that the Liberal Government passed the Maori Councils Act in 1900. This proposed elected committees to supervise Maori community and tribal affairs with powers comparable to those exercised by Pakeha local authorities.

The tribal committees were expected to supervise sanitation and to suppress those customs that Young Maori Party leaders regarded as pernicious. It was hoped too that they would provide accurate information on births, deaths, marriages and population movements. General conferences were to bring together elected representatives from all over the country, thus doing under official auspices what the Kotahitanga movement had proposed unofficially. In this way the Liberals hoped to diffuse Kotahitanga support; and in this they succeeded. The structure provided by the act itself was not a success, however. The councils were embraced with temporary enthusiasm in some districts and ignored in others. Even in areas where they had met initially they eventually lapsed through a combination of lack of enduring local interest, unfamiliarity with Pakeha committee procedure and lack of commitment to inter-tribal cooperation. By 1910 most councils had ceased to function.

The Tohunga Suppression Act of 1907 was devised by Carroll and Ngata (by then in Parliament) to eradicate what they saw as charlatanism in Maori folk medicine, and to undercut the mana of prophets such as Rua Kenana in the Urewera and Hikapuhi of Te Arawa. Its intention was worthy. The rapid spread of Pakeha-introduced diseases and the profound anxieties they introduced into Maori life had spawned an army of amateur tohunga, untrained in esoteric rites and lore. Maoris suffering from illnesses such as influenza, measles and whooping cough sometimes died as a result of immersion in water by 'healers'. But this measure was a more conspicuous failure than the Maori Councils Act. Few prosecutions were brought under it, victims could not or would not give evidence, tohunga practices continued in all Maori districts and the act was eventually repealed in the 1960s.

Some historians and Maori leaders contributed to the view that the programmes and activities of the Young Maori Party were the major factors ensuring the survival of the Maori race and culture. Reweti Kohere, for example, said the party's efforts had 'turned the tide in the history of the Maori People'. That process of survival has even been referred to as a 'Maori Renaissance'. Certainly the Maori population did recover spectacularly from the nineteenth to the twentieth centuries. From the estimated low point of 42 113 in 1896 it rose to 45 549 in 1901, 56 987 in 1921, and increased steadily to more than a quarter of a million by the 1980s. The dying race whose pillow the Victorian liberals had sought to smooth had not merely recovered; it had taken up its bed and walked.

If the claims of the proponents of the Young Maori Party are to be accepted, however, it needs to be shown that the population recovery was a consequence of Young Maori Party activities. And this cannot be established. In his book *The Maori Population of New Zealand 1769-1971,* D. Ian Pool has demonstrated that the Maori birth rate towards the end of the nineteenth century was in fact not low. It was increasing even at a time when the population itself was still decreasing, because fertility was improving. What brought about a steady increase in life expectation from the early 1890s was a decline in the mortality rate. This was based on steady acquisition of immunity to diseases that had previously taken a heavy toll; and to the related reduction in the incidence of epidemics. It is not clear to what extent Pomare's and Buck's sanitation and vaccination programmes from 1900 arrested infection rates; nor what effects the erratic supervisory activities of some Maori councils had on their communities. Pomare reported proudly that by 1908 he had been responsible for the destruction of 1 057 substandard whare and the construction of 1 183 new ones and 839 latrines. As other observers such as Elsdon Best noted, however, the existence of such latrines did not mean that they were used; they were most often abandoned once the medical officer had moved on.

Undoubtedly, Buck and Pomare's activities had some influence on the reduction of the mortality rate, especially in checking the influence of typhoid in some areas. But the more significant causes of the Maori population recovery were an increase in fertility, the decline in epidemics, the related acquisition of immunity through exposure to disease and as a result of marriage with Europeans, and a consequent steady increase in the child-bearing age group. It has to be remembered that Buck and Pomare themselves were often disappointed at the lack of acceptance of their proposals at community level. Indeed, this lack of progress was a reason both cited for entering national politics. The population recovery only became fully apparent after they had become politicians. Their own efforts to assign cause and effect and credit to themselves for the 'renaissance' were largely retrospective exercises in propaganda.

In the field of literacy and education the Young Maori Party leaders made little impact. The models they represented were remote and unattainable for most Maoris of their time. Maori educational achievement beyond primary school remained minimal until after the election of the first Labour Government. Legislation that touched Maori life intimately — that relating to land development, income, social welfare, housing and the settlement of land claims — was not passed until Ngata's pre-eminence from the late 1920s and the formation of the Ratana-Labour alliance from the mid-1930s.

Young Maori Party leaders did not even succeed in communicating with their own people at community level. Buck noted that he was aware of speaking to them as a stranger. Outside their own electorates the Young Maori Party parliamentarians wielded little influence; even within them — with the exception of Ngata — their role was limited. In the two-cosmology view of life that many Maoris came to adopt in the twentieth century, parliamentarians were elected to deal with taha Pakeha, the Pakeha aspects of life, not taha Maori. Their experience of frequently being in an adversary role against community spokesmen from their own electorates (especially in the case of Pomare) and yet not necessarily being rejected by those electorates, was a reflection of this. The subsequent rapid spread of the Ratana Movement in the 1920s and 1930s was a mark of how little the Young Maori Leadership and programmes had touched Maori life, and how much the Maori electorates felt their political leaders had still to deliver.

There is a further antidote to the view that Maori affairs in the early twentieth century were dominated by the Young Maori Party. It is the fact that as the incidence of epidemics diminished and families and hapu regained some of their former dimensions and cohesion, Maori community life was far more vigorous than most Pakehas realised. And these communities were in most instances led by immensely able tribal or regional leaders whose qualifications were traditional, local and genealogical. For the most part these men and women were not acknowledged by Pakeha officialdom, nor were they known to Pakehas in general. Unlike the Young Maori Party leaders they did not receive acclamation and knighthoods. But they built up the resources of their communities steadily and regulated the intake of Western elements in a manner that strengthened Maori values and institutions.

They were people such as Eru Ihaka in the far north, Te Puea Herangi in Waikato, Mita Taupopoki of Te Arawa, Numia Kereru of Tuhoe, Te Hurinui Apanui of Ngati Awa, Mihi Kotukutuku of Whanau-a-Apanui, and Teone Taare Tikao of Ngai Tahu on Banks Peninsula. All these and others like them exercised the most effective and most enduring influence over Maori community life up to World War Two. They remained solidly and proudly tribal in orientation. They were able to represent their own local interests fairly and to harness community effort. From the 1930s, as a result of Ngata's initiatives in government, some were able to form symbiotic relationships with parliamentarians. There had to be Ngata-type figures in the House of Representatives, to take an overview of what was beneficial and to acquire sufficient expertise and mana to bend the Westminister-based system of legislation and administration towards Maori needs.

Tribalism, however, remained the most potent reality in

Maori rural life. To implement his later programmes for cultural and land development, Ngata needed strong allies at hapu and kainga level. Local leaders found that they in turn could strengthen their positions by tapping the resources that Ngata offered, without having to abandon their local power base in a manner that parliamentarians risked. In this way figures like Te Puea, Whina Cooper of Te Rarawa, Hone Heke Rankin of Ngapuhi, Taiporoutu Mitchell of Te Arawa, Rima Whakarua of Taranaki, Hoeroa Marumaru of Rangitikei and Te Kani Te Ua of Ngati Porou were able to increase their influence substantially, successfully supervise local land development and marae building programmes, stimulate community cultural activities and generally raise both standards of living and morale in their own territories. They were not necessarily popular among their own people — in some instances their very lack of popularity was a measure of their bullying success. Some of them such as Te Puea, Marumaru and Whina Cooper, would eventually become national figures in the process of extending their tribal work into wider fields.

The rise of Te Puea Herangi as a Waikato leader and ultimately a force in national Maori affairs is worthy of special consideration. She was born at Whatiwhatihoe in the King Country in 1883, a grand-daughter of the second Maori King Tawhiao. She achieved prominence within the Kingitanga when she led a campaign against Waikato Maori conscription in World War One. Her claims to leadership as a member of the Kahui Ariki were strengthened greatly by a sharp intellect, quick wits, a high degree of articulateness in Maori and a near-ruthless determination. All these qualities were in evidence when she established Turangawaewae marae at Ngaruawahia from 1921. In the late 1920s the coincidence of her need for further resources with Gordon Coates' and Ngata's plans for Maori cultural and agricultural development brought her into fruitful contact with the governmental and public service network. From this time she was a national Maori figure, Turangawaewae began to take on the character of a national marae, and Te Puea had access to additional resources with which to consolidate her objectives and heighten her mana at home. Ngata's land development scheme* was the most dramatic example of this process — it offered a means by which Waikato rural communities could subsist on their own territory and conserve their traditional living patterns. In association with this she developed a calendar of Kingitanga activities in the 1930s and 1940s.

Te Puea used a number of devices to consolidate and extend her programmes. Like other successful local leaders she was an innovator who appealed to precedent. It is difficult to judge the extent to which she chose this or to which the role assumed her.

What is apparent is that having decided on a course (moving to Ngaruawahia, building a new meeting house, re-establishing carving and rivercraft, returning to farming) she would always find justification in precedent and tradition, most often in the sayings of her grandfather Tawhiao. Even when breaking with tradition — by standing and speaking in public, for example, which Maori women did not do conventionally — she always made it clear that her own actions should not be taken as reason for discarding tradition. When she devised new programmes — such as raising money by concert tours or inviting political and public service participation in her hui to open Mahinarangi meeting house in 1929 — she cloaked them with traditional Maori activities so as to arouse, quite deliberately, nostalgic memories of past achievements.

While she was succeeding as an innovator appealing to tradition, her innovations themselves became precedents to which she could subsequently appeal to sustain the momentum of her reforms. Hence the Mahinarangi inter-tribal hui presaged and made easier the one to open Turongo House nine years later; and her makeshift hospital shelters and primitive attempts to cope with smallpox and influenza at Mangatawhiri anticipated and helped win acceptance for her fuller health and sanitation programmes in the 1930s and 1940s. She even succeeded in making Western education acceptable as a means of strengthening Maori ties rather than (as conservative Waikatos feared) weakening them.

Te Puea's natural aptitudes — in particular her perceptiveness about tactics and the quick-wittedness with which she wrong-footed rivals — were strengthened greatly by her unusual mastery of the arts of organisation and delegation. Her meticulous keeping of records of her activities ensured that she was always well-informed and often better armed than her adversaries. She knew instinctively when to persist in one tactical direction and when to alter course. She was adept at extending her own talents and compensating for skills she lacked by choosing lieutenants to act for her in specialised ways. Her use of Maori and Pakeha mediators made valuable inroads for her in both worlds to an extent she could not have achieved on her own. And at points where people were no longer useful or let her down she was rarely handicapped by sentiment; she simply discarded them.

The immediate consequences of Te Puea's leadership in Waikato can be judged by comparing the legacy she left with the conditions she inherited. She began tribal work in 1910 when Waikato people were largely fragmented and demoralised. In 40 years of relentless effort she found ways for them to return to a system of rural-based extended families, communal patterns of living, the influence of traditional leadership and a calendar of distinctively Maori cultural activities. In addition to these more general goals she was largely responsible for the considerable measure of Pakeha acceptance that the Kingitanga had won by

---

* See page 200.

164

the early 1950s, and she helped mitigate the pain of the land confiscation issue by persuading the Labour Government to pay some compensation to Tainui in 1946. She had also established a model pa and a system of Kingitanga organisation that would eventually survive her. She has been called the most influential woman in New Zealand's political history, and it is difficult to dispute this assessment.

Some Young Maori Party objectives did eventually come to fruition as a result of Ngata's long tenure of political office. In the 1920s he became a close friend and confidant of the Reform Government Prime Minister Gordon Coates, although they belonged to opposing parties (Ngata remained a Liberal until the party changed its name to United in 1928). Coates was Native Minister from 1921 and Ngata persuaded him to set up the Maori Purposes Fund Board to provide grants for Maori educational, social and cultural activities (the money came from unclaimed interest earned by Native Land Boards). Together they devised the Maori Arts and Crafts Act 1926 to set up a carving school in Rotorua and to encourage Maori art in general. They also collaborated in the establishment of the Board of Ethnological Research to finance the recording and investigation of Maori oral and material culture, and Ngata himself undertook a study of Maori waiata eventually published in three volumes, and with additional editorial work by Pei Te Hurinui Jones, as *Nga Moteatea*.

Once Ngata replaced Coates as Minister of Native Affairs after the change of government in 1928, the same kinds of measures continued with increased momentum. He made use of large huis — such as that organised by Te Puea for the opening of Mahinarangi meeting house in 1929 — for inter-tribal discussion on broad questions such as how Maoris could best share in the kinds of opportunities offered by Pakeha society and on specific topics such as social welfare, land development and the future of Maori language, arts and crafts. In this manner he was able to prepare people for his programmes, gauge reaction, and often shrewdly plant initiatives so that they appeared to come from the people rather than from the Government or the Department of Native Affairs.

The effect of Ngata's cultural policies, allied to his programmes for land development*, was a florescence of aspects of Maori culture. There was a sharpening and a strengthening of the arts of Maori oratory on marae throughout the country. Haka and action song were revived for competitive display at the inter-tribal huis. Maori sports meetings intensified competitiveness and strengthened hapu and tribal cohesion. New meeting houses and dining rooms were built in large numbers in the 1930s and 1940s, many of them carved impressively by pupils and graduates of the Rotorua Carving School, such as Pine Taiapa.

* See page 200.

Grants from the Board of Ethnological Research laid the foundations for Maori social and cultural research, particularly in association with the work of the Polynesian Society, of which Ngata was an enthusiastic member.

In alliance with Ngata and drawing from the resources which he made available, many tribal leaders began cultural revival programmes of their own. Te Puea, for example, established a carving school at Turangawaewae (after her leading carvers had been trained at Rotorua), built a series of meeting houses and other community facilities throughout Waikato and the King Country, revived the construction and ceremonial use of canoes, and composed waiata and action songs and trained her TPM concert party for performances throughout the North Island. The effect of all this, she noted, was 'to make Waikato a people again' — to enchance tribal identity and cohesion.

In the early years of the twentieth century there were reactions against both the elitism of the Young Maori Party and the conservatism of traditional Maori leadership. One was Rua Kenana's Wairua Tapu movement. Rua, a member of the Tamakaimoana hapu of the Tuhoe tribe, was born at Maungapohatu in the Urewera in 1869. His father had died some months earlier fighting alongside Te Kooti Rikirangi. After a series of visions in about 1904, Rua came to believe that he was the brother of Jesus Christ and also the leader that Te Kooti had prophesied would arise to succeed him in the leadership of the Ringatu Church. As a result of the visions he preached a Maori millenium: everlasting life for Maoris who would follow him; and eventual removal of Europeans from New Zealand soil. From 1905 Rua began to carve a 'New Jerusalem' out of the bush at Maungapohatu, one of the most rugged locations for a settlement in the country. Within three years he had attracted over 1000 Tuhoe, Ngati Awa and Whakatohea followers.

Like other Maori prophets before him, Rua was strongly influenced by the Old Testament, especially by the revelations of God to His chosen people. He identified the Maori people with the Israelites and interpreted scripture accordingly. He also sought complete economic, social and political independence from Pakeha officialdom, believing that the days of the Pakeha occupation of New Zealand were numbered. His community and his preaching were regarded with distaste and suspicion by most Europeans and by Maori leaders such as Carroll and Ngata. An opportunity to exert discouraging pressure on the prophet and his community came in 1911 when he was found to be supplying alcohol to his followers. Between 1911 and 1915 Rua was convicted several times of sly-grogging. When he refused to appear in Court on one of these charges police were sent to arrest him. Rua, misunderstanding the charges and believing he was being persecuted, declined to accompany the police and made provocative remarks about the Germans winning the war in which the country was then engaged. A charge of treason was then added to those relating to liquor and resisting arrest.

The climax came in April 1916 when a force of 70 armed police converged on Maungapohatu to arrest the prophet. In the confusion that followed their arrival shots were exchanged for half-an-hour, and when they ceased two Maoris were dead (including one of Rua's sons), three were wounded, and four policemen were injured. The ensuing trial was the longest in New Zealand's legal history to that time. Rua was sentenced to 12 months hard labour and 18 months reformative treatment. He was released after serving only nine months of these terms.

Rua never recovered completely from the loss of mana which resulted from arrest and imprisonment. His community disintegrated as most of his former followers returned to their previous homes and to the practices of the Ringatu Church (or to the Presbyterian Church, which had begun to evangelise in the Urewera about this time). Rua himself continued to lead a smaller group of Iharaia (Israelites) until his death at Matahi in 1937. The movement had been a further example of an attempt to find a Maori path to the Judaic-Christian God that excluded the Western trappings of European Christianity. It also represented an attempt to establish rangatiratanga or separate Maori government in New Zealand.

The movement founded by Tahupotiki Wiremu Ratana had different roots from those of the Young Maori Party and Rua's Wairua Tapu religion. It was neither elitist nor traditionalist in origin, although it did draw on Maori precedents for prophetic movements. It arose from the leadership vacuum that developed in some Maori communities in the early years of the twentieth century. On the one hand there were the Young Maori Party 'modernisers', working at parliamentary and public service level to try to improve the lot of Maoris nationally. At community level there were the local leaders operating according to traditional conditions and conventions. Increasingly, however, there was a group of Maoris who were not touched by either of these brands of leadership: people who lived in communities in which traditional leadership structures had fallen into disuse, or people who had moved to communities outside their own tribal territory. Many such Maoris were utterly unmoved by and uncomprehending of the kind of directions offered by the Young Maori Party. They were leaderless and yet seeking leadership, but of a kind that was Maori rather than tribal, and populist rather than elitist. And they found it in T. W. Ratana.

Ratana was a ploughman from the Rangitikei district south of Wanganui. He began his spiritual mission in November 1918 when he was 45 years old. He said subsequently that he was sitting on the verandah of his family home looking out to sea when a small cloud arose from the water and hovered over the house. From it Ratana heard the voice of God telling him that He had selected the Maori to be His chosen people, and that Ratana's mission was to unite them and turn them to God. In the wake of this experience Ratana prepared himself for this role. He read the Bible closely, and a book called *Health for the Maori* by J. H. Pope (which had been one of the texts most valued by members of the Young Maori Party). Then he began to preach the kotahitanga or essential unity of the Maori people and to practise faith healing, initially among his own family and then among a wider congregation. People began to visit him from all over the country as his reputation spread.

Unlike other Maori leaders of the time Ratana was not of rangatira status and did not have a recognisable hapu or tribal base; nor was he well educated in the Western sense; nor, even, especially charismatic. He was a man of ordinary appearance and mannerism driven by an extraordinary mission. Much of his success can be understood in the light of the social climate in which he preached, and from the fact that the Maori people at large were then reeling from the physical and psychological effects of the influenza epidemic, which took five times as many Maori lives as non-Maori.* Further, many Maori servicemen had returned from World War One impatient with the conservatism, the inertia and the technological backwardness of rural Maori communities. They sought leadership that offered material progress for Maoris.

Ratana provided leadership that met these diverse needs. From his reading of the Bible he offered an Old Testament explanation for the displacement and suffering of the Maori people as God's chosen race, and he promised deliverance from these tribulations. Although he was emphatically Maori in his use of language and metaphor, he rejected many traditional practices and values such as tribalism, tangihanga, tapu, tohungaism and carving. His faith-healing successes were so spectacular that a settlement grew around his house and came to be called Ratana Pa. The museum there took on the appearance of a New Zealand Lourdes as it filled with discarded crutches, wheelchairs and spectacles. Ratana, now called the Mangai by his followers, began to travel and carry his preaching and healing to all parts of the country. He had a special appeal to those he called the Morehu — the growing number of detribalised, non-chiefly common people, most of them subsistence farmers, farm labourers or rural town workers.

From 1922 the Ratana Movement that had formed around the Mangai became preoccupied increasingly with politics. It campaigned for statutory ratification of the Treaty of Waitangi as a panacea for Maori difficulties, and it circulated a petition (which eventually collected over 30 000 signatures) calling for this measure. When the Mangai's oldest son Tokouru contested Western Maori in the 1922 General Election, he astonished political observers by coming to within 800 votes (3037 to 3835)

* See page 200.

of unseating the experienced Pomare. Clearly the face of Maori affairs was changing; Ratana and his followers constituted a political force as well as a spiritual one. In 1928 Ratana declared the end of his spiritual mission and the beginning of his temporal one. He vowed to place his chosen representatives — the Four Quarters — into all four Maori parliamentary seats.

Support for the movement fell away nationally in the 1928 and 1931 General Elections. But Eruera Tirikatene took Southern Maori in a 1932 by-election. With the intensification of the Depression the Ratana bandwagon gathered momentum. Candidates made much of the fact that unemployment benefits for Maoris were lower than those for Europeans and far more difficult to obtain. They continued to use the Treaty of Waitangi as a symbol for Pakeha breaches of faith with Maoris. And they adopted American-style campaign techniques in the form of brass bands, rosettes and rallies.

The movement struck an informal alliance with the New Zealand Labour Party for the 1931 election. Ratana candidates, although nominally independent, would vote with labour if elected; Labour in turn would not put up official candidates against them. When Tirikatene took his seat in Parliament the following year he was escorted by the Labour whips. In the 1935 election he was joined by Tokouru Ratana in Western Maori. Labour, in becoming the Government with a landslide majority, increased its appeal in the eyes of the Ratana Movement. The Mangai visited the new Prime Minister Michael Joseph Savage and formalised the association between the two movements in a manner that was characteristic:

'Ratana . . . placed on the table before him four objects: a potato, a broken gold watch, a greenstone tiki and a huia feather. The Mangai explained their meaning. The potato was the ordinary Maori, needing his land. The watch was the law relating to the lands of the Maori. Only the machinery of the law could repair the law. The greenstone tiki stood for the traditions and mana of the Maori. And the huia feather, the sign of a paramount chief, would be worn by Mr Savage if he would look after his Maori people. The Prime Minister accepted the proposal. . . .'

Ratana electoral support gathered further momentum from this time. Paraire Paikea took Northern Maori in 1938. And in 1943 Tiaki Omana did what most observers believed was impossible: he toppled Ngata in Eastern Maori. The Ratana hegemony was now complete: the Four Quarters held the four Maori seats; the prophecy of the Mangai was fulfilled. And Labour was able to count on retaining those seats for the next 30 years. The alliance between the two movements was cemented by the policies of the Labour Government and by the continuing success of Ratana candidates at the polls, partly as a consequence of those policies.

Labour legislation introduced the secret ballot for Maori electors, equalised unemployment benefits and opportunities for housing finance, raised expenditure on Maori health and education, provided social security and the first Maori welfare officers, and addressed contentious land claims in the South Island and Waikato. These latter negotiations did much to consolidate support for Labour in the areas that benefited. It was not simply a matter of monetary gain; it was also a public acknowledgement that many of the Maori grievances from the nineteenth century had been justified. In addition, Maori workers shared in the resumption and expansion of post-Depression economic activity — more spectacularly than Pakehas in many instances because their previous plight had been more acute.

The result of these measures was that although Ratana Members of Parliament were less conspicuously able than some of their predecessors and their political opponents, they were nonetheless able to point to a body of legislation that had improved the material circumstances of the Maori people dramatically. As one Maori writer has noted, 'it was inevitable that Ratana MPs should present these developments as . . . a delivery of their election promises . . . Because these benefits persisted, the Ratana claim to have substantially lifted the Maori standard of living has been self-perpetuating and self-justifying.'

Leadership

Of the Maori religions established in the nineteenth century, the Ringatu Church of Te Kooti Rikirangi Te Turuki proved the most durable. Founded as a consequence of visions Te Kooti experienced while in prison on the Chatham Islands in 1866, the church was still a force in Maori life in the 1990s, especially in the Bay of Plenty, Urewera and East Coast districts of the North Island. Te Kooti himself was restricted in his movements after the New Zealand Wars. Exiled in the King County from 1872, he was pardoned by the Government in 1883. He spent most of his remaining years among his followers in the King Country and the Bay of Plenty. This meeting house at Te Karaka in Poverty Bay was one of a group built to commemorate the prophet's return there in 1889 (his own tribe, Rongowhakaata, was based in the district). The Government and police refused to allow the visit, however, in case it provoked retaliation from Maoris and settlers who had fought against him and this crowd waited in vain for his arrival. Te Kooti died at Ohiwa Harbour in 1893.

Henare Te Maire (sitting) was one of the last survivors of the Ngai Tahu heke up in the Waitaki Valley in 1877. This migration was led by the South Island Maori prophet Te Maiharoa, who wanted to conserve Maori values and to establish a community completely independent of Pakeha influence. He believed that the inland of the South Island had never been sold to Europeans and that it therefore remained Maori land. The settlement he established near Omarama was broken up the following year as a result of a combined police and army raid which came close to bloodshed. Te Maiharoa lived out his last years at settlements close to the mouth of the Waitaki River. This building at Waihao near Morven is a remnant of one of them.

PARIHAKA.   726.

Parihaka Pa in Taranaki represented another
Maori attempt in the late nineteenth century to
conserve Maoriness in the face of
Westernisation. Led by the prophets Te Whiti O
Rongomai and Tohu Kakahi, the community
was devastated by an Armed Constabulary raid
in 1881, led by the Native Minister John Bryce.
Hundreds of Parihaka men were arrested over
several years for occupying and ploughing
unused land that had been confiscated by the
Government in 1865 after the Taranaki War.
The pa was rebuilt and modernised in the late
1880s and 1890s.

Like Te Kooti, Te Whiti would not allow photographers to photograph him. He believed reproduction of his image would diminish his mauri, and that commercialisation of himself or his religious beliefs would be injurious. This is thought to be the only picture of him taken. According to the traditions of his Otakou followers, he was caught unaware while imprisoned in the South Island between 1881 and 1883. The photographer set up his equipment while Te Whiti slept in the sun and allegedly snapped the shutter as somebody else called to the prophet to wake him. The chair on which he was sitting and the hat he was wearing have been touched out of this print.

One of the tenets of Te Whiti's religion was that great emphasis should be given to manuhiritanga, the care of visitors. Here is his dining hall, Te Niho-o-Te-Atiawa, set elegantly in preparation for guests. The most important huis at Parihaka were held on the eighteenth day of each month, Te Whiti's holy day, and on 5 November each year to commemorate the invasion of the pa by Bryce's forces.

At his tangi in November 1907, Te Whiti's body lay in this tent in front of Te Raukura, the meeting house of his followers. His tomb, raised after the burial, included the inscription: 'He was a man who did great deeds in suppressing evil so that peace may reign as a means of salvation to all people on earth. His emblem, the white feather...signifies glory to God on high, peace on earth and goodwill to all mankind...' Te Whiti's lieutenant Tohu Kakahi, from whom he had become estranged, died only nine months before. Thus Parihaka lost both its leaders in the space of one year.

One of the last of the great rangatira of the nineteenth century. Wahanui Huatare was paramount chief of Ngati Maniapoto of the King Country when this photograph was taken at his house in Alexandra (later Pirongia) in 1885. He was a man of herculean proportions standing six feet six inches. Educated at the Wesleyan College in Auckland, he had originally been destined for the Methodist ministry. He became a leading supporter of the newly formed King Movement in 1858, however, and he fought against the Government in the war of 1863-64. By the 1880s he had supplanted Rewi Maniapoto as the principal leader of Ngati Maniapoto, with whom the Government was then negotiating for the opening of the King Country so as to allow the continuation of the Main Trunk Railway. Wahanui's house at Alexandra was built by the Government in part settlement of those negotiations. He died in 1897 at about the age of 70.

Patara Te Tuhi of Ngati Mahuta, photographed at Mangere in about 1908. Patara was the product of an arranged marriage between a son of Te Wherowhero and a niece of Hongi Hika. This union in 1824 settled the Waikato-Ngapuhi blood feuds, which had earlier led to savage fighting and thousands of casualties. He was educated at mission schools in Waikato and in 1863 was appointed editor of *Te Hokioi*, King Tawhiao's newspaper that was printed on the press given to two visiting Waikato chiefs by Archduke Maximilian of Austria. A gentle man, Patara was greatly upset by the outbreak of the Waikato War. He accompanied his cousin Tawhiao into internal exile, and in 1884 travelled with the King to England in an unsuccessful attempt to put Maori grievances before the British Government and the Crown. He settled on Waikato land at Mangere in the 1890s and in the early 1900s was the last fully tattooed Maori living near Auckland, which made him a favourite subject for the artist Charles Frederick Goldie. He died in 1910.

The last attempt by traditional Maori leaders to rectify Maori grievances with a direct appeal to the Crown was this mission to England in 1914. The members are the Maori King Te Rata (back centre), the Kingmaker and Maori 'Premier' Tupu Taingakawa (front), and secretaries Mita Karaka (left) and Hori Tiro Paora. They stayed in London hotels and outfitted themselves in the most expensive London suits for an audience with King George V and Queen Mary, arranged for them by the New Zealand High Commissioner, Sir Thomas Mackenzie. This was the first meeting between Maori royalty and a British monarch, and it was not to be repeated for another 40 years. A condition of the audience, however, was that nothing contentious was to be raised, including the Waikato plea for the return of land confiscated in 1865 that was the major reason for the visit. The delegation returned to New Zealand with nothing to show for their mission other than bills from a London lawyer for the preparation of an illuminated document on parchment entitled 'Maori Rights'. Tupu died in 1929, Te Rata in 1933.

Many Maori traditional leaders remained outside general Pakeha notice, and did not dress or behave in a manner that Europeans would have recognised as 'chiefly'. Nevertheless they were decisively influential figures in their own communities, among their families and hapu. One such rangatira was Te Whenua, chief of Te Anu hapu of Ngati Tawhakei and Ngati Rongo, which were themselves sub-tribes of Tuhoe. He poses for a visitor's camera in a traditional attitude of assertion outside Mataatua meeting house near Ruatahuna in 1930.

Maori representation in Parliament was established in 1867, initially to help balance the North-South Island distribution of seats (the general population was still larger in the South at that time but the bulk of the Maori population lived in the North). The first Members of Parliament tended to be nominees of the Native Minister and therefore pawns of the government of the day. Mete Kingi Terangi Paetahi of Wanganui, first member for Western Maori, was one of them. He was a kupapa chief who had supported government forces during the wars of the 1860s and who was rewarded subsequently with preferment. Nicknamed 'the General', Mete Kingi led kupapa Maoris against the Hauhau forces, even though many of his own people had joined the rebels. Later he was active in trying to break up Te Whiti's settlement at Parihaka. For such actions many of his fellow tribesmen regarded him as a turncoat. Successive settler governments thought highly of him, however, and he was a particular favourite of Native Minister Donald McLean. This photograph shows him spooning grapes in Dr A. C. Barker's garden in Christchurch in the course of an expenses-paid visit there in 1869.

A different style of parliamentary leadership was established by Hori Kerei (George Grey) Taiaroa. Taiaroa was a son of Te Matenga Taiaroa, leading chief of the Otakou Peninsula at the time of the European colonisation of Dunedin. He decided that his father and other Ngai Tahu chiefs had been out-manoeuvred in land negotiations with government purchasing officers, and he instigated the Ngai Tahi Claim for the full honouring of earlier agreements, particularly the clauses which guaranteed reserves for South Island Maoris. The prosecution of this claim took him twice into Parliament, from 1871 to 1878 and from 1881 to 1885, as anything but a friend of the Government. Two of his sons were star rugby players in the Otago, New Zealand Natives and New Zealand teams. He died in 1905.

Henare Kaihau, Member of Parliament for Western Maori from 1896 to 1911, was chief of the Ngati Teata of Waiuku. A brother-in-law of King Tawhiao, he was highly influential in the upper echelons of King Movement leadership. He entered Parliament as the personal nominee of King Mahuta, Tawhiao's son. Kaihau built himself a large homestead at Tahuna near Waiuku, where this photograph was taken with his daughters. His second wife Maerewa acquired fame in her own right as the composer of the internationally known Maori tune 'Now is the Hour'. By 1910 Kaihau had lost Kingitanga money in unsuccessful land speculation ventures and Mahuta switched his patronage to Maui Pomare of Taranaki, who won Western Maori the following year.

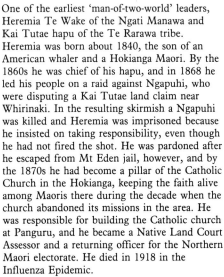

One of the earliest 'man-of-two-world' leaders, Heremia Te Wake of the Ngati Manawa and Kai Tutae hapu of the Te Rarawa tribe. Heremia was born about 1840, the son of an American whaler and a Hokianga Maori. By the 1860s he was chief of his hapu, and in 1868 he led his people on a raid against Ngapuhi, who were disputing a Kai Tutae land claim near Whirinaki. In the resulting skirmish a Ngapuhi was killed and Heremia was imprisoned because he insisted on taking responsibility, even though he had not fired the shot. He was pardoned after he escaped from Mt Eden jail, however, and by the 1870s he had become a pillar of the Catholic Church in the Hokianga, keeping the faith alive among Maoris there during the decade when the church abandoned its missions in the area. He was responsible for building the Catholic church at Panguru, and he became a Native Land Court Assessor and a returning officer for the Northern Maori electorate. He died in 1918 in the Influenza Epidemic.

Teone Taare Tikao of Rapaki was leader of the Banks Peninsula section of Ngai Tahu in the early years of the century and a major authority on South Island Maori tradition. He was born near Akaroa around 1850. In the closing decade of the nineteenth century he became totally committed to the concept of Kotahitanga or a supra-tribal Maori parliament, and he joined forces with Tamahau Mahupuku of Ngati Kahungunu to establish a meeting place for such an organisation at Papawai in the Wairarapa. When the Maori Federated Assembly met there in 1897, he was its first chairman. Tikao was the major claimant in the Ngai Tahu Claim, and he fathered a large family from two marriages, including five daughters from the second, who were all active in Banks Peninsula Maori affairs. He died in 1927.

A series of huis to discuss the disposal of Maori land in general and Waikato land in particular were held at Waahi Pa, headquarters of the King Movement, in the late 1890s and early 1900s. They were set up by James Carroll, who became Minister of Native Affairs in 1899. The major purpose was to persuade Maoris to accept the Liberal Government's policy of greater sale and lease of Maori land to Pakeha farmers on small units. Pictured at the first of these meetings in April 1898 are (front from left) Prime Minister Richard Seddon, Government Land Purchase Officer P. Sheridan, King Mahuta (holding the straw hat he liked to wear on such occasions), James Carroll and Resident Magistrate Gilbert Mair, who had remained involved in Maori affairs after leading the Flying Arawa Column in the New Zealand Wars.

The Ngai Tahu Claim which had been originally and unsuccessfully pressed in Parliament by H.K. Taiaroa was carried on in the early 1900s by a series of regional claim committees. These defined what settlement should be sought and (equally important) who the beneficiaries should be. In the course of this work they compiled one of the most comprehensive collections of genealogies in the country, under the supervision of the Native Land Court. This meeting of the combined claim committees at Tuahiwi in January 1925 sought to finalise the list of beneficiaries. The mounted block of greenstone in the foreground was presented to Robert Noble Jones, head of the Native Affairs Department and Chief Judge of the Native Land Court. He sits behind it next to Henare Uru, Member of Parliament for Southern Maori. The claim was still being prosecuted in the 1990s, after a lengthy Waitangi Tribunal hearing had found largely in Ngai Tahu's favour.

A Maori success story. James Carroll, a Ngati Kahungunu born in Wairoa in 1858, broke through many early barriers to Maori achievement. After election to the parliamentary seat of Eastern Maori in 1887, he became the first Maori to win a European seat, Waiapu, in 1894 (later Gisborne); the first Maori Minister of Native Affairs; the first Maori to be knighted, in 1911; and the first Maori to serve as acting-Prime Minister. His philosophy was to compete with Europeans on their own terms and to beat them. His example provided an inspiration and a blueprint for the later members of the Young Maori Party. Carroll is also credited with coining the expression 'Maoritanga' to describe Maori culture and identity. He is pictured here at home in Gisborne with his wife (centre). The Carrolls had no children of their own but adopted others. He died in 1926.

The Young Maori Party was a loose association of Western-educated Maoris who believed that the key to the survival of their people lay in the progressive adoption of European technology, sanitation, literacy and values. Most were products of Te Aute College in Hawke's Bay in the 1880s and 1890s. Here three of them, Timutimu Tawhai and Rewiti Kohere of Ngati Porou and Maui Pomare of Te Ati Awa relax in the course of a walking holiday through Hawke's Bay in June 1889. On this occasion the students visited maraes and lectured the inhabitants on the need to adopt Christian values, sobriety and sanitary habits.

The outstanding member of the Young Maori Party was Apirana Turupa Ngata of Ngati Porou. Also educated at Te Aute, Ngata was the first Maori to graduate from a New Zealand university. He gained a B.A. in 1893, an M.A. in 1894, an LL.B. in 1896, and subsequently an honorary doctorate. Ngata's political activities began as a full-time secretary for the Young Maori Party. His lobbying was responsible for the passing of the Maori Councils Act of 1900, and he was appointed to supervise the setting up of Maori committees under that act. He entered Parliament as Member for Eastern Maori in 1905 and held the seat continuously for the next 38 years.

Maui Pomare left Te Aute in 1892 and the following year travelled to Michigan in the United States, where he studied medicine at the Seventh Day Adventist College at Battle Creek. He emerged in 1899 as the first Maori doctor. Back in New Zealand he was appointed a Native Health Officer under the Maori Councils Act and spent the next 10 years attending to the health of Maori communities. In particular he vaccinated patients against contagious diseases and campaigned for the building of latrines. He entered Parliament as Member for Western Maori in 1911 and became a cabinet minister in 1912.

Te Rangi Hiroa or Peter Buck was another Taranaki Maori who studied at Te Aute. He left the college in 1898 and won a scholarship to Otago University College, where he too studied medicine. He graduated in 1904 and followed Pomare into the Native Health Service, practising mainly in Northland, South Auckland and Waikato. In 1909 he accompanied the body of Northern Maori Member of Parliament Hone Heke to Kaitaia for the tangi. There Heke's mother proposed that a chief from the south be nominated to take her son's place, and James Carroll put forward Buck's name. He was elected. In 1912 he sat briefly in Cabinet as Member Representing the Native Race, and in 1914 he decided on war service overseas in preference to another term in Parliament. This picture is reputed to show his acceptance of the parliamentary nomination in 1909.

The Maori Councils Act of 1900 promoted by Carroll and members of the Young Maori Party was not a success. The European committee structure it proposed did not transplant easily into Maori communities and districts, where competitiveness among hapu tended to be the dominant social feature. One committee which did meet regularly for a time, however, was the Takitimu Maori Council, seen here at the Poho-o-Rawiri meeting house in Gisborne in June 1902. Its members include representatives of rangatira families from the Poverty Bay and East Coast districts.

One reaction to the elitist and modernising style of leadership offered by the Young Maori Party was an advocacy by some other leaders of more traditional Maori lifestyles. Such a leader was Rua Kenana, who established a community away from direct Pakeha influence at Maungapohatu in the heart of the Urewera in the early 1900s. The passing of the Tohunga Suppression Act of 1907, sponsored by Carroll and Ngata, was in part aimed at restricting Rua's influence among other Maoris. Here Rua and some of his Tuhoe, Ngati Awa and Whakatohea followers meet Prime Minister Sir Joseph Ward at Whakatane Beach in March 1908. This gathering was called by Ward in an attempt to reconcile differences among the Tuhoe and to convince Rua of the Government's power. 'I told Rua,' Ward reported later, 'that in New Zealand King Edward is King, and is represented here by the Government. There can be no other Government or King...there can't be two suns shining in the sky at one time.'

A view of the settlement Rua carved out of the bush at Maungapohatu, taken in 1908. It accomodated up to 1 000 people at the peak of Rua's popularity. The double-gabled building at left is Rua's house Hiruharama Hou (New Jerusalem). At right is Hiona, Rua's round courthouse and meeting house, which was decorated with designs from playing cards. The dwellings between these were occupied by Rua's family and intimates, and the less substantial ones in the foreground by other followers.

Rua's arrest on 2 April 1916, after a shoot-out between his followers and a party of 70 armed police. He is handcuffed to his son Whatu. Other captives are handcuffed at left and right. One of them, Awa Horomona (second from right) has blood running down his face from a police baton wound. Two of Rua's followers were killed in the shooting including Toko, one of his sons, three were wounded, and four policemen were injured. As a result of this incident Rua was sentenced to 12 months hard labour after what was the longest trial in New Zealand's memory to that time. The community at Maungapohatu began to break up while he was serving his term and it was never fully re-established. Rua died at Matahi in 1937.

The prophet Tahupotiki Wiremu Ratana shortly after he began preaching and faith-healing in 1918. Ratana, a ploughman from the Rangitikei district, has been described as 'a man of ordinary appearance and mannerism driven by an extraordinary mission'. He believed that Maoris were the Chosen People of God, and that it was his task to unite them and rid them of sin and weakness, especially to eliminate what he regarded as debilitating traditional practices such as tangis and the observation of tapu. With these goals achieved, he told his followers, Maoris would gain control of their own destiny in their own country. Those followers called him the Mangai or mouthpiece of God. He died in 1939.

The Whare Maori at Ratana Pa near Wanganui, with dramatic evidence of the success of Ratana's faith-healing. It contains crutches, spectacles and wheelchairs discarded by people the Mangai cured. Pictures, cloaks, carved objects and other artifacts were placed there too because Ratana said they contained atua or spirits that were injurious to health. It is significant that such a museum was set up inside a carved meeting house. This symbolised Ratana's rejection of much Maori tradition.

In 1924 Ratana led a mission overseas, hoping to lay Maori grievances before King George V as King Te Rata and his party had tried to do 10 years before. It was symptomatic of an enduring faith in the fairness of the British Crown, even when trust of Pakeha governments in New Zealand had been exhausted. The problem was that protocol and political tacticians at home and in London prevented Maori submissions actually reaching the Crown. The Mangai had even less success than Te Rata, however, even though he was accompanied by Tupu Taingakawa who had organised the previous mission. The Ratana delegation did not manage to speak to anyone of any importance in England. Here three of its members pose for a London photographer, dressed in their visiting clothes: (from left) Tokouru Ratana, the Mangai's eldest son who was elected to Parliament in 1935, Tupu Taingakawa, and Te Rewiti, a Taranaki elder. During the visit Ratana is said to have prophesied the bombing of London in World War Two and the eventual election of a Labour Government in New Zealand.

The Ratana Movement took an active part in national politics from the late 1920s. The Mangai vowed to place four chosen followers — The Four Quarters — in the Maori seats. His organisers adopted flamboyant electioneering techniques reminiscent of American campaigns. Here Ratana publicises his presence in Taupo, for example, by flying one of his flags from his car. The movement had captured all four Maori seats by 1943.

The Maori King Movement led by Te Puea Herangi declared total opposition to the religious and political proselytising of the Ratana Movement, and a great deal of mutual hostility was expressed by spokesmen from both groups. There were moments of truce, however. Here Ratana leads his followers on to Waahi marae, Huntly, for the tangi of King Te Rata in October 1933. The Mangai had previously hoped to win the King over to his cause, and he made a determined but unsuccessful effort to convert Te Rata's successor, King Koroki.

While his Young Maori Party colleagues Ngata and Pomare gave themselves almost wholly to politics after World War One, albeit in different political parties, Peter Buck became progressively more interested in ethnology and anthropology. Although he was appointed Director of Maori Hygiene in the Health Department in 1919, he was frequently away from his duties for long periods collecting Maori traditions and information on the technology of Maori material culture. Here he places a fish-trap in a weir on the Waiapu River on the East Coast, having first helped to make the trap under the direction of a Ngati Porou elder. This passion for understanding and recording Polynesian culture was to take him away from New Zealand in 1927, when he went to work for the Bishop Museum in Hawaii. He subsequently became its director. He was knighted in 1946 and died in Honolulu in 1951.

Maui Pomare gloried in the trappings of office of a government minister. He held the portfolios of Health, Internal Affairs and Minister in Charge of the Cook Island in the Reform Government of 1912 to 1928. His geniality appealed greatly to Pakeha Members of Parliament, who knew him as 'Pom'. For his part in releasing further Maori land in Taranaki for Pakeha leasehold he was knighted in 1922. He was far more popular in Pakeha circles than in Maori ones, and came close to losing his seat to T. W. Ratana's son. He died while holidaying in California in 1930.

The colossus of Maoridom in the twentieth century was Apirana Ngata, seen here characteristically leading the haka at the opening of Waitangi meeting house in the Bay of Islands in 1940. Ngata devised schemes for the consolidation and development of Maori land, and he was able to put these into operation nationally after he became Minister of Native Affairs in 1928. Previously, in an unprecendented gesture of bi-partisan respect, his political opponents had arranged for his knighthood while he was still in opposition. Ngata resigned from Cabinet in 1934 after a Royal Commission had investigated his administration of the Department of Native Affairs. But he remained the dominant figure in Maori politics and culture until his death in 1950.

Ngata was a master at making politics the art of the possible. Realising that the development schemes would never take root without the active cooperation of community leaders, he invited such leaders from all over the North Island to observe the successful operations of the earlier development programmes. In this way he showed people rather than told them what could be done, and he invariably won them over. Such leaders then went home and launched and directed similar schemes in their own districts. This group of Northland, East Coast and Ngati Tuwharetoa chiefs was summoned by Ngata to Rotorua in July 1932, to inspect the schemes being carried on there by the Arawa tribe. It includes Whina Gilbert (later Cooper), front centre with dark hat, who was to lead Hokianga land development; left of her Hoani Te Heuheu, paramount chief of Ngati Tuwharetoa; and Ngata at left behind him.

Ngata's most valuable contribution to Maori life at community level was his legislation to allow loans for the development of Maori land. Previously Maori farmers and potential farmers had had no access to finance to improve land and bring it into production. Under Ngata's direction development schemes went into operation all over the North Island and enabled thousands of Maoris to derive a living from farming, especially dairying. These pictures show activities on one such scheme at Panguru, Hokianga, in the early 1930s. In one, workers take delivery of potatoes provided by the Government in part-payment for development work. And (below) a team of men pause in the course of clearing and ploughing a block in preparation for sowing grass.

Ngata's legislative programme also promoted cultural development. The Arts and Crafts Institute at Rotorua was designed to train carvers and craft workers. Ngata also organised a meeting house building programme throughout the country and provided assistance with finance for construction and carvers from the Rotorua school. Many of these community buildings were erected in association with land development schemes, a process Ngata described as 'putting back the mana'. At top the ridgepole goes up for the Porourangi meeting house at Waiomatatini on the East Coast in 1936, a job personally supervised by Ngata (it was his home marae). And (below) final work is carried out on Mahinarangi meeting house at Turangawaewae marae, Ngaruawahia, in 1929. Ngata helped raise funds for this building, directed the carvers, and provided workers to complete the decoration of the interior. The house became the focal point for subsequent King Movement functions.

Ngata's association with other Maori leaders also
extended their own programmes for Maori
recovery and cultural revival. He was especially
close to Te Puea Herangi of Waikato, seen here
at Turangawaewae (with white head scarf) in
1938, moving forward to accept her CBE from
the Governor-General for services to the Maori
people. Behind her stands the TPM concert
party in their distinctive long piupius and skirts.
Ngata sits in the foreground at left. Over the
previous decade he had persuaded Te Puea to
bring Waikato and the King Movement out of
isolation and into fruitful association with
government ministers and the Department of
Native Affairs.

Part of Te Puea's programme for making Waikato 'a people once again' was the re-establishment of traditions that linked them to a past of which they could be proud. In the nineteenth century they had been known above all else as a river people, and their rivercraft was both an important means of transport and a source of morale-boosting ceremonial displays. In the 1930s Te Puea sent workers into virgin bush near Lake Taupo to fell enormous totara trees and rough out hulls for new canoes (above). All this was done with the observance of traditional ritual. Then the hulls were brought to Turangawaewae for detailed work and assembled under the supervision of master carver Piri Poutapu (below, at left).

One of the three canoes Te Puea completed was *Te Winika*, restored from a vessel broken up by the Forest Ranger Gustavus von Tempsky on the lower Waikato River in 1863. Te Puea had it rescued and rebuilt, and had new carvings done for the prow, stern post and sides. The head at the front is a stylised representation of the Tainui fighting chief Te Rauparaha, carved by the singer Inia Te Wiata.

Te Puea also experimented with architecture. She had this house, Turongo, built for her nephew King Koroki at Turangawaewae in the 1930s. It blends Maori and European building styles and is decorated inside and out with the work of Waikato carvers. The pataka or storehouses in the roof contain Waikato taonga or tribal relics. Koroki declined to live permanently in the house, to Te Puea's disappointment, but it became the headquarters for Maori monarchs staying at Turangawaewae for ceremonial occasions.

The face of Maori politics changed considerably in the 1930s with the rise to power of the Labour Party and the alliance between Labour and Ratana. Here some of the major political figures come together at Waahi Marae for the funeral of King Te Rata in October 1933. They are (from left) Kepa Ehau of Te Arawa (interpreter); Gordon Coates, Prime Minister and Minister of Native Affairs in the Reform Government; Harry Holland, leader of the Labour Party; Frank Langstone, later acting-Minister of Native Affairs in the Labour Government; and Ngata, Minister of Native Affairs. Shortly after this photograph was taken Holland collapsed and died as a result of climbing Taupiri Mountain to observe Te Rata's burial. Waikato Maoris regarded this as an indication that Labour would win the subsequent election, because the life of the party's leader had been paid as a price for such a victory.

The first Labour Prime Minister and Native Affairs Minister Michael Joseph Savage meets the Maori King at the opening of Raukawa meeting house at Otaki in March 1936. Pei Te Hurinui Jones and King Koroki stand left of Savage, and Ngata is on the far right. Savage was ill with cancer at this time and most administration of the portfolio was done by the acting-minister, Langstone. He died in 1940 after having cemented an alliance with the Ratana Movement which ensured that Ratana Members of Parliament would vote with Labour when they were elected. Labour in return undertook not to put up candidates against them.

The first Ratana Member of Parliament was
Eruera Tirikatene of Ngai Tahu (left),
representing Southern Maori. Tirikatene came
within one vote of winning the seat in 1931, and
finally took it in a by-election in 1932. He is
seen here with Taranaki elder Rima Whakarua
and Akonga Mohi of Ngati Mihiroa. He was
joined in Parliament by Tokouru Ratana in
Western Maori in 1935, Paraire Paikea in
Northern Maori in 1938, and Tiaki Omana in
Ngata's Eastern Maori seat in 1943. Thus
Ratana members came to hold all four seats,
fulfilling a prophecy made by the Mangai in
1928. Tirikatene became a member of Cabinet
in the first and second Labour Governments. He
was knighted in 1960 and died in 1967,
succeeded in the seat by his daughter Whetu
Marama.

CHAPTER FIVE

Two Nations?

For the first half of the twentieth century the Maori population remained located largely where it had been in the late nineteenth century.* This meant that in effect there were two New Zealands, one Maori and one Pakeha. They were insulated from one another geographically, socially and culturally. As a consequence race relations were initially a far less dominant feature of New Zealand life in the twentieth century than they had been in the nineteenth: they were a less noticeable aspect of day-to-day life and they did not require (or receive) anything like the same degree of attention from the architects of government policies.

The reasons for this are not difficult to understand. In addition to the location of Maori population there was its size and its relationship to the population of the country as a whole. In 1850 there had been some 50 000 Maoris in a total population of less than 100 000. By 1857 Maoris still represented 48.6 percent of the total. At the same time a large number of them were armed and in effective control of large sections of the central North Island.

By 1901 the Maori population had dropped to about 45 000 and represented only 5.6 percent of the total — a percentage drop of more than 40 in 50 years. Even with the subsequent recovery in Maori numbers the proportion did not rise to more than eight percent. By the turn of the twentieth century, therefore, there were fewer Maoris than there had been previously; and they were to remain a far smaller percentage of the total population than they had been at mid-nineteenth century.

Further, Maori who had survived were not considered the threat — whether visible or latent — to European settlement and civilisation that some of their parents and grandparents had seemed to be. By 1900 they were no longer armed on a large scale. And, although they were largely in settlements remote from centres of Pakeha population, the Queen's law was established unequivocally throughout the country. At the slightest suggestion of Maori intransigence — at Waima in 1898 or at Maungapohatu in 1916, for example — the authorities moved swiftly to meet threatened force with greater force and to deter other would-be aggressors. When Rua Kenana was eventually tried on charges relating to seditious language and sly-grogging, the judge presiding made it clear that the real issue at stake was one of authority:

'You have learned that the law has a long arm, that it can reach you, however far back into the recesses of the forest you may travel, and that in every corner of the great Empire to which we belong the King's law can reach anyone who offends against him. That is the lesson that your people should learn from this trial.'**

There had also been a degree of Maori withdrawal from contact with Europeans. In 1900 the bulk of the Maori population of 45 000 lived in scattered rural communities that were Maori in composition and orientation. Some who had formerly seen a good deal of Pakeha and traded with them

---

* See page 76.

** 'Your people' and similar judicial references at this time seemed to suggest that when Pakehas were on trial it was as individuals; when Maoris were before the courts it was as representatives of their race. This too illustrated a gap between the two peoples.

extensively — such as Waikato and Bay of Plenty tribes — were seeing far less of them by 1900 in the still-bitter wake of defeat in war and land confiscations. The tendency throughout the country was for Maoris to get on with their lives in their own territories; and for non-Maoris to get on with theirs in other territories.

The general view of Pakeha officialdom in national and in local body administration was that it was better for Maoris to be living in rural districts than in towns; and that this location gave them an opportunity to live off the land and not be a drain on the public purse, and to practice aspects of their lifestyle (huis, tangis, Maori values) that Europeans found distasteful.

In fact, however, the rural distribution of the Maori population was not necessarily advantageous for Maoris themselves. The Maori work force in the early twentieth century could best be described as a rural proletariat, part of it land-owning but not land-using; part of it disinherited by alienation of land. Only on the East Coast of the North Island and in Northern Hawke's Bay was Maori farming carried on in an organised and sustained manner. And these operations had come about in part because sympathetic Pakehas such as the Williams family had been prepared to help finance such operations in the absence of government assistance. Few Maori individuals at this time could be described as wealthy in European terms. Those who could have been — rangatira families who held title to large tracts of land or who had leased or sold such land — had strong community and tribal demands made upon their monetary and other material resources. Aroha and mana gave status to distribution, not to accumulation.

Maori individuals and communities without land had lost it as a consequence of confiscation (Waikato, Bay of Plenty and Taranaki tribes); as a consequence of what was later deemed to be unfair purchase (the Ngai Tahu and Ngati Mamoe tribes of the South Island); or by the orthodox temptations of lease and sale. Even where they had inherited land interests, however, these were frequently uneconomic because that land was often marginal (which was why Pakeha purchasers had overlooked it in the first place); because it could not be brought into production without heavy capital investment; or because of the administrative divisions brought about by multiple ownership. Sometimes all three handicaps applied. And Maori farmers, unlike Pakeha farmers, were not eligible for assistance from public funds.

Maoris, then, were geographically, socially and administratively segregated from contact with Pakehas; and — in the case of non-rangatira who could not attend inter-tribal hui — from contact with Maoris from other districts and tribes. There was no social and cultural interaction between Maori and Pakeha on a wide scale. Such contact as there was, was limited largely to land dealings, and to the minimal effort of governmental authorities to implement policies on Maori health and

education.* These latter involved only a small number of Europeans and very little expenditure of public money.

With few exceptions, Europeans in New Zealand did not want to draw from the cultural and emotional reserves of Maori life. The only asset Maoris held that interested non-Maoris was land. And it was the continuing need to acquire Maori land by sale or lease for an expanding Pakeha population and agricultural economy that shaped most governmental policies towards Maoris.** Maoris for their part were forced to accept what they had not appreciated in 1850: that the European colonisation of New Zealand was permanent and irreversible. For many of them this was a source of trauma and depression, an additional reason to withhold themselves from non-Maori aspects of New Zealand life.

One way of charting the gulf between two people*** is to survey the writing by Europeans about Maoris from the turn of the century. Such literature tended to be either hostile or patronising. Expressions of hostility in newspaper articles and (especially) letters-to-the-editor were often undisguisedly racist and employed terms such as 'blacks' and 'niggers', and favoured such adjectives to describe Maoris as 'dirty', 'degraded', 'lazy' and 'immoral'. Articles and cartoons were sometimes almost xenophobic in their views of the Maori being Maori — as if such people had no right to live in a country colonised by Europeans. (Similar feelings were directed against other non-Anglo-Saxons such as Jews, Chinese and Dalmatians.) Coon humour, which portrayed Maoris as simpletons who were comic in their inability to cope with Western civilisation, was common on postcards, in newspaper cartoons and in photographic journals such as the *Auckland Weekly News*.****

The patronising writers were at least motivated for the most part by humanitarianism and compassion. Many of them had a *fin de siecle* interest in characters described in terms such as 'the last of the old type of better Maori'. The leading practitioner of this perception and style was historian and journalist James Cowan, who felt considerable regret about the extent to which Western intrusion in New Zealand had fragmented Maori culture.

According to this view, there had been much about the pre-European Maori that was noble and dignified. There had been

---

* See pages 200 to 201.

** See page 200.

*** It could be argued that Pakeha New Zealanders with their varied backgrounds did not constitute 'one people' at this time. For the most part, however, they were British; and they submerged minor differences in class, occupation and ethnic traditions to participate in a British political, legal and administrative system with a facility and willingness that Maoris could not match.

**** See page 3.

old world courtesies, codes of honour, psychic and spiritual perceptions, handsomeness and virility in 'pure-bred' chieftains and warriors and dusky beauty in maidens of similar pedigree. According also to this view, contact with Western things had tainted these qualities and manners. Throughout the nineteenth century Maoris had been in physical, cultural and moral decline as a consequence of abandoning old ways and of prolonged contact with alcohol and disease. Cowan tended to view his elderly informants as survivors from a pristine age, as men and women who exemplified the most worthy features of their culture that were destined for extinction. One of them, Hauauru of Araikotore near Kihikihi, he described in this manner:

'[He] is a picturesque figure who, in my memories of the past, personifies much of the departed savage glory of the Maori race. He typified the splendid dying manhood of his people. Born in the New Zealander's Stone Age, he survived to near the end of the miracle-working white man's nineteenth century, flotsam of the primitive world stranded on the shores of modern progress...A Homeric personality was that of this old cannibal warrior, a savage but a gentlemen, full of courteous friendly feeling for the whites whom he had once fought and bitterly hated, and full of the hospitable generosity of the true Maori *rangatira*...'

Such a view was limiting on several counts. First, it sentimentalised Maori life to the point of unreality. At whatever point writers chose to 'freeze' history there would always have been Maoris whom they regarded as 'good' and 'bad', courteous and discourteous, traditionalists and innovators, activists and idlers. Secondly it suggested that everything worthwhile about Maori life lay in the past and would soon be lost irretrievably. And thirdly it tended to blind observers to many of the fascinating and innovative phases of adaption that Maoris were experiencing in local communities in the early years of the twentieth century.

Again reflecting the conventions of his time, Cowan invested his Maori work with a mystique that was not present when he was writing about the same period of non-Maori history and experience. His information, he noted, had been gathered 'around the camp fire on summer nights on the shores of one or other of the beautiful lakes in the Rotorua country, in the Taranaki bush, in the settlements of the King Country and Taupo, in the houses of the Waikato canoe-men, in the bark-roofed *wharepunis* of the Urewera.' The italicisation of Maori words, a convention for the use of 'foreign' concepts and words, exemplified the extent to which Maori things were then viewed by Europeans as exotic in the land of their origin.

All this was undeniably well-intentioned. It did at least place some value on Maori perceptions and customs. It suggested Maoris displayed worthy qualities abandoned by rationalist, acquisitive and individualistic Western communities. And it suggested this at a time when racism was rife in some pockets of New Zealand life. Yet Cowan's views, with their gauze of romanticism, also served to place Maoris and Maori considerations into a kind of never-never land, safely beyond the political and social preoccupations of contemporary New Zealand life. According to such a vision Maoris would not be seen as claimants on the national purse and conscience, their social and economic difficulties would not be viewed as the responsibilities of the country as a whole. They receded to being merely a colourful element from New Zealand's past, surviving in the mountainous and rural hinterlands.

The imaginative equivalent of Cowan's writing was the fiction of authors such as Alfred Grace, William Satchell and F. O. V. Acheson. They depicted romantic Maori figures — noble heroes, beautiful and tragic heroines, unrequited love — through a haze of poetic imagery. These figures bore little relation to life and conditions in twentieth century Maori communities; and for the most part they made no distinctions between Maoris of different regions, tribes and hapu — distinctions that would have been crucial in Maori eyes and in fact.

From the 1930s more able writers (Frank Sargeson, Roderick Finlayson, Maurice Shadbolt and others) devised far more credible Maori characters and situations, and ones that were closer to the realities of Maori life. There were still elements of unconscious patronisation, however, 'the temptation...to find in the Maori virtues that are missing in the Pakeha and to use him as a criticism of Pakeha society.' There was also a continuation of stereotyping ('happy-go-lucky, lazy people, mostly not too bright...or the big-brown-eyes and little-bare-feet touch'), and severe difficulties in conveying Maori English. Fiction involving Maoris did not lose these elements of awkwardness nor reflect the variegated patterns of Maori experience until imaginative writers who were also Maori, most notably Witi Ihimaera, Patricia Grace and Keri Hulme, emerged in the 1970s.

In non-fiction, apart from the able ethnologists such as Elsdon Best and Peter Buck*, the earliest perceptive writers on Maori matters were the journalist Eric Ramsden, who made earnest and frequently successful attempts from the 1920s to interpret Maori preoccupations to non-Maori audiences and to Pakehas in authority; and I. L. G. Sutherland, New Zealand's first recognised social scientist. Sutherland and his successors Ernest Beaglehole and James Ritchie highlighted reasons for lack of Maori advancement in socio-economic terms as well as in cultural ones. With Ramsden, they deserve much of the credit for public discussion and policies in the 1940s and 1950s that were related towards Maori needs, while at the same time recognising the intrinsic worth of Maori ritual and values. Such

---

* Both of whom, like Cowan, tended to equate Maori adaptation to Western influences with pollution of a formerly pure stream of culture.

discussion eventually gave weight to the concept of New Zealand as a bi-cultural rather than a purely Anglo-Saxon society.

There was no comparable body of literature to mirror Maori views of Pakehas over the same period. But what has been published by way of reminiscence by writers such as Amiria Stirling and Reweti Kohere suggests that there was a Maori stereotype of the Pakeha as someone who was self-centred, materialist, acquisitive, unfeeling about his extended family and callous about his treatment of the dead. By highlighting and caricaturing European qualities distasteful in Maori eyes, Maori commentators such as Te Puea Herangi also communicated indirectly the qualities they valued most according to their own *mores*. And these too suggested a wide and a continuing cultural gap between most Maoris and most Pakehas.

Throughout the first half of the twentieth century there were a few aspects of wider New Zealand life in which Maoris sought to participate, and in which they were accepted by the Pakeha majority. The most notable (and noticeable) was warfare. Traditional Maori communities had, for the most part, placed high value on prowess in battle. This valuation persisted through the periods of the musket and the New Zealand Wars. After the 30-odd years of peace that followed the Te Kooti campaign, some Maoris actively sought opportunities to keep the warrior tradition alive. James Carroll believed it could be a factor that would restore vigour to languishing Maori communities. He himself had fought in the Te Kooti skirmishes and he was keen to lead a force of 300 Maoris to put down an apparent uprising in difficult terrain in Samoa in 1899. After the outbreak of the South African War that same year a large meeting at the Basin Reserve in Wellington, dominated by Tamahau Mahupuku, called on the Government to dispatch a Native Contingent to the war. Neither of these proposals were accepted. Up to 1914 the Imperial Government in London refused to allow the use of coloured colonials alongside or against white troops. A number of Maoris with European names succeeded in enlisting for the South African War in the New Zealand contingents, however, and they served with distinction.

With the outbreak of World War One 15 years later, the Imperial Government at first allowed recruitment of Maoris for garrison duties; and then, with the Gallipoli campaign, for combat. To Maori Members of Parliament, and to Pomare in particular, it was essential that Maoris show themselves to be the equals of Pakehas in recruitment and casualty rates. Only this, they believed, would prove that Maoris were worthy of equal consideration in civilian life. The members formed a recruitment committee and stumped the country to raise volunteers for what eventually became the Pioneer Battalion. Peter Buck sailed with the first contingent to Egypt. Once casualties began to occur in Gallipoli and later in France, the committee redoubled its efforts

to enlist reinforcements to obtain utu and to sustain the battalion's strength.

The campaign was not an unqualified success, however. Although some 2200 men volunteered for service (about 20 percent of the eligible group) and almost half this number became casualties, the committee found it extremely difficult to maintain the promised reinforcement quotas. Some tribes — Te Arawa, Ngati Porou, Ngai Tahu — contributed disproportionately well (they tended to be the kupapa ones). Others, such as Taranaki with a confiscation grievance, gave scarcely any men. Later drafts had to be swollen by Rarotongans and Niue Islanders, and even then they did not come up to strength. The Waikatos in Pomare's own electorate refused to enlist at all and were conscripted towards the end of the war as a punishment (conscription was not applied to Maoris in general).

The overall Maori contribution to the war effort, however, especially the combat record, had the effect sought by the Maori Members of Parliament. It showed the Maori to be, Pomare suggested, 'the peer of any man on earth', and it made it more difficult for the country's Pakeha leaders to argue in favour of excluding Maoris from full participation in national life. It also raised hopes among ex-Battalion members that conditions of wartime equality with Pakeha soldiers would continue into peacetime. They did not. Legislation forbidding Maoris to buy alcohol and excluding them from housing and farm development finance persisted after the war. Few Maori soldiers were eligible for rehabilitation assistance. These conditions were among those that drove many ex-servicemen into the ranks of the Ratana Movement.

The Maori response to World War Two was even more wholehearted and showed the extent to which the race had become more integrated into the national life in the intervening 25 years. Without conscription (which was again applied to Pakehas only) and with no organised opposition to recruitment, over 17000 Maoris enlisted for combat and 11500 took places in essential industries, many of the latter moving into towns from rural districts to do so. The Maori Battalion covered itself in glory as a combat unit in North Africa and Italy, and individual soldiers such as Victoria Cross winner Moananui-a-Kiwa Ngarimu and battalion commander Arapeta Awatere were regarded as heroes by all New Zealand troops.

At home the Maori contribution to the war was coordinated in the Maori War Effort Organisation, which was designed specifically to overcome some of the difficulties experienced in the previous war (remembered by Ngata, who was still in Parliament). It was officially recognised by the Government and the Member for Northern Maori, Paraire Paikea, was co-opted into Cabinet as Minister in Charge of the Maori War Effort. Under Paikea's direction and with the support of the other Maori members, the organisation appointed recruiting and liaison officers at tribal level. It also set up 407 tribal committees and 60 executives to encourage enlistment, to mobilise men and women for work in essential industries, to direct the growing of crops specifically needed for the war effort, to raise funds for the Red Cross and to collect comfort items for Maori prisoners of war and troops at the front.

The effect of both battalion service and the success of the Maori War Effort Organisation was to increase Maori consciousness over tribal feeling, and to enlarge Maori confidence. Maoris as a recognisably separate ethnic group with distinctive ways of organising themselves had contributed intertribally to a successful national effort. Again servicemen returned home expecting and this time demanding equality of treatment with their Pakeha compatriots, and this time they were far more successful in achieving it. Maori land development schemes were expanded significantly as a rehabilitation measure, and Maoris were also eligible for business loans, tools-of-trade loans, trade training and other educational assistance.

Throughout the period Maoris also attended Agricultural and Pastoral shows in districts where they lived in proximity to Pakeha farmers. They were especially keen to engage in sport amongst themselves, and against Pakeha individuals and teams. A and P show competitions (athletics, tug-of-war) were among the most popular; there were also horse racing, cycling, hockey, tennis, golf, basketball and river regattas.

But apart from warfare, the one national activity to which Maoris contributed in a meaure resembling their full potential was rugby football. The first Maoris to represent New Zealand overseas went on a tour of Britain and Australia in 1888-89 as the 'New Zealand Native Team'. Other tours followed from 1910. Within New Zealand there were Maori clubs, internal Maori tours, a Maori Advisory Board of the New Zealand Rugby Football Union from 1922, and from 1928 the country was divided into four Maori districts to compete annually for a trophy provided by the Prince of Wales.

Maoris were also welcomed into the country's national representative team, the All Blacks. Those who distinguished themselves — George Nepia, Lui Paewai, Ben Couch, Pat Walsh, Waka Nathan, Sid Going — acquired the status of national heroes during their playing days. In this sphere at least there was no reluctance to recognise or accept Maori talent, except in the case of tours of the other great rugby-playing nation South Africa. On such occasions Maori players were stood down, the first time being from a New Zealand Army Team in 1919. This created some ill-feeling throughout the country although not, apparently, among the Maori players themselves. The differences between New Zealand and South Africa were highlighted in 1921, however, when a Maori team played the Springboks at Napier. A South African journalist filed a report for his own paper that was intercepted and published by the local *Daily Telegraph*:

'. . .it was bad enough having to play a team officially designated New Zealand natives, but the spectacle of thousands of Europeans frantically cheering on a band of coloured men to defeat members of their own race was too much for the Springboks, who were frankly disgusted.'

When protests against such attitudes and against the participation of New Zealand players in a racially segregated system within South Africa were finally made, they came from the wider New Zealand community, not from rugby players or the New Zealand Rugby Union. Until 1960, however, the vast majority of New Zealanders continued to tolerate South African dictation of the racial composition of All Black teams to tour that country.

Participation in rugby within New Zealand did much to enhance a positive sense of Maoriness in Maori communities; and it offered one of the few occasions on which Pakehas could view a Maori activity that they understood and approved of wholeheartedly. The only other occasions on which Maoris were 'on display' to citizens who would not otherwise encounter them as a group were Royal Tours, and National Exhibitions such as those held in Christchurch in 1906, in Dunedin in 1925 and in Wellington for the centennial of British sovereignty in 1940.

The Royal Tours were those of the Duke and Duchess of Cornwall in 1901, the Prince of Wales in 1920, the Duke and Duchess of York in 1927 and the Duke of Gloucester in 1935. For all these visits Maoris were assembled at Rotorua for a single national welcome and display of loyalty and Maori culture. Most tribes went along with this arrangement, albeit with reservations. Many were scornful of the extent to which the Arawa hosts had oriented their Maori activities around the entertainment of tourists; some, such as successive leaders of the Kingitanga, boycotted the function on the ground that they wanted to welcome Royal visitors on their own territory, as Pakeha New Zealanders were able to do. Tour organisers believed that one Maori welcome was as much as Royal Personages could endure, and they were worried about the risks of food poisoning. Disagreements over such matters were always between Maoris and Pakeha officialdom, never with Royalty. Maori loyalty to the British Crown and its representatives was a constant feature of Maori-Pakeha relations up to the 1980s.

The National Exhibitions also highlighted Maori culture but — concentrating as they did on carving, costume and action songs — they did so in a manner that was nostalgic and decorative. They may have helped win acceptance of Maori material as pleasingly exotic elements from New Zealand's past. But, like the displays for tourists at Rotorua and the haka and action song performances of itinerant concert parties, they gave non-Maoris little indication of the nature and day-to-day strengths of Maori values for those who were committed to them.

The preoccupations of government policies relating to Maoris remained land, health and education; and by far the greatest of these was land. Between 1892 and 1911 the Liberal Government purchased a total of 1.2 million hectares of Maori land, leaving about 2.8 million hectares in Maori ownership. The Reform Government which came to office in 1912 was farmer-dominated and its two Native Affairs Ministers were also farmers: William Herries and Gordon Coates. Not surprisingly it too sought to continue the acquisition of Maori land and did so with the support of its sole Maori Member, Maui Pomare. Between 1912 and 1920 Maori holdings were further reduced from 2.8 million to 1.8 million hectares; and of that 1.8 million 310 800 were unsuitable for development and 300 000 were already leased to Pakeha farmers.

Throughout this period, as a member of the Opposition, Apirana Ngata worked virtually on his own to explore organisational and legislative measures that could surmount the difficulties of Maori land development and administration. With his own Ngati Porou people he evolved management of land by incorporated committees (of which the Mangatu Incorporation was later the most successful), and a system of consolidation that allowed exchanges of interests to group land blocks into economic holdings. These experiments were limited largely to the East Coast and the Urewera until the mid-1920s, when other tribes began to adopt them with the encouragement of the Native Land Court. By that time Ngati Porou owned nearly a quarter of a million sheep and had their own dairy company, a finance company and a cooperative store.

When Ngata became Native Affairs Minister in 1928 he was able to devise legislation to assist Maori farmers on a national basis for the first time. His Native Land Amendment and Native Claims Adjustment Act allowed the advance of public money for clearing and development work on Maori farms — up to three-fifths of the value of the property, allocated through local land boards. These loans were repaid from subsequent agricultural production. The schemes were operated largely by Maori labour under Maori leadership, and Ngata was assiduous about recruiting the talents and mana of energetic local leaders such as Te Puea Herangi and Taiporoutu Mitchell.

In 1934, Ngata's administration of his portfolio was investigated by a Royal Commission. This found him guilty of disregarding accepted channels of communication, of not adequately accounting for the expenditure of State funds, and of using State funds in the interest of his own family and tribe. None of these were criminal matters. But, unsupported by his colleagues and under fierce attack from the Labour Opposition, Ngata resigned from Cabinet. He never regained ministerial office. The land schemes themselves were regarded as being sufficiently successful to be carried on by subsequent administrations, however, and they remained a permanent feature of rural Maori life.

Throughout the period of Ngata's ministry New Zealand moved steadily into the grip of worldwide Depression. Maori rural workers began to suffer as Pakeha farmers and local bodies laid off their contract workers. In rural towns the small number of Maori salaried employees were the first to be displaced by staff reductions. There was a feeling in Government and among the public at large that, unlike Pakehas, Maoris could simply 'go home to the pa' for food and shelter. By 1933 they made up an estimated 40 percent of the total unemployed and they were paid lower benefits than non-Maoris.

The situation was relieved after the election of the Labour Government in 1935. One of its first measures was to abolish the unequal benefit rates; and the expansion of economic activity in the late 1930s brought a degree of temporary prosperity to many of the land development schemes and created additional employment in rural areas. Social Security greatly increased the spending power of extended families with its provision of additional income for children and for the aged. Labour modified earlier requirements that had made it difficult and frequently impossible for Maoris without adequate documentation of birth to secure child allowances and old-age pensions. A study in one district noted that, 'From the Maori [Social Security] has removed some of the fear of grinding poverty which has been...the major anxiety of their lives.'

Reports on health and sanitation in most areas of Maori population remained critical of conditions until well into the 1930s. This was an embarrassing blot on the record of a nation that claimed racial equality. The one major element of progress was that the incidence of the kinds of epidemics that had mown down the Maori population in the nineteenth century was kept low. The last major one was the Influenza Epidemic (the 'Great Flu') of 1918 in which at least 1 130 Maoris died, a rate 4.5 times greater than that for Europeans. The actual death rate for Maoris was higher, because figures were not collected in many communities. Peter Buck called it 'the severest setback the race has suffered since the days of Hongi Hika.'

In the 1930s tuberculosis, typhoid fever, dysentery, diarrhoeal and respiratory diseases persisted and were taking a disproportionate toll on Maori life. The Maori death rate per 1 000 people in 1938 was 24.31; that for non-Maoris 9.71. The Maori infant mortality rate was 153.26 per 1 000 live births as against 36.63 for others. No real progress was made in reducing these figures until the Labour Government drastically improved Maori housing in the 1930s and 1940s; and until Maori health was made the responsibility of the Health Department's district medical officers. This last measure succeeded because it presented 'a direct challenge to bring the state of Maori health to a standard more comparable with that of Europeans, and medical officers could no longer look to anyone else as being responsible for doing this.'

The individual most responsible for lifting standards of Maori health was Dr H. B. Turbott, first as South Auckland Medical Officer and later as Director of School Hygiene. He lobbied the Labour Minister of Health (and later Prime Minister) Peter Fraser for special appropriations for Maori health projects. Turbott's most efficacious programmes were persuading the Government to provide tanks and privies for Maori homes, installed by local labour; and persuading Maoris on a wide scale to seek treatment for tuberculosis and to agree to a degree of isolation for this treatment, often in well-ventilated portable huts provided by the Health Department. Turbott also directed Disrict Health Nurses towards preventative work, especially with children, and he developed good working relations with local leaders such as Te Puea.

The combination of all these measures along with the general lifting of Maori incomes in the post-Depression years brought spectacular improvements in Maori health over two decades. The death rate from tuberculosis dropped from an estimated 50 per 10000 of population in 1933 to 10.06 in the early 1950s, and 3.82 in 1956-60. The incidence of typhoid dropped right down. Infant mortality rates fell, though less dramatically. And the general life expectancy for Maoris rose from 46.6 years for males and 44.7 for females in 1925-27 to 57 and 59 in 1956-57.

Apart from geographical isolation, one reason Maoris remained conspicuously absent from most areas of national life in the twentieth century was that the numbers receiving secondary and tertiary educational qualifications were low. Hence Maoris were poorly represented in the professions and in business. This was caused in part by rural-urban segregation of the races, which meant that Maori families often lived considerable distances from State secondary schools, in part by cultural and sociological factors which discouraged Maori parents from placing a high value on educational qualifications, and in part by the policies pursued by successive governments.

Up to the 1930s Maori education in both denominational and State-run schools reflected the ideology that had led to official acceptance of Ngata's land schemes in 1929: that the future life of Maoris was to be worked out in rural areas. This view was reflected in 1931 in a major policy statement by the Director of Education: '...the best means for [Maoris] to realise the full benefits of civilisation is through the cultivation of land...These considerations lead us to the final conclusion that in the system of Maori education...we should provide fully a type of education that will lead the lad to be a good farmer and the girl to be a good farmer's wife.'

A consequence of this policy was that the curriculum in Maori schools emphasised agriculture and (to a lesser extent) manual and vocational training, and domestic training for girls. Few Maori pupils moved beyond primary level (about 8.4 percent in 1935), most of them defeated by the lack of specifically Maori-oriented secondary schools, the need to pay fees, the requirements of the proficiency exam, or parental discouragement.

The situation changed under the Labour Government. Expenditure on education was increased after a period of entrenchment under the previous government. Rural schools were consolidated, their facilities improved and school transport organised. Secondary education was made free for every pupil, the proficiency exam was abolished, and the school leaving age was raised to 15.

It also became apparent that land alone would not provide livings for the entire Maori population, and that training for alternative occupations was urgently needed. The movement of Maori workers and later families into rural towns for essential war work underlined this fact. The Government's response was to build Native District High Schools that placed greater emphasis on vocational training such as wood- and metalwork. As a result of these efforts the number of Maori pupils at secondary schools increased, to 30 percent of those eligible by 1951. But the rate of training for skilled manual work remained low, and there was still a lack of emphasis on academic education and on preparation for the professions. Consequently few Maoris entered white-collar occupations in the post-war years. Most remained farm workers. And a growing minority was joining the unskilled labour force in rural towns and in cities.

Another consequence of the segregation of Maori and Pakeha populations throughout the early years of the twentieth century was a continuing commitment on the part of Maoris to Maori values and practices, and to specifically Maori religious observances, even though most Maoris belonged at least nominally to a Christian Church. Most denominations had separate Maori missions with Maori clergy and Maori congregations. Although it has been noted that formal church attendance tended to be lower than that for non-Maoris, religion permeated Maori life far more intimately. Services were frequently held in the course of huis and tangis; committee meetings opened and closed with prayers; and the very status of training for the ministry or ordination tended to convey kaumatua rank in Maori situations.

The Church of England claimed the strongest Maori following throughout the first half of the twentieth century: 34 percent in 1926 and 32 percent in 1951 (the latter figure representing some 37000 members out of a total of 115600 declared religious adherents). The Ratana Church increased its membership spectacularly in the 1920s and 1930s to claim second place and a proportional peak of 20 percent in 1936. In the 1940s it dropped back to third place behind the Catholic Church, which held a steady 13 to 14 percent adherence. The other major affiliations in order of size were Methodist, Latter Day Saints and Ringatu.

Of the specifically Maori churches Ringatu was the strongest after Ratana with six percent in 1926, dropping to four percent in 1951. Numbers for the smaller denominations — Pai Marire, Wairua Tapu, and the followers of Te Whiti O Rongomai and Tohu Kakahi at Parihaka and elsewhere — fell away sharply to total less than 400 people by 1951. In one sense the statistics for the Maori churches are misleading, however. They do not show that many people belonged to a Christian denomination *and* a Maori church. In the Urewera, for example, many Tuhoes were Presbyterian and Ringatu; in Waikato Pai Marire practitioners were often also Methodist. Declared affiliation would usually depend on whether the circumstances were judged to be Maori or Pakeha; and the collection of census information was decidedly Pakeha.

Among the Maori sections of the Christian churches, denominational differences tended to be less defined and less important to members than among non-Maori sections. They were regarded far more as a reflection of the earlier spheres of influence decided upon by the Churches' missionary arms (and, indeed, the major denominations retained the expression 'mission' to designate their Maori pastorates). Ecumenical services were a commonplace feature of tangis long before they achieved acceptance among Pakeha churchgoers.

Membership of a Christian denomination in no way precluded the observance of Maori values and religious practices. The Anglican, Methodist and Presbyterian Churches incorporated concepts such as tapu, noa and wairua into their liturgy because they had close Christian equivalents. With the exception for a time of Ratana and the Latter Day Saints, all churches allowed their rituals for the dead to be absorbed into the institution of the tangihanga; and tangis for the dead continued to be held throughout the twentieth century. Indeed for most Maoris, tangihanga provided more regular opportunities for the observances of Maori ritual and marae ceremonial than any other occasion. All denominations devised prayers for circumstances in which traditional tohunga would have recited karakia: for sickness, death, misfortune, exorcism, setting out on a journey, blessing newly made objects. Water for blessing and ritual cleansing continued to be used in the manner it had been traditionally.

Adherence to Maori values persisted in other contexts to an extent that surprised Pakeha observers. Mana continued to be the quality that determined leadership status, though increasing weight was given to mana that was earned by achievement rather than that which was purely hereditary. The personal tapu of persons of rangatira rank continued to invite respect in Maori communities. People continued in Maori situations to place weight on personal identification through their genealogy. Muru took place in appropriate circumstances into the 1950s. And certain kinds of disputes between individuals and tribes were still settled by tatau pounamu, gifts of greenstone.

Discussion at huis continued to be held almost exclusively in Maori, to be structured according to the conventions of whaikorero, and to centre on the continuous preoccupation with whenuatanga, rangatiratanga, whakapapa, mana and mana motuhake. Such discussions were surrounded and protected by marae ceremonial conducted according to the kawa of the tangata whenua. Whatever demographic and cosmetic changes the Maori people underwent in the first half of the twentieth century, they cloaked persistent commitment to traditional beliefs and practices, especially in the vicinity of turangawaewae or established marae.

Tribalism continued to be a dominating feature of Maori life, to the joy of those who *felt* tribal, and to the exasperation at times of those who felt Maori or who were Pakeha. Hence tribal rivalry led to disputes over authority and occasional slander in the Maori Battalion; Maori officials in the Department of Native Affairs had the greatest difficulty persuading people to adopt departmental policies if they (the officers) were from another tribal district; and well-meaning Pakehas who tried to get Maori information as distinct from tribal propaganda were often doomed to frustration. After spending half a lifetime compiling the *Dictionary of New Zealand Biography*, G. H. Schofield said in 1940:

'Maori history is sadly distorted and vitiated by the highly developed tribalism and the intense rivalries of the generations that the Maoris have spent in New Zealand... the spirit of tribal pride moves even the broadminded Maori to ignore, if possible, and to gloss over if not, the vicissitudes of their own tribes and chiefs.'

What was a debilitating and destructive handicap from one point of view (in the above case a Pakeha one) could be a source of strength from another. Tribalism was the source of much of the group vitality and competitiveness of Maori life. And most Maori individuals continued to draw their identity and strength not from being Maori, but from being a known member of a particular hapu or tribe, and from being embraced by the people, history and traditions of that tribe. John Rangihau of Tuhoe, born into such a situation at Waikaremoana in 1919, expressed it in this way:

'These feelings...are my Tuhoetanga rather than my Maoritanga. Because my being Maori is utterly dependent on my history as a Tuhoe person...It seems to me there is no such thing as Maoritanga because Maoritanga is an all-inclusive term which embraces all Maoris...I have a faint suspicion that [it] is a term coined by the Pakeha to bring all the tribes together. Because if you cannot divide and rule, then for tribal people all you can do is unite them and rule. Because then they lose everything by losing [the] tribal history and traditions that gave them their identity.'

Maori and Pakeha

Maori life retained elements of mystery and romanticism for many Europeans in the early years of the twentieth century. The more remote from centres of Pakeha population Maori communities were, the more they fascinated Pakeha observers, especially anthropologists. Tuhoe Maoris in the Urewera and the tribes of the Wanganui River attracted particular attention in these years from people hunting for cultural and physical remnants of the 'old-time Maori'. This picture was taken in 1921 in the course of an expedition up the Wanganui River that included the self-taught anthropologist Johannes Andersen and Elsdon Best. It shows the chief Rangi Tahua, grasping a mirror, having his beard trimmed for a photograph.

The only view most Europeans had of Maoris up to World War Two: men and women sitting on the footpath in a provincial North Island town. Such people, dressed up in their best clothes, were most likely to have come to town for a sitting of the Native Land Court. While male Maori clothing was likely to be indistinguishable from that of Europeans, Maori women often wore men's hats and smoked pipes.

A Maori family 'in town' in Wairoa in 1897. Maoris were a far more visible part of rural settlements such as this one, founded on Pakeha commerce and the servicing of primary industry, but located alongside Maori centres of population — in this case, Ngati Kahungunu kaingas.

Maori and Pakeha mingle outside the Geyser Hotel in Rotorua. Rotorua provided something of an exception to the general pattern of New Zealand race relations. Maoris here were part of the attraction for tourists, along with geysers and mineral baths. They tended to mix with visitors, to transport them, and to escort them around the thermal sights. It led to the epithet of 'penny-diving Arawas' from Maoris in other parts of the country, a reference to the willingness of Maori children to dive off the Whakarewarewa bridge for coins which tourists tossed into the Puarenga River. The woman second from right is Guide Sophia.

Maori culture was very much on display in the Rotorua Maori communities (primarily Ohinemutu and Whakarewarewa) from the close of the nineteenth century. Indeed, the need to keep up Maori appearances for Pakeha visitors and for other Maoris, assembled for gatherings such as Maori welcomes to Royalty, was a strong incentive for Arawas to keep their traditional material culture alive and visible. These pictures, all dating from the late ninteeth century, show (above) poi performers lined up in front of the carved meeting house at Whakarewarewa; (middle) master carvers Anaha Te Rahui and Wehe Kapua at work at Ohinemutu; and (below) a tukutuku worker making a decorative panel for a meeting house interior. Te Arawa carving traditions, which produced deep, three-dimensional figures, were especially strong and pervasive at this time, more so than those of any other part of the country. This was the major reason why Apirana Ngata located the national carving school at Rotorua some two decades later.

The Native Land Court was a major institution in Maori life. Sittings to validate titles or to arrange transfers were the only reason many Maoris had for coming to urban areas or provincial centres. Whole families tended to congregate, and the sittings became huis in their own right. Here a group of Hokianga Maoris wait outside a Northland courthouse for a court sitting in the late 1920s.

Officials and major witnesses pose outside a sitting of the Native Land Court in the South Island, also in the 1920s. They include (centre) Henare Uru, Member of Parliament for Southern Maori.

Royal Tours presented one of the few opportunities for Pakehas to witness Maori activities. Tribes from all over the country were invited to Rotorua for a single Maori display of loyalty to the Crown and performances of action songs and haka. This one was held in 1920 to welcome the Prince of Wales. There were three other tours between 1901 and 1953. For Maoris such visits were a rare excuse for an inter-tribal hui on a national scale. Some such as the Waikato people, however, refused to attend. They held that it was an insult to themselves and to Royal visitors to have to welcome them on the territory of another tribe.

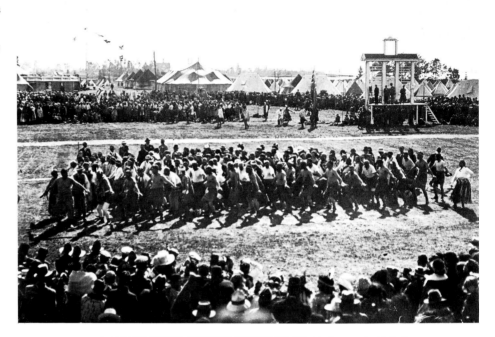

National Exhibitions (in 1906, 1925, and 1940) were another occasion on which Maoris and Maori activities were on display to New Zealanders and to visitors from overseas. At this one in Christchurch in 1906 the action song performers include Apirana Ngata (left) and Peter Buck (front row left). Such displays tended to reveal the superficial aspects of Maori life and gave non-Maoris little idea of the real strengths of Maori values and institutions.

Another group at the Christchurch Exhibition demonstrate house-building methods using traditional materials. At this time skills such as this one were practised by people who had been brought up in dwellings of this kind. But such houses were already outmoded by the availability of pit-sawn timber and corrugated iron, and had become ethnological curiosities.

Annual regattas on the Waikato River in the early years of the century provided additional opportunities for Pakehas in country centres to observe Maori activities. At this one at Ngaruawahia around 1901, Maori women contestants take part in the taxing but popular canoe hurdle race.

Here Sir John Gorst and his party are ferried
across the Waikato River at Ngaruawahia in
December 1906. Gorst, who had been Resident
Magistrate in the district at the outbreak of the
Waikato War in 1863, was revisiting the area
from England as a guest of King Mahuta.

Rural work

Flax was one of the first commodities to bring Maori and Pakeha together in a trading relationship, and many hapu relocated their settlements in the nineteenth century so as to be near both flax and suitable anchorages for trading vessels. Maoris continued their involvement in the flax trade in the twentieth century. By this time the plant was largely processed in New Zealand, in Pakeha-owned factories. The Maori role tended to be that of cutter and processor and such employment was taken on a seasonal basis. Here Maori workers under Pakeha supervision recover flax that has been left soaking prior to processing in Northland, about 1910. Some of it is already stripped. A wagon on rails transports the material to the adjacent factory.

A mill in the Bay of Plenty, possibly at Te Puke. Here flax was made into items such as sacking and rope. Many families and hapu relied on work of this kind as a major source of cash income until the industry went into sharp decline in the 1930s. In some places, such as Turangawaewae marae in Ngaruawahia, workers would vacate their communities for a whole season to work in distant mills. The trade mark visible on the corrugated iron walls is Redcliffe.

Another major source of cash income for Maori hapu in the early 1900s was gum digging, carried out largely on the site of prehistoric kauri forests in Northland, South Auckland and the Coromandel Peninsula. The digging itself was demanding and uncomfortable work, and bad for health (as were conditions in many of the camps in which the diggers ate and slept). The group here is working as a team in the Sweetwater swamp near Kaitaia in 1914. Spears are used to probe the peat for gum nuggets, which are then dug out with spades. The use of flax baskets to carry the gum enabled the worst of the surface dirt to be washed off by immersion and agitation in water.

The second part of the process was cleaning and grading the gum. Here (from left to right) it is sieved, sorted according to purity and condition, broken up and boxed. This industry was yet another controlled by Pakeha entrepreneurs. The bulk of the digging and collecting was done by Maoris and Dalmatian immigrants, resulting in a large number of marriages between the two groups in Northland. Buyers paid them for the gum according to its quality and then exported it to Europe for use in the manufacture of varnish and linoleum. The market for gum was strong until the Depression of the late 1920s, and subsequently it was outmoded by the use of synthetic materials.

Maoris throughout the country relied heavily on seasonal work on Pakeha-owned or leased farms, particularly before loan finance became available to develop Maori farms from the 1930s. Often whole hapu would specialise in particular jobs and acquire large contracts to complete them. Here Waitaki Maoris harvest a potato crop near Morven in 1913; and Ngai Tahus Edward Gregory and Kaik Tipa beside a steam-driven threshing machine help with a grain harvest at about the same time. In the second photograph, because of the need to be in the fields all day, the women have brought infants with them in pushchairs.

Maori farmers were often competitors for prizes at Agricultural and Pastoral Shows in the smaller centres. Such events provided further opportunities for limited Maori-Pakeha contact in rural districts. Here Whina Gilbert of Panguru receives a cup for her Jersey cows at the Broadwood Show in Northland in 1932.

Early A. and P. Shows also provided a variety of entertainments and sports in which Maoris and Pakehas competed against each other for titles and trophies. Tug-of-war was one of the most popular of these. This South Island Maori team is believed to have come from Arowhenua Pa near Temuka in 1902. The hats worn by two men at the back were a feature of Maori ceremonial costume in some areas in the early years of the century.

Maoris were heavily involved in the timber industry, which remained one of the country's major sources of export throughout the twentieth century. This too was Pakeha owned and controlled by large companies such as Ellis and Burnand, and the Maori contribution tended to be seasonal and contracted. Here (above) Hokianga Maoris manoeuvre a large log over a trestle for pit sawing in the 1930s; and (below) Richard Gilbert of Panguru operates a log hauler in the bush above Hokianga Harbour.

Sheep shearing was another seasonal job in which Maoris remained heavily involved in the twentieth century. This too was carried out by gangs on contract, mainly for Pakeha farmers (although some Maori land owners ran sheep on the East Coast and in Hawke's Bay). These Ngati Porou shearers are working in a woolshed near Ruatoria on the East Coast in the early 1960s.

War

From the close of the New Zealand Wars in 1872, many Maoris were keen to enlist for service in Imperial wars abroad. Tribal offers of troops were made for fighting in the Sudan in 1884, in South Africa in 1896 and in Samoa in 1899. For the Boer War, Maoris were prevented from forming their own contingent by an Imperial Government edict that Coloured troops should not be used against Whites. Many Maoris enlisted in the New Zealand contingents as individuals, however, and served with distinction. Here a group in uniform is featured at Papawai Pa in the Wairarapa in about 1901. Native Minister James Carroll stands in the centre, and Prime Minister Seddon reclines at right under a korowai cloak.

With the outbreak of World War One in 1914, most tribes were keen to contribute soldiers to the country's Expeditionary Force. Some 2 200 enlisted, mainly Ngapuhi, Arawa, Ngati Porou and Ngai Tahu. After 1916 they were kept together in the Pioneer Battalion. This group trains for overseas service at the Narrow Neck Military Camp on Auckland's North Shore.

Princess Te Puea Herangi of Waikato led a campaign against Maori conscription, which was applied to Waikato and Maniapoto tribes only, because of their refusal to enlist voluntarily. She gathered together all men of conscriptable age at her pa at Mangatawhiri near Mercer. Police made arrests there in 1918 and many of her followers were sent to prison. This campaign brought Te Puea to national prominence for the first time.

Apirana Ngata (left) and the Minister of Defence Sir James Allen (centre) try fruitlessly to talk Waikato into enlisting for war service. This meeting was one of several held at Mercer and Waahi Pa in which government spokesmen tried to change Waikato's policy, which was based on the teachings of King Tawhiao, and on the refusal of successive governments to return Maori land confiscated in 1865. On another occasion the Chairman of the Maori Recruitment Committee, Maui Pomare, was subjected to an abusive bare-bottomed haka.

Under the direction of the Maori Members of Parliament, tribes other than Waikato, Maniapoto, Taranaki and Tuhoe threw themselves into the war effort with enthusiasm. This group at Tuahiwi in the South Island encouraged local recruitment and raised funds to buy comfort items for Maori troops abroad. It was called the Lady Liverpool and Mrs Pomare's Maori Soldiers Fund Committee, named after the wives of the Governor-General and the chairman of the Maori Recruitment Committee. It included members of well-known South Island rangatira families, such as the Tainuis and Tirikatenes.

These Arawas enter a marae displaying the money they intend to contribute to the Maori war effort (a total of £1300). Huis for this purpose, organised by Member of Parliament Apirana Ngata, were held throughout the North Island during the war. Ngata encouraged intense competition among tribes and hapu to contribute more than their rivals. Such proceedings took on the character of an auction, with mana for the highest contributors being the prize.

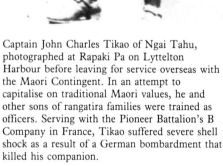

Captain John Charles Tikao of Ngai Tahu, photographed at Rapaki Pa on Lyttelton Harbour before leaving for service overseas with the Maori Contingent. In an attempt to capitalise on traditional Maori values, he and other sons of rangatira families were trained as officers. Serving with the Pioneer Battalion's B Company in France, Tikao suffered severe shell shock as a result of a German bombardment that killed his companion.

A familiar tableau of World War One. Prior to seeing action for the first time at Gallipoli in August 1915, five members of the Maori Contingent led by Captain Pirimi Tahiwi (left) pose on donkeys in front of the Sphinx and the Pyramids. A quarter of a century later sons of many of the same men posed in the same place for identical pictures as they trained for combat in World War Two.

The first contingents of Maori troops sent
abroad went straight to training camps in Egypt.
The impact on Maoris of the organisation of
such complexes, including this one at Mena, was
considerable. Many of them had come from
small hapu settlements in remote rural districts.
Captain Peter Buck wrote: '...our wonder grew
as we studied this city under canvas, so
complicated in the various parts that composed
it, and yet with everything working smoothly
and without a hitch along a system where
provision is made for the minutest detail...it is
no wonder that one of our full-blooded Maoris
shook his head sadly and said : "Yet some of the
Maoris ask for mana motuhake, the right to
govern themselves. Let them travel with the
Expeditionary Force, and they will never open
their mouths again!" '

In France in 1916, after combat at Gallipoli, the Maori Contingent was re-formed as the Pioneer Battalion. Its main duties were the digging and repairing of trenches and the maintenance of roads. Even in this role it suffered casualties from German bombardments: in total the battalion lost 336 killed and 734 wounded. Here members perform a haka at Bois de Warnimont on the Western Front in June 1918. The occasion is a visit by the New Zealand Prime Minister William Massey (right) and his deputy standing next to him, Sir Joseph Ward.

Chopping firewood and meat were among the Pioneers' other duties. Here three members of the battalion sharpen their hatchets at Bayoncourt in July 1918. The man at left displays his identity disk hanging from his braces. The puttees and boots were standard issue for trench conditions in World War One.

Leave and recreation for Maori troops abroad presented the authorities with difficulties. Many of the soldiers had never before experienced town life, let alone cosmopolitan cities the size of London. There were also fears that they might encounter racial discrimination and — being unaccustomed to such treatment — react violently. Some Empire-minded welfare groups such as the Aboriginal Protection Society and the medical one shown here came to the rescue and provided supervised hospitality of an 'approved' kind; mainly tea, cakes and genteel company. This might not have been much fun for the troops themselves, if their expressions are any indication.

War's end in November 1918 and the promise of the return of troops from overseas inspired jubilation throughout the country. This group, largely Maori, poses at Moeraki in the course of celebrations. Items of festivity include flags, masks, funny hats and clackers.

Sport

In the early years of the twentieth century South Island Maoris were proportionately more involved in competitive sport with Pakehas than those in the North. Henare Uru (left) of Tuahiwi was a champion cyclist. He also played rugby and won trophies for wrestling. Later (1922-28) he was Member of Parliament for Southern Maori. The champion athlete, photographed at Ashburton at about the same time, is not identified. A. and P. shows and sports meetings often offered large cash prizes for such events.

In other areas where Maori-Pakeha contact was congenial, such as the Hokianga District, some Maoris also took up boxing with considerable enthusiasm. Here the figure at right looks more Aboriginal than Maori. But he is nevertheless identified as a Maori fighter posing with a Pakeha pugilist in the Hokianga, early 1900s.

Cricket was another popular sport in some North Island Maori communities, including — again — those in the Hokianga. But it was not conducted according to rules that Englishmen would have recognised. It was played more often for fun than for serious competition. Teams included men and women, frequently without limitations placed on numbers. Few Maoris took the game sufficiently seriously to play it at representative level. This Maori-Pakeha group has paused in the course of a game at Motukaraka on the Hokianga Harbour in 1906.

Maori tennis was taken far more seriously. One player, Ruia Morrison of Rotorua, achieved international distinction (she reached the quarterfinals at Wimbledon in 1957). Separate Maori tennis championships were organised throughout the country in the 1920s and 1930s. Many maraes at this time including Turangawaewae at Ngaruawahia and this one at Panguru had tennis courts that were in constant use.

The sport that brought Maoris to national and international attention was rugby. From the time the game spread through New Zealand in the 1870s, Maoris embraced it with enthusiasm and played in rural clubs with Europeans and in separate Maori competitions. This New Zealand Native Team toured Britain and Australia in 1888-89. It played a prodigious 107 games, winning 78, losing 23 and drawing six. Members scored a total of 772 points and had 305 scored against them. They included four Europeans, and four Maoris who also represented New Zealand: Joe Warbrick, Pony Gage, Tabby Wynyard and Tom Ellison. Ellison, a forward from the Otakou settlement near Dunedin, was the outstanding New Zealand player of his day and captained the New Zealand team in 1893. His cousins John and Dick Taiaroa also played in national teams. The Native Team is shown here in Sydney in 1889. The front row includes three Aboriginal supporters.

With room for individual flair within a framework of team cooperation, rugby was an ideal vehicle for the expression of Maori physical qualities of speed and strength, and imagination. Maori teams quickly developed a reputation for fast unorthodox play that made them favourites with New Zealand crowds. It was also an outlet for Maori competitiveness and — according to Bishop Frederick Bennett — for Maori aggression. Specifically Maori competitions were introduced in the 1920s, in which teams competed for a cup donated by the Prince of Wales. This team, the South Island Tu Ahuriri Club, was joint winner of the North Canterbury Rugby Union competition in 1918.

New Zealand Maori sides were formed to play teams visiting from overseas from the time of the 1904 British tour. On that occasion the Maoris won 8-6. Maori teams also travelled abroad again in 16 tours between 1910 and 1982. Most of these trips were to Australia, with some to the Pacific Islands and two to the United Kingdom. Some were arranged to compensate for the exclusion of Maoris from New Zealand teams to tour South Africa. In this picture the Maori team to play the British Lions at Athletic Park in Wellington in 1930 performs the traditional pre-match haka. On this occasion they lost, 13-19.

Some Maoris became national heroes for their skills and match-winning propensities. One such player was George Nepia, a Ngati Kahungunu from Wairoa, seen here at the Maoris versus Lions game in 1930. Nepia played his first first-class game at the age of 16, his last when he was 45. He is regarded as one of the best full-backs the country has produced and he was at the peak of his form when he toured the United Kingdom with the 'Invincible' All Black team in 1924-25. He was excluded from the New Zealand tour of South Africa in 1928 because of the colour bar in that country.

Another national figure in his playing days was Ben Couch, regarded as the country's best five-eighths in the late 1940s. A Ngai Tahu from Rapaki on Banks Peninsula, Couch began his representative career playing for Wairarapa in 1945. He first played for New Zealand in 1947 and for New Zealand Maoris in 1948. Like other Maori players he was excluded from the All Black tour of South Africa in 1949 because of his race. His popularity as a rugby player and administrator went a long way towards securing his election to Parliament as member for Wairarapa in 1975. Three years later he became Minister of Maori Affairs in the National Government.

Schools

From 1867 Maori education was carried out in government-sponsored Native Schools in addition to the small number of church schools still in existence. By 1870 30 such schools had been established with a total of 219 pupils. They were built in Maori communities that expressed an interest in education, and offered instruction in English to primary level only. In the early years they were administered by the Native Department, later by the Department of Education. This one pictured in the late nineteenth century is at Tuahiwi near Kaiapoi and the sole teacher, Mrs Reeves, stands at right. There were no Maori teachers outside of church schools at this time.

Inside a Native School in the 1930s. The Wairewa School at Little River displays the basic props of education: desk, blackboards and pictures. The core of the syllabus was English, arithmetic, spelling, writing and geography. There was little teaching in Maori or about Maori culture at this time.

A geography lesson at Te Hapua School in Northland in 1907. In addition to communicating basic primary skills, such education was also designed to give pupils a view of New Zealand's place in the world and in particular its place in and its responsibilities to the British Empire (England was always at the centre of world maps and countries of the Empire marked in red.)

Girls learning dressmaking, also at Te Hapua in 1907. The philosophy of education at this time was based on the assumption that Maori boys would become farmers or rural workers, and that girls should be trained to be versatile wives and mothers. There was no encouragement and little opportunity for Maoris to go on to secondary or tertiary education, unless they were wealthy enough or lucky enough to secure a place in a church-run secondary school such as Te Aute College for boys or St Josephs Maori Girls College, both in Hawke's Bay. Hence few Maoris considered business or professional occupations.

Pupils at Te Hapua 25 years later, assembling outside the school to greet a visitor. Little had changed in Maori education over the preceding quarter of a century. Even by this time only 4.8 percent of Maori students went on to secondary schools and general encouragement of Maori students to attend them was still a decade away.

Churches

Christian ritual and Maori values continued to interact to produce Maori churches that combined Polynesian ingredients with Judaeo-Christian forms of worship. One of these churches, the Ratana Movement, grew spectacularly in numbers, becoming for a time the third largest denomination with Maori membership. Others such as this sect known as the Church of the Seven Rules of Jehovah declined after brief bursts of popularity. The photograph was taken at the opening of the church's new place of worship at the Tinui Valley near Masterton in about 1900.

The Church of England attracted the largest number of Maori adherents throughout the first half of the twentieth century. This was a continuing reflection of the fact that their missionaries had been first in the field in New Zealand and had evangelised over a wider territory than other denominations. The Maori and Pakeha sections of the church remained administratively separate, although it was not uncommon for some Pakeha clergymen to serve in both sections. Here an Anglican minister talks with his Maori congregation outside the church at Temuka. The soldier in the lemon-squeezer hat indicates that the photograph was taken in the later years of World War One.

233

The Anglican Church was especially assiduous in its recruitment and training of Maori clergy, and in its linking of Maori cultural activities to church programmes. This concert party, trained by the Rev. Frederick Bennett (centre), performed around the North Island to raise money for the building of churches at Awahou, Te Ngae and Mourea. Members also contributed in 1914 to the cast of one of the first feature films made in New Zealand, a depiction of the love story of Hinemoa and Tutanekai of Te Arawa. In 1928 Bennett was appointed first Bishop of Aotearoa, a bishopric without a territorial diocese, making him the leader of the Maori section of the church.

Among the established denominations, the Catholic Church had the second largest Maori congregation. But it had noticeably fewer Maori clergy than other churches (only one up to the 1950s). Its membership also tended to reflect earlier spheres of missionary influence. The west coast of Northland, for example, had been traditionally a Catholic area since the arrival of French priests there in the late 1830s. Here Father Richard Bressers, a member of the Mill Hill order, conducts a burial service at Waihou Pa on Hokianga Harbour in 1931.

The Methodist Church, with its system of 'home missionaries', had the largest number of Maori clergy. These men were lay preachers, neither theologically trained nor ordained, who acted as ministers in rural districts, preached, conducted services, weddings and funerals, and were entitled to be addressed as 'Reverend'. Most of them were not paid by the church for this work and had to find their income from other sources. Here a group of such clergy gathers with ordained ministers at Kawhia for the laying of a stone commemorating 100 years of Wesleyan mission work there. Members include (from second left, front row) the Rev. A. J. Seamer, who was in charge of the church's home and Maori missions, Queen Te Atairangikaahu and her husband King Koroki, and the Rev. Robert Tahupotiki Haddon.

The Anglican, Catholic and Methodist Churches continued to operate secondary boarding schools for Maori students. Pupils from such schools tended to do well in later life, apparently because of the confidence acquired as a result of learning in a distinctively Maori atmosphere (which State schools did not provide) with other Maoris. Up to the 1950s most of the small number of Maoris who entered the professions were the products of such schools, which also made provision for the teaching of Maori language in many instances. This group poses at Hato Petera, St. Peter's Maori College in Auckland, in the early 1930s, with two of the school's benefactors, Whina and Richard Gilbert of Hokianga. Hato Petera was at that time staffed by the Catholic Mill Hill order.

Music

Most Pakehas associated Maori culture with action song and haka because these were the only manifestations of Maoritanga that they saw, however intermittently. Here a group of girls performs a poi dance at about the turn of the century, watched by Maori and Pakeha spectators. The picture appears to have been taken in Waikato, possibly at one of the Mercer regattas.

There was an enormous interest among Maoris in brass band instruments and music in the late 1890s and early 1900s. This band performed under Pakeha direction at civic functions in Rotorua in the late 1890s. It was one of the features that gave the town a Maori character, which was in part designed to attract tourists to the region.

These performers, known as The Band, were a sub-group of Te Puea Herangi's Te Pou o Mangatawhiri concert party. They toured the North Island in the 1920s to raise funds for Turangawaewae marae. After the Maori section of their concerts, The Band would appear in European dress with guitars, violins, banjos and mandolins to play dance music, the floor would be cleared, and concert goers would take their partners. Players include (middle row, left) Te Puea's husband, Tumokai Katipa. The backdrop is marked with symbols of King Tawhiao's Tariao religion, an offshoot of Pai Marire which the King Movement had reinstated as Waikato's 'established' religion during their anti-conscription campaign in the course of World War One. The Tawera referred to is the planet Venus, an object of special veneration in Tawhiao's cosmology.

This member of Te Puea's TPM party wears the group's distinctive costume: a piupiu over a long taniko-bordered skirt, and a finely woven taniko bodice and headband. The widespread performances of the TPM throughout the North Island had the effect of reviving interest in haka and action song in Maori districts where the practice of these arts had previously lapsed, especially on the west coast of the island. They also made Pakehas in Auckland and Wellington aware of the work that Te Puea had undertaken at Turangawaewae, particularly her building programme which was advertised as being the reason for the TPM tours.

The Waiata Methodist Maori Choir, which toured Australia in 1935 and the United Kingdom in 1937. Members of this group were Maoridom's most successful ambassadors abroad in this decade. In England they gave a Royal Command performance at Buckingham Palace for King George VI, and they took part in one of the first transmissions for British television. The star of their Australian tour was the young bass Inia Te Wiata, later a world-famous opera and concert performer. Those pictured here include (back left) Te Uira Manihera, subsequently a Waikato elder and spokesman for the King Movement; and (reclining at front right) Airini Grennell of Ngai Tahu , one of the country's first Maori radio announcers.

Inia Te Wiata (left) on tour with the Waiata Choir through New Zealand in about 1933, when he was 17. He is pictured with another choir member, Te Aku, at a house where they were billeted. Two years later, in Australia, agents for the musical company J.C. Williamson's tried to lure him away from the Methodist Choir with the promise of a full-time performing job. When he gave his first broadcast on New Zealand radio in 1938, Te Wiata's voice was mistaken for that of the American bass Paul Robeson. He eventually went to London to study singing in 1947 and did not return to live in New Zealand. He was followed there by another Tainui singer 20 years later, soprano Kiri Te Kanawa.

The enormous popularity of radio after its
introduction in the 1920s carried Maori music
into almost every New Zealand home for the
first time. This group of performers, believed to
be from the Rangitikei district, is about to go to
air on the national programme from the
Wellington Town Hall in the late 1920s.
Incongruously, it appears to have an
instrumental backing.

War

Back to North Africa in 1940, where many of their fathers had trained a quarter of a century earlier. Members of the 28th (Maori) Battalion fought in World War Two with a gusto that at times exceeded that of their Pakeha compatriots. This time there was no coercion to enlist and no conscription for Maoris. Over 17 000 were recruited between 1939 and 1945. Here a group performs a morale-raising haka at Maadi Camp in Egypt.

Maori troops were sometimes determined to the point of recklessness. Brigadier Howard Kippenberger noted that they needed strong leadership to prevent them over-running their objectives. Here two infantrymen advance with bayonets fixed on German and Italian positions in the North African desert.

The Maori Battalion moves into the firing line with rifles and mortars at Faenza, Italy, in 1944. After being held up at Cassino, the advance of the New Zealand Army up the Italian peninsula in late 1944 and early 1945 was one of the most rapid and successful operations of the war, and one in which the 28th Battalion took a full share of fighting and casualties.

Battle-weary troops in a forward area unwrap Christmas presents in December 1944. The heavy coats and improvised brazier combat the effects of a severe Italian winter.

Although given equal treatment with other New Zealand troops, Maori soldiers had some special needs. The Maori War Effort Organisation raised funds for comfort items such as these barrels of South Island mutton birds. When a similar consignment was intercepted by the Germans in Africa it led to accusations that British forces were reduced to rations of salted seagull.

Far from the battle fields, at Ruatoria on the East Coast of the North Island. Hamuera Ngarimu and his wife learn that their son Moananui-a-Kiwa has been awarded the Victoria Cross posthumously for heroism at Tebaga Gap in Tunisia on 26 March 1943. In the words of the citation, 'he led his men with great determination straight up the face of the hill, undeterred by the intense mortar and machine-gun fire, which caused considerable casualties. Displaying courage and leadership of the highest order, he was himself first on the hill crest, personally annihilating at least two enemy machine-gun posts. In the face of such a determined attack the remainder of the enemy fled...'

The hui at Ruatoria in October 1943 to celebrate Ngarimu's Victoria Cross was an opportunity to commemorate the contributions and sacrifices of troops from all tribes, and was a highlight of the Maori war effort at home. On this occasion Sir Apirana Ngata announced the establishment of the Ngarimu Scholarship Fund, used subsequently to help Maori students achieve education beyond primary level.

The presence of American troops also brought the war home to New Zealand. Some 100 000 were accommodated and trained there between 1942 and 1944. There were accusations that a number of marines discriminated against Maoris generally, mistreated Maori women in particular, and encouraged prostitution in Auckland and Wellington. In an effort to put Maori-American relations on a better footing, Princess Te Puea invited these officers to Turangawaewae marae in November 1942.

After resisting Maori conscription in World War One, Te Puea and Waikato got right behind the war effort. In addition to entertaining troops at Turangawaewae, she grew food for the Army, supervised the making of camouflage nets, made comfort items for men at the front, and raised over £30 000 for the Red Cross. More than 400 tribal committees in other parts of the country undertook similar activities. These groups became the basis for a post-war Maori welfare organisation.

Mrs Ripeka Love (centre) and other members of the local Maori community mourn fallen soldiers as the Maori Battalion arrives back at Wellington after the war. Of 17 000 recruits the battalion lost more than 600 men killed and another 2 000 wounded. Tangis were held at marae all over the country as the returning soldiers, in accordance with Maori custom, 'carried' the deaths home. Mrs Love's son, Colonel E. Love, had been an Ati Awa chief and the first Maori to command the Maori Battalion. He was killed at Ruweisat Ridge in the North African desert in 1942.

Maoris made up a large section of the
1 500-strong volunteer Kay Force that New
Zealand sent as part of the United Nations
action in Korea in 1950. Members of this group
come from North Auckland, Thames, the Bay of
Plenty and Dunedin.

Maoris were also strongly in evidence with New
Zealand volunteer troops in South Vietnam from
1965 to 1972. In this Army propaganda
photograph a medical officer attends to a
wounded Maori soldier in camouflage. Even
outside years of combat the New Zealand Army
continued to attract a large proportion of Maori
enlistment.

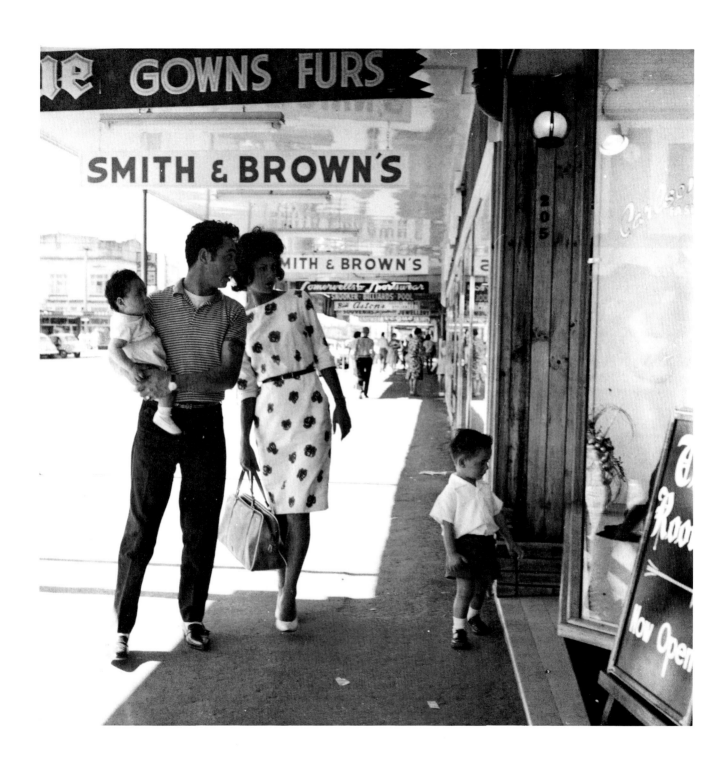

CHAPTER SIX

Te Ao Hou

Te Ao Hou is one of those resonant Maori expressions whose force comes from simultaneous meanings, literal and metaphorical. Its fundamental meaning is 'new dawn' or 'new day'. It also has connotations of freshness, of budding, of brightness and light as opposed to darkness. It is an expression that Maori leaders came to apply symbolically to the experiences that entirely reshaped the contours of Maori life in the wake of World War Two.

Most tribes retain traditional recollections of one or even two migrations: that which brought their ancestors to New Zealand from the ancestral homeland Hawaiiki; and that which took them from an earlier place of settlement to the one in which the hapu is now based around its meeting houses and waahi tapu. From the time of the Second World War, however, most Maori families underwent a third migration: that which took its members from small, largely rural Maori communities into the towns and cities of the nation, where the conventions of living were Pakeha-defined. It was a shift that brought compensations and trauma; eventual security and wider opportunities for some and cultural and emotional dislocation for others. It brought Maori and Pakeha into widespread contact for the first time since the wars of the 1860s; and with that contact came new demands, conflict, and a long apprenticeship of adjustment in which both peoples were forced for the first time to begin to know one another. By the latter half of the 1990s that readjustment had led to a reassertion of mana Maori and a need to renegotiate the social contract between Crown and Maori, and Maori and Pakeha.

The relocation of the Maori population began in earnest during the Second World War when manpower regulations and the Maori War Effort Organisation opened up a diversity of labouring and manufacturing jobs not previously available generally to Maori men and women. In addition, the recreational options of city life created in some country areas what one observer called a 'fantasy contagion'. In 1936 only 11.2 percent of the Maori population had lived in urban areas. By 1945 this had risen to 19 percent, and by 1971 to 68.2 percent. In the 1980s the figure rose to over 90 percent and Maoris had become an overwhelmingly urban people. The impact can perhaps be best visualised by consideration of the figures for individual cities. There were 1766 Maoris in Auckland in 1935, for example. By 1945 there were 4903, and by 1951 7621. In the same period the Wellington Maori population jumped from 341 to 1570.

There was no single cause for the momentum which this migration built up. In periods of national prosperity the ready availability of well-paid but unskilled work was one attraction. It led to Maoris taking manual jobs in large numbers in provincial towns and cities (in labouring, construction sites and freezing works, for example) — the kinds of jobs that would leave them vulnerable to unemployment in times of national economic difficulty. Nor was it simply a case of the positive appeal of such work. There was also a negative factor in the economic decline of Maori rural communities brought about by the inability of Maori land alone to provide a living for a burgeoning population.

Ngata's land legislation had helped to sustain Maori communities in the 1930s and 1940s. It had come nowhere near 'solving' all the problems associated with Maori land, however.

And with the population explosion that became apparent in the wake of World War Two the deficiencies of that land as a source of employment and income became more obvious. Much of it was characterised by steepness, remoteness, high rainfall, unstable surfaces and other unfavourable features. Further, many of the dairy farms developed under Ngata's schemes proved to be uneconomic because of their size; many scheme workers found they could make considerably more money from casual labour on larger adjacent units, usually Pakeha-owned. These became steadily more profitable as a result of progressive mechanisation, which most Maori farmers could simply not afford.

In some areas land which had been on short-term lease to Europeans, with no provisions for compensation for improvements, was returned to Maori owners 'unscrupulously milked', in the words of one commentator. And, as if these difficulties were not enough, there were also those 'associated with ownership and control, grounded in a recent history of rapid and thorough cultural change, and related to a system of values which does not accord total priority to the Pakeha goals of efficiency and productivity.'

This is not to suggest that Maori farming as a whole was a failure. Far from it: some incorporations and individual farmers did spectacularly well. Nor was Pakeha farming by contrast an unqualified success. But the situation did create a circle of circumstances that led to unforeseen problems in town and country: uneconomic Maori farming was an incentive for workers and families to move to towns and cities; and this process of depopulation made rural communities even less viable and urban migration by contrast still more appealing. And the combination of rural population displacement, urbanisation, and a relative lack of educational qualifications among Maori workers produced a brown proletariat in New Zealand cities, a situation that some commentators viewed as a dangerous ingredient in urban race relations.*

Another major contribution to the urban migration was the monetary, recreational and lifestyle attractions of city life. These offered more choices, far more options for entertainment and hence — in the eyes of many — opportunities for a richer and fuller life. (In the eyes of a minority these same facts were tantamount to confirming that cities were dens of temptation and iniquity.) Related to this was the feeling that opportunities for

what was generally referred to as 'success' or 'betterment' lay in the city, not in the country.

There was also a follow-on process at work. A single member of a family might move to a city and experience immediate work and recreational advantages. He would report back to other members of the extended family, who would then join him over a period of time. These would in turn communicate with other members of the hapu or rural home community and set further migrations in motion. And so on. This was all part of the 'fantasy contagion'. It was not unlike older rural myths such as that about the streets of London being paved with gold. The reality rarely lived up to full expectations; but that did not stop either the fantasies or the migration.

The social and cultural consequences of this relocation were considerable. They brought a need for dramatic changes in the management of both Maori and wider national affairs. Urbanisation presented migrants newly arrived from rural areas with a set of Pakeha surburban *mores* not evident in Maori communities; there were difficulties associated with managing salaried incomes, budgeting, savings and investments; with accommodation, hire purchase and door-to-door salesmanship; there were instances of overt discrimination in employment, accommodation and hotel bars that arose from Maori and Pakeha becoming visible to one another and having to interact on a broad basis for the first time.

Urbanisation also brought a need to redefine aspects of Maoriness: the nature of the extended family in the urban context; how to hold huis in the city; whether to take tupapaku 'home' to rural maraes or to conduct tangihanga and burials in the city. There was also a need, for the first time outside war conditions, for people from differing tribal backgrounds to devise ways of cooperating with one another to solve specifically Maori problems. Differences of kawa had to be resolved, traditional suspicions and antagonisms discarded or submerged. Tangata whenua already swallowed up by urban expansion were at first unwilling to let people from other tribal backgrounds use existing marae facilities (Ngati Whatua in Auckland, for example, and Ngati Toa in Porirua). This fact and the absence of maraes in new suburbs led to the conception and development of urban maraes. In the process of addressing themselves to these problems Maoris discovered that detribalisation could lead to multi-tribalism, and an intensification of a sense of Maoriness grew out of urban marae projects such as those at Maraeroa in Wellington and Hoani Waititi in Auckland. For many Maoris this experience was an unexpected joy and a source of additional strength and optimism.

Urbanisation brought to light aspects of Maori vulnerability in relation to non-Maoris. In 1951, 57 percent of the Maori population was 20 years old and younger (as against 34.8 percent of the Pakeha population), which indicated a greater proportion of young dependents and non-wage earners. In addition the

---

* J. G. A. Pocock, for example: '. . .we may be going to have ghettoes — the current term for urban areas where a distinctively pigmented minority have to live with bad houses, bad schools and unrewarding jobs — and, when faced with such ghettoes, the Pakeha may find that he is more prejudiced than he likes to believe. . . *whakama* may cease to be the mere feeling of shyness and inadequacy which it is now, and become instead a truly bitter sense of rejection; ideologies of alienation and ambivalence may arise, and the voice of some Maori (or Islander) James Baldwin may some day be heard.'

Maori birth rate was considerably higher than that of the non-Maori: 43.6 per 1000 in 1955 as against 26. Most significantly, the vast majority of the Maori work force was in unskilled and lower income employment, especially agriculture and related industries (33 percent in 1951) and manufacturing (23 percent). Only 3.36 percent of Maori workers at that time earned £700 or more per year compared with 18.6 percent of non-Maoris. Conversely, in 1956 only 6.56 percent of the Maori work force held professional, managerial and clerical positions as against 26.69 percent of non-Maoris.

All these factors combined to make Maori families more vulnerable as a group than Pakehas when wool prices fell a decade later and ended full employment. They created a circle of circumstances that was self-reinforcing and difficult to break: lower standards of educational attainment led to lower-income jobs or unemployment, which led to lower standards of housing and health, which led to higher rates of Maori crime, which led back to lower educational attainment and so on. Attempts to define these factors and their magnitude, and to devise new policies to deal with them, were not made until well into the 1960s.

In addition all the conditions mentioned — especially poorer educational performance, lower incomes, poorer standards of housing and higher rates of crime — were ingredients for racial tension. They were seen by the wider community as 'Maori problems', and Maoris were physically identifiable as a racial group. Pakeha were viewed by the media as individual New Zealanders; Maoris as representatives of a race. And this, along with instances of overt discrimination against Maoris in employment and accommodation, underlined why race relations had seemed relatively good in New Zealand from 1900 to the 1950s: not because of enlightened legislation or Pakeha altruism or even the Maori's capacity for adaption; but because the two races had been kept largely apart from one another.

Changing social and economic conditions in Maori life led to continued experimentation with different styles of leadership. The rangatira or hereditary basis for hapu leadership survived, but largely in rural areas. An increasing number of leaders such as Whina Cooper, whose basis for authority had originally been tribal and rural, made the transition to leadership in urban, multi-tribal Maori life.

Born Josephine Te Wake at Te Karaka on the Hokianga Harbour in 1895, she was the daughter of a leading Te Rarawa chief, Heremia Te Wake. From Heremia, Whina inherited mana, considerable ability, and an expectation that she would assume a leadership role among the Kai Tutae and Ngati Manawa hapu of Te Rarawa. After education at Whakarapa Native School and St Joseph's Maori Girls' College in Napier, Whina was in succession a teacher, a storekeeper and a farmer in the Hokianga district. She took her father's place after he died in the Influenza Epidemic of 1918, and by the late 1920s, based at Panguru, she was known as the most forceful Maori leader in the northern Hokianga.

When Ngata was seeking community support for his land development programmes, Whina was an obvious ally and she introduced and supervised the schemes in her area. She extended her expertise and her influence as a consequence of a second marriage in 1935 to William Cooper, a Ngati Kahungunu friend of Ngata who had represented the Maori people on the Royal Commission investigating Maori land in 1925.

After Cooper's death in 1949, Whina moved to Auckland to begin voluntary welfare work among Maoris who had been moving steadily to the cities after World War Two. She was elected first president of the Maori Women's Welfare League in 1951, a position she held for five years. After establishing local branches of the league throughout the country, and making a considerable impact in the education of Maori mothers in such matters as child-rearing and household budgeting, Whina Cooper turned the league into the only national Maori forum for discussion then in existence, and into the major non-political pressure group for representations to governments. (Both these roles were later assumed by the New Zealand Maori Council, established in 1962.) She was also especially active in securing adequate Maori housing in Auckland, in building urban maraes, and in fund-raising for voluntary welfare programmes, especially those organised by the Catholic Church.

In 1975 she established Te Roopu O Te Matakite and led the Maori Land March from Te Hapua in the far north to Parliament in Wellington, dramatising a national Maori determination not to lose any further land to Pakeha ownership. She remained a prominent Maori protest figure in the 1980s and 1990s, still adopting new causes and formulating representations to the Department and the Minister of Maori Affairs as she approached 100 years of age. She had departed from traditional patterns of Maori leadership in that her influence in the later years of her life sprang from her reputation as an urban and national Maori figure — as Te Whaea o te Motu or 'Mother of the Nation' — rather than from her localised or tribal position. She died in 1994 in her ninety-ninth year.

Another major training ground for non-tribal Maori leadership, in addition to preparation for church ministries, was the Public Service. There had been few Maori public servants prior to World War Two, although those few exercised considerable influence: Raumoa Balneavis, a Ngati Porou, was for over 20 years secretary to successive Ministers of Native Affairs and became the most powerful force in his department; Pei Te Hurinui Jones of Ngati Maniapoto received his administrative training in the Native Land Court and later turned it to impressive use in land incorporation and development work; and Tipi Ropiha of Ngati Kahungunu, after a highly successful career in the Departments of Lands and Survey and Native Affairs, was appointed first Maori to head the Department of Maori Affairs in 1947. Later ministerial secretaries, especially Michael Rotohiko Jones of Ngati Maniapoto and John Grace of Ngati Tuwharetoa, were also major sources of influence behind the political scene.

After World War Two, a large group of former Maori Battalion officers moved into Maori-related posts in the Public Service (men such as Jim Henare, Arapeta Awatere, Rangi Royal, Charles Bennett, Bill Herewini, Fred Baker, Moana Raureti and John Rangihau). Many of them completed university degrees with rehabilitation assistance after war service. Some, such as Henare Ngata and Harry Dansey, stayed outside the government and public service but dealt frequently with both in the course of tribal and incorporation administration. These men were an extension of the Young Maori Party model in the sense that they accepted the need for Western education and administrative skills so as to function within the bureaucracies of the government system. But, unlike their predecessors, they had seen the survival of Maori language, ritual and values into the second half of the twentieth century; and they were impatient with anything less than full equality with Pakeha citizens. One of their number, Rangi Logan, was to voice their feeling in the 1946 election campaign: 'We did more than our share at El Alamein and elsewhere...we shed our blood in two world wars.' If this had done nothing else, he declared, it had at least purchased the right to equality.

They accepted the *raison d'etre* for the Department of Maori Affairs and the hierarchical structure by which it functioned, largely under Pakeha direction at district officer level. They accepted the basic concepts behind the land development schemes, incorporations, and the post-war welfare services. They also accepted that — to make a significant impact on the Pakeha-dominated systems of party politics and Public Service — they had to lobby as Maoris stating Maori *takes* (causes); to be Waikatos stating Waikato views or Ngapuhis representing Ngapuhis would have been to exercise relatively little influence over policy and legislation. In this they were assisted by their Maori Battalion background, which had helped them to view Maoris as a people rather than as a group of competing tribal units; and by the process of detribalisation that accelerated after World War Two as more and more families abandoned home maraes and increasingly intermarried in cities with Maoris from other regions.

These same Maori bureaucrats were to be challenged a generation later by a group of largely urban-based Maori dissidents, most of whom had backgrounds in tertiary education. They included Ranginui Walker and Pat Hohepa of the Auckland District Maori Council, Robert Mahuta of the Waikato kahui ariki, Koro Dewes and Sidney Mead of Victoria University, Tipene O'Regan of Ngai Tahu, and some leaders of Maori protest groups. These spoke out for Maori interests more emphatically and more abrasively than their predecessors, and they were to question whether the public service and local authority structures, with Pakehas reserving for themselves key policy-making positions, were the most appropriate ones to deal with the needs and aspirations of an indigenous Pacific people.

A major source of discontent among all Maori leaders in the wake of World War Two was that successive governments were slow to perceive the changing conditions brought about by Maori urbanisation, and to respond to the representations of Maori pressure groups. Labour made some concessions by passing the Maori Social and Economic Advancement Act in 1945, which established tribal committees and the first Maori welfare officers. Labour also dropped the expression 'Native' from all official usage in 1947 and substituted 'Maori'.

When National came into power in 1949 they did so without any previous interest or conspicuous expertise in Maori affairs. They assisted with the setting up of the voluntary Maori Women's Welfare League in 1951, and in 1962 they passed the Maori Welfare Act which set up the New Zealand Maori Council (over the system of tribal committees established by Labour) and acted upon some of the recommendations of the Hunn Report of 1961. This latter had been commissioned but not actioned by the second Labour Government.

The Hunn Report was a milestone for its time. It was the first official act of recognition of the process of Maori urbanisation and it suggested policies to cope with the conditions that urbanisation presented. It assumed that the future of the two races and cultures was to blend, and that this was a desirable goal. Articulate Maori opinion attacked it on the grounds that Maoris did not want to blend with Europeans and would not; and that Maori leaders had not been canvassed in the course of its preparation. The Government accepted its recommendation that Maori houses should be 'pepper-potted' among general State housing, but this policy was later abandoned; Maoris, even in cities, preferred to live in Maori surroundings, and many Europeans turned out to be unenthusiastic about the prospect of Maori neighbours. The report's most successful consequences were the setting up of the Maori Education Foundation to help pupils through secondary and tertiary education, the extension of trade training facilities for Maoris, and the provision for hostel accommodation and pre-employment courses for young Maoris new to city life.

From the time of the publication of the Hunn report, Maori spokesmen became increasingly aware that although Pakeha governments now spoke of integration as the ideal cultural blueprint for New Zealand, few Pakehas were actually prepared to tread the two-way street of integration by learning Maori language and customs. Assimilation and integration both required Maoris to become Pakehas. The Maori had to learn everything about the English language and Western ways of living; there was no serious pressure on Pakehas to reciprocate. As a result Maori values and institutions had a lower status in New Zealand life than their Western equivalents.

Frequently when cases were made to government or the Public Service for things such as the teaching of Maori language, a larger Maori content on radio and television, greater recognition of oral literature and provision for Maori methods for dealing with Maori offenders, these proposals were subject to what one Maori commentator called 'the Pakeha veto'. Maoris were in many respects prevented from pursuing Maoriness because Pakeha-oriented institutions could see neither the value of nor the necessity for such measures; they were frequently dismissed as a potential source of social divisiveness. The agencies of the New Zealand system of government — in education, in law, in public works and in other branches of the public service bureaucracy — were committed to reflect Western values, criteria, practices and priorities rather than Polynesian ones. The more these factors were recognised and articulated in Maori quarters, the more they were resented. They led to the rise of urban protest groups: Maori organisations that articulated Maori considerations and needs, but which adopted Western rather than traditional modes of expression, such as demonstrations, picketing, petitions to Parliament and press releases.

The first such group to make its influence felt in the late 1960s was formed in Auckland, where Maori numbers were greatest and where the unpreparedness of government, local bodies and Pakeha individuals for Maori urbanisation was most apparent. Nga Tamatoa (the young warriors) grew out of the leadership of the Auckland University Maori Club; but its membership included young manual workers. Like the Maori Organisation On Human Rights established in Wellington slightly earlier, it was initially a reaction to the National Government's 1967 Maori Affairs Amendment Act, which gave the Maori Trustee additional powers to take control of Maori land, and which provided for land owned by fewer than four persons to pass into individual titles. It was immediately attacked by Maori opinion as a high-handed (if well-intentioned) measure that lacked the support of the very people it purported to help.

Rapidly, however, both protest groups widened their campaigns to include the teaching of Maori language in schools, Maori control of Maori land and Maori finance, assistance for Maori offenders appearing unrepresented before the courts, an end to annual celebrations of the signing of the Treaty of Waitangi, and the severance of sporting links with South Africa. They were joined by Te Reo Maori, centred on Victoria University, which concerned itself primarily with the promotion of Maori language and literature and with the performance of the media, especially television, in dealing with Maori issues.

Te Roopu O Te Matakite (later Te Matakite O Aotearoa) grew out of the Maori Land March of 1975, which dramatised a determination not to relinquish further Maori land. Separate protests groups formed to campaign for the return of the Raglan golf course to Maori ownership (it had been seized by the Government and a community displaced for the building of a landing strip during World War Two); and for the return of Bastion Point in Auckland to Ngati Whatua ownership. This last led to a 17-month occupation of the point in 1977-78, and the arrest of 200 protesters in May 1978 after the largest police operation in the country to that time. In 1979 the Labour Member for Northern Maori Matiu Rata resigned his seat and contested it as leader of the Mana Motuhake Movement, which presented a comprehensive policy for Maori self-determination. He did not regain the seat but Mana Motuhake achieved second place behind Labour in all four Maori electorates in the 1981 General Election, the most spectacular launching of a political party since the appearance of the Ratana Movement.

The cumulative effect of the activities of these groups was to focus media attention on Maori issues, to gradually radicalise such establishment organisations as the New Zealand Maori Council and Maori parliamentary representation, and to bring about major changes in the operations of the Departments of Education, Justice and Maori Affairs. Additional Maori language courses were introduced in schools, Kohanga Reo or 'language nests' were set up for pre-schoolers, one-year teacher-training courses were established for native speakers of Maori, public funds became available for the renovation of marae, legal aid was offered for Maori offenders, a Race Relations Act was passed outlawing discrimination and a Race Relations Conciliator's office was opened to deal with complaints about discrimination and to mitigate racial and cultural conflict.

Most importantly, the Waitangi Tribunal was established in 1975 to deliberate and rule on alleged breaches of the Treaty of Waitangi; in 1985 its powers were made retrospective to 1840. From this time it became the focus of Maori resource claims.

The National Government's major Maori policy measure was the establishment of the Tu Tangata (stand tall) programme in the late 1970s, a crash course to equip young Maoris with additional vocational and living skills. By the early 1980s the Government had accepted the call for greater Maori determination of Maori issues and had assigned the redrafting of the unsuccessful Maori Affairs Act to Maori representatives and organisations. It made additional funding available for the promotion of Maori culture and literature. It had appointed a Maori to head the Department of Maori Affairs, Kara Puketapu, and a Maori Minister, Manuera Benjamin Couch of Ngai Tahu. It also appointed a Maori chairman of the Parliamentary Select Committee on Maori Affairs.

From the mid-1980s the Lange Labour Government took reform of Maori policy even further. The Department of Maori Affairs was split into a slimmed-down policy advice ministry, Manatu Maori, and the Iwi Transition Authority, created to transfer former departmental functions to Maori groups and other Crown agencies. This restructuring was completed when the Ministry of Maori Development, Te Puni Kokiri, was established in 1992 with former senior Army officer Wira Gardiner at its head.

Another aspect of State sector restructuring also had far-reaching consequences for Maoris. The 1986 State Owned Enterprises Act had given the Waitangi Tribunal power to adjudicate on the status of land being transferred from government departments to SOEs. The following year, in a case arising out of this process, the Court of Appeal ruled that 'the principles of the treaty override everything else in the State Owned Enterprises Act, and these principles require the Pakeha and Maori treaty partners to act towards each other reasonably and with the utmost good faith.' This decision, and the references to the Treaty of Waitangi grafted on to amendments of such legislation as the Education and Conservation Acts, gave the treaty an explicit place in New Zealand jurisprudence for the first time.

In 1993 the Bolger-led National Government offered Maoris the Sealords Deal, by which the Crown in effect purchased 20 percent of the nation's fishery for allocation to Maori tribes. The actual distribution was to be carried out by the Waitangi Fisheries Commission. In return, Maoridom was asked to drop its treaty-based claims to fisheries resources. This action was controversial enough. But the Government went further.

In 1994 it produced its so-called Fiscal Envelope proposals to settle all Maori resource claims by the year 2000 and to budget a total of one billion dollars of public funds for this purpose. The scheme was rejected decisively by most Maoris at a series of regional huis in 1995. Instead, most tribes opted to continue pursuit of claims through either the Waitangi Tribunal or direct negotiation with the Crown (and the Tainui tribes settled their raupatu or confiscation claim in this manner in 1995). They rebuffed both the Government's suggested timetable for settlement and the notion that there should be a one billion dollar cap on such spending.

Because of the divisiveness of these proposals, Maori protests against Crown actions and proposed actions built up a head of steam not seen since the more acrimonious Waitangi Day protests of the early 1980s. Compared with the conditions of earlier years, however, major and irreversible adjustments had been made within New Zealand society by the 1980s. Maoris were a far more visible component of every aspect of the country's life, although still under-represented in the professions and in higher-income suburbs. Maori elements were increasingly apparent in the arts, literature and rituals of the nation. And, for the first time, its institutions were bending slowly but decisively towards Maori needs and aspirations. Nothing seemed more certain than that the momentum of these changes would increase.

Te ao hou

After World War Two many Maoris such as Kirikino Epiha of Honikiwi remained in rural communities. Like her, some still lived in earth-floor whares, cooked on an open fire, dried eel over the fireplace and plastered cracks in the walls with pages from the *Auckland Weekly News*. But the number of people retaining this lifestyle was diminishing rapidly. The movement to the cities which had begun in earnest with manpower direction during the war accelerated from the mid-1940s.

Another centenarian, Karu Mohiti Wilson, lived out her last days at Muriwai near Gisborne like a relic from a former age. In her youth she had known Te Kooti Rikirangi, founder of the Ringatu Church. Her husband was believed to be the last man to have the *rape* pattern tattooed on his buttocks. Both she and the grandson shown here died within weeks of this photograph being taken in 1970.

Rititia Irihei was another survivor from the nineteenth century. Although she too refused to move to the town, the town caught up with her. She resisted all efforts to buy her property and the house in which she had lived most of her life. Taupo township grew around her until she was the only link with its pre-urban past. She died in 1976.

Many Maori homes were without facilities that most Pakeha families regarded as essential, right up to the 1960s. The 1961 census showed that 29.9 percent had no hot water, 38.1 percent cooked without electricity or gas, and 44.4 percent had no flush toilet. This Ngati Porou woman prepares the family dinner on a wood range at Ruatoria in 1963.

With the steady movement of the rural Maori population into towns and cities, many country marae fell into disrepair. Some, however, increased in vitality and activity and regularly attracted visitors back from the cities for major huis. Here two kuias perform at the fiftieth anniversary of the foundation of Turangawaewae marae, Ngaruawahia, in 1972. This pa remained the ceremonial headquarters of the Maori King Movement.

The amenities of the towns, and the jobs and educational and recreational opportunities they offered, attracted Maori families in large numbers in the post-war years. These new city immigrants are pictured shopping in Rotorua in 1962.

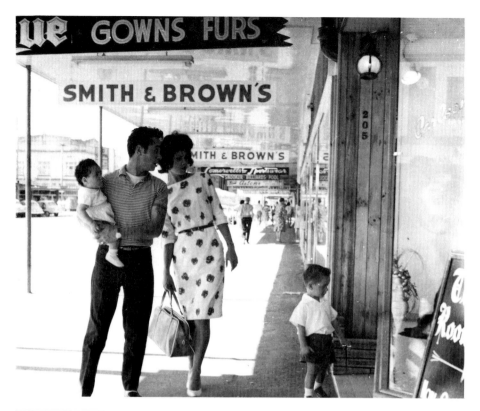

The greatest problem facing new Maori city-dwellers in the 1940s and 1950s was lack of suitable accommodation. The Maori Women's Welfare League did a survey of Maori housing for the Auckland City Council in 1955 to highlight the problem. It found that a large number of families lived in conditions that were unsanitary, overcrowded and unjustifiably expensive. Here the league's foundation president, Whina Cooper (centre), records details of one such household in Pitt Street.

A crash Maori-housing programme which followed publication of the Hunn Report in 1960 brought dramatic changes to Maori communal landscapes, and to the standard of accommodation. Whare and meeting house gave way to Maori Affairs dwellings in city suburbs. Some planners criticised these areas for the featurelessness of the houses and the lack of plants and trees. For thousands of families, however, like this one at Otara, they represented well-equipped homes and were a considerable advance on the accommodation that had been available previously.

Unlike rural communities, New Zealand cities were not equipped with meeting houses and marae for traditional Maori activities. Nor could such facilities have a tribal base in mixed tribal areas. The answer was multi-tribal urban marae, often set up in buildings that were not specifically Maori in character. This one is the Kokiri centre at Otara, established with assistance from the Department of Maori Affairs.

Some urban marae were used for specifically tribal purposes as tribal organisations attempted to keep in touch with members in cities. Here Irihapeti Ramsden, a Ngai Tahu leader in Wellington, prepares food for a South Island Maori function at Te Mangungu marae in Naenae.

Bright lights and a chance for recreation with large numbers of others were attractions for gregarious people brought up in quiet country communities. Options were extended and there were more opportunities to be communally involved with other Maoris. This dance was held at the Auckland Maori Community Centre.

Not everybody found warmth and satisfaction in the city. Those without lifelines into Maori organisations or community activities sometimes found cities to be lonely places. Increasingly the streets became the haunts of displaced young people, especially those who were unable to find work. This group mills about on late-shopping night at St Kevins Arcade off Karangahape Road in Auckland.

Many young Maoris who were not part of an established urban tribal network sought tribal-type bonds in gangs. Members' exuberance in behaviour and flamboyance of dress tended to offend more conservative elements of the community, Maori and Pakeha. Warrior traditions were transposed to another context. These Black Power Gang members are pictured in Wellington.

Gang activity was by no means all violent and anti-social, nor was it exclusively Maori. For many it was a means of establishing steadying roots in the communities in which they lived. Here a Maori member of the Highway 61 Club in Auckland enjoys club facilities with a Pakeha friend.

In the 1970s and 1980s a greater media interest in the Maori being Maori was both a reflection of a higher Maori profile and a cause of further public interest. Broadcasting media moved from an almost exclusive concern with concert-party performances towards a more searching coverage of Maori affairs. Here a film crew at Raglan records a discussion among Maori elders of the Tainui Awhiro tribe for television.

Cityscapes brought changes in Maori art forms — a move away from traditional materials and motifs into experimental areas. Selwyn Muru, painter, sculptor, writer and broadcaster, was one of the first whose work was affected by new locations and new media.

The 1970s saw the emergence of a phalanx of active Maori writers and artists. Here poet Hone Tuwhare, founder of the annual Maori Artists' and Writers' Hui, talks to a kuia at Te Kaha during the first such hui in 1973. Other prominent members of the group included writers Witi Ihimaera, Patricia Grace and Bruce Stewart, and artists Para Matchitt and Cliff Whiting.

A section of the Maori Writers' and Artists' Hui at Wairoa in 1974. Here a group rises to sing a waiata in Takitimu meeting house in the course of evening discussion. Huis such as this continued to be held on established marae within a framework of traditional protocol.

Part of a massive mural designed by and built under the supervision of artist Para Matchitt. Using non-traditional materials such as particle board, this work of art was installed by the local community in the Kimiora Hall at Turangawaewae marae, Ngaruawahia. One observer has called the result New Zealand's Sistine Chapel.

Experience of the Maori Land March of 1975 and of the Bastion Point dispute spawned a radical Maori theatre group, Maranga Mai. It dramatised Maori and Pakeha views of land and other instances of racial and cultural conflict. Performances in Auckland schools in 1980 brought protests from some education authorities who believed that the group would polarise racial feeling.

The late 1940s and early 1950s saw a changing of the guard in Maori leadership. Old faces and styles disappeared, new ones took their place. Here survivors of the Young Maori Party, Sir Peter Buck, Bishop Frederick Bennett and Sir Apirana Ngata, meet for the last time in 1949. Buck was making a farewell visit from Hawaii, where he was director of the Bishop Museum. Within two years all three were dead.

Many of the new directions in Maori Leadership were established by these men, seen at a Maori welfare meeting immediately after World War Two. They are (from left): John Grace, later knighted, Secretary to the Minister of Maori Affairs; George Shepherd, Chief Judge of the Maori Land Court; Peter Fraser, Prime Minister and innovative Minister of Maori Affairs; Michael Rotohiko Jones, ministerial secretary; and Tipi Ropiha, first Maori to head the Department of Maori Affairs.

One of the most pervasive innovations in Maori life after World War Two was the establishment of the Maori Women's Welfare League. This addressed itself to new social problems. But it also provided for the first time a network for the thousands of women engaged in voluntary Maori community work throughout the country. It became the first national Maori pressure group. At the league's first conference in Wellington in 1951, Mira Petricevich stands behind Whina Cooper, who became the first president.

War service brought a variety of post-war work in the Public Service for ex-Maori Battalion officers. Moana Raureti, as welfare officer based in Hamilton, had to travel widely throughout a mixed rural-urban district. John Rangihau, major spokesman for the Tuhoe tribe, was welfare officer in Rotorua and a close adviser to successive Pakeha Ministers of Maori Affairs. For his unsurpassed knowledge of Maoritanga he was known in some quarters as 'Mr Maoridom'.

The increased Maori presence in New Zealand national life was apparent in a variety of organisations and institutions. Here Charles Bennett of Te Arawa is elected President of the Labour Party in Wellington in 1969. Son of Bishop Frederick Bennett, he was subsequently knighted.

Archbishop Paul Reeves in 1980 became the first Maori to head the Anglican Church in New Zealand. Here he is flanked at Turangawaewae marae by the Maori Queen, Dame Te Atairangikaahu, and her husband Whatumoana Paki. In 1985, as Sir Paul, Reeves was appointed first Maori Governor-General of New Zealand.

268

Matiu Rata caused the biggest upset in Maori politics since the establishment of the Ratana Movement. He resigned from both the Labour Party and his Northern Maori seat in 1979, and contested the electorate as leader of the Mana Motuhake Party. Although he failed to win his way back to Parliament, his party was runner-up in all Maori seats in the 1981 General Election. A decade later Rata took Mana Motuhake into the Alliance group of political parties led by the New Labour Party's Jim Anderton.

The first urban Maori protest group to employ 'Pakeha' tactics such as demonstrations, petitions and press releases was formed in Auckland in 1970. Members called themselves Nga Tamatoa — the Young Warriors. Here one of their leaders, Syd Jackson, welcomes anti-Apartheid campaigner Dennis Brutus to New Zealand in 1969. Nga Tamatoa's activities concentrated on what its members regarded as racism and cultural imperialism in New Zealand — in government, in the Public Service, and in education in particular.

Herepo Rongo of Raglan, seen here with a grandchild, was a tattooed Maori kuia who spoke little English. In 1973 she sparked off demands for the return of the Raglan Golf Course to its original owners. The area had been the site of a community until World War Two, when it was seized for a temporary aircraft landing strip. Mrs Rongo was one of several dozen people displaced by the move.

Eva Rickard, who took up the Raglan Golf Course dispute on behalf of the Tainui Awhiro people of Waikato. Arrested for trespass on the course in 1975, her prosecution was overturned on appeal. Eventually the Muldoon National Government restored the course to its previous Maori owners.

Discontent with progressive Maori disinheritance led to the largest Maori protest, the Land March of 1975. This symbolic pilgrimage began in the far north in September 1975, when octogenarian Whina Cooper and one of her grandchildren Airini led about 100 marchers on to the road from the Te Hapua marae.

Several thousand additional demonstrators joined forces with the original members of the Maori Land March for their walk across Auckland Harbour Bridge.

At Parliament Buildings in Wellington the
marchers presented a Memorial of Rights to the
Labour Government asking for the protection of
Maori land and culture. Toby Kameta of
Rotorua addresses the politicians who came to
meet the protestors, including Prime Minister
Bill Rowling. Above flies the flag of Te
Matakite O Aotearoa, the group that inspired
and organised the march.

The Bastion Point protest began in 1977 when the Government decided to subdivide Crown land in Auckland for high-cost housing. A group representing many of the former owners of the land, Ngati Whatua, occupied the point to prevent development. Members built communal facilities, a meeting house, planted crops, welcomed sympathisers and imposed a strict code of conduct.

Left, an enormous force of police drawn from all over the North Island completely surround the Bastion Point squatters to prevent further people joining them before their eviction in May 1978. Below, police and squatters confront one another peaceably prior to the enforced removal of the protesters.

Maori protests outside the country's courts became a feature of the 1970s and 1980s as prosecutions followed demonstrations over land issues, Waitangi Day celebrations and the 1981 Springbok Tour. A common element of such proceedings was a refusal by Maori defendants to recognise the jurisdiction of the New Zealand legal system, which judges and magistrates usually defined as a 'not guilty' plea. This gathering outside the Auckland Magistrates Court was occasioned by the Bastion Point prosecutions.

Maori faces were to the forefront of anti-Springbok Tour demonstrations in the winter of 1981. As the tour proceeded demonstrators took on a more military appearance, arming themselves in many instances with protective shields and helmets so as to confront police baton charges. This group was assembling at Fowlds Park in Auckland on the day of the Third Test in September.

One effect of the 1981 Springbok Tour was to push subsequent demonstrations towards a new threshold of violence. The results were seen in February 1982 in Waitangi Day protests in and around the Bay of Islands. Confrontations between protesters and tangata whenua took place on the Waitangi marae, incendiary devices were thrown at police and missiles hurled at the Governor-General. The same year the Catholic Church became embroiled in a controversy over whether or not it should give financial support to the Auckland-based Waitangi Day Action Committee.

By the mid-1980s much of the urgency and anger drained from the Maori protest movement after the Waitangi Tribunal was given powers to hear cases which allegedly breached the treaty dating back to 1840. As long as the tribunal was seen to be addressing grievances and delivering decisions whose integrity could not be challenged, it offered Maoris hope of regaining lost resources through the country's system of government and judiciary. The sitting members pictured here are Sir Graham Latimer (long time chairman of the New Zealand Maori Council), Chief Maori Land Court Judge Eddie Durie and Paul Temm QC. They were taking evidence from Ngati Whatua at Orakei Marae in 1984. As a result of this hearing Ngati Whatua regained ownership of disputed land around Bastion Point.

Maoris also began to regain lost cultural ground as the Kohanga Reo (language nest) movement spread in the early 1980s. This Maori initiative introduced pre-school children to learning in Maori. Typically, mothers and grandmothers fluent in the reo taught their youngsters the basic ingredients of Maori language and culture in a wholly Maori environment. Later, some of these children would go to Kura Kaupapa, schools which taught the primary and secondary curricula in Maori.

Sir James Henare of Tai Tokerau and Ngati Hine was one of the founders of Kohanga Reo. Because of the universal respect in which this former commander of the 28th (Maori) Battalion was held, he was a serious contender for the post of Governor-General of New Zealand in 1985 (the appointment instead went to Anglican Archbishop Paul Reeves). Sir James died at his home in Motatau in 1990.

Another traditional leader with high national standing was Robert Te Kotahi Mahuta of the Tainui kahui ariki (seen here working in gardens at Waahi Marae). As adopted son of King Koroki he was a step-brother to the Maori Queen, Dame Te Atairangikaahu. In the 1980s and 1990s he was major spokesman for the Kingitanga and chief negotiator for Tainui in their raupatu claim against the Crown. In 1995, on his recommendation, Tainui accepted an offer of land, cash and other assets worth $170 million in settlement of their 130-year long confiscation grievance.

Decisive Maori rejection of the Fiscal Envelope proposals is illustrated by this Rotorua protest march in February 1995. The mainly young demonstrators were led by two wheelchair-bound kuia and a Maori Battalion veteran. In a succession of hui around the country, tribal leaders told National Government ministers that the proposals ought to have been developed in consultation with Maori and that the billion dollar cap on settlement expenditure was unacceptable to Maoris.

Sir Hepi Te Heuheu, Ariki of Ngati Tuwharetoa, was another tribal leader with a national profile. The National Maori Congress, an umbrella grouping based on tribe, was formed as a result of a hui called by Sir Hepi in 1989. He also led Maori opposition to the National Government's 1995 Fiscal Envelope proposal to settle all Maori claims. Sir Hepi is seen here (in white suit) attempting to negotiate with police at a Waitangi Day protest at Waitangi in 1984.

Tribal Location Map

Traditional tribal areas and locations resulting from nineteenth century tribal migrations (based on Appendices to the Journal of the House of Representatives, 1870).

1 Aupouri
2 Rarawa
3 Ngapuhi
4 Ngati Whatua
5 Ngati Paoa
6 Ngati Maru
7 Ngati Haua
8 Waikato
9 Ngati Toa
10 Ngati Maniapoto
11 Ngati Raukawa
12 Ngai Te Rangi
13 Arawa
14 Ngati Awa
15 Whakatohea
16 Whanau a Apanui
17 Ngati Porou
18 Rongowhakaata
19 Tuhoe
20 Ngati Kahungunu
21 Ngati Tuwharetoa
22 Ngati Tama
23 Ati Awa
24 Taranaki
25 Ngati Ruanui
26 Ngarauru
27 Wanganui
28 Muaupoko, Ngati Raukawa, Ngati Apa
29 Ngati Toa, Ati Awa, Ngati Ira
30 Ngati Kuia
31 Ngai Tahu
32 Poutini Ngai Tahu
33 Ngati Mamoe

NORTH ISLAND

SOUTH ISLAND

Sources and Acknowledgements

An overview history such as this one is gleaned from more Maori informants, books, institutions and documents than I could list individually. Nevertheless, I shall mention those to whom I am most indebted.

For assistance over a period of time I wish to thank Sally Marshall-Tuwhangai, Robert Mahuta, Te Uira Manihera, Heeni Wharemaru, Whina Cooper, Joseph Cooper, Alex McKay, Marjorie Rau, Bill Parker, Mairatea Tahiwi, Marie Smith and Sweet and Whenua Rehu; and, for special assistance with South Island Maori material, Irihapeti Ramsden and Sir Tipene O'Regan. E hoa ma, nau i waka aua te kakahu, he taniko taku.

Among colleagues whose work I have drawn especially from are Ann Parsonson, Janet Davidson, John Owens and M. P. K. Sorrenson (all contributors to *The Oxford History of New Zealand*), Keith Sinclair, Judith Binney, W. H. Oliver, Dick Scott, Rangi Walker, Pat Hohepa, Ngahuia Te Awekotuku, Father E. R. Simmons and David Simmons.

Advice on photographs and photography was given to me by William Main, John Turner, Leonard Bell, John Sullivan of the Alexander Turnbull Library, Gordon Maitland of the Auckland Institute and Museum, Sheila Robinson of the Gisborne Museum, and Ian Rockel of the Rotorua Museum. I am grateful for the expertise of such people, but they should not be held responsible for the final expression of views in this book. I also received considerable assistance from staff members of the Hocken Library, the Canterbury Museum, the National Museum, the Auckland Public Library and the *Northern Advocate* newspaper. Stephen O'Regan arranged for use of photographs from the Ngai Tahu Archive, University of Canterbury.

I am greatly indebted to individuals and families who lent photographs or who gave permission for them to be used. Among them are Irihapeti Ramsden, Whina Cooper, Sir Henare and Lady Ngata, Tumokai Katipa, Heeni Wharemaru, Gwen Howe, Cathy Baker, Sir Tipene O'Regan, Mairatea Tawhiwi, Meri Taka, Raukura Gillies, Ben Tewake, Norman Nicholls, F.O. Bradshaw, Te Uira Manihera, R. G. H. Manley, Bert Roth, Alan Baldwin, Barry Mitcalfe and Kirby Wright. Malcolm Burdan and Colin Salt assisted with the photographing of pictures from private collections.

I am grateful to my parents, Eleanor and Lewis King, for continuous support; to Jonathan and Rachael King for putting up with prolonged absences; to Terry and Toni King for shelter and for cooperation in a variety of ways; and to Maria Jungowska for assistance and encouragement.

The following are among the major publications I have consulted and in some instances quoted from:

For the book as a whole, I have drawn from *The Oxford History of New Zealand*, W. H. Oliver (ed.), Oxford University Press, Wellington, 1981; and *The Maoris of New Zealand, Rautahi*, Joan Metge, Routledge and Kegan Paul, London, 1976.

Introduction. *Maori in Focus: a selection of photographs of the Maori from 1850-1914*, William Main, Millwood Press, Wellington, 1976; *The Maori in European Art*, Leonard Bell, Reed, Wellington, 1980; *New Zealand Photographers, a selection*, Hardwicke Knight, Allied Press, Dunedin, 1981; *Burton Brothers, Photographers*, Hardwicke Knight, John McIndoe, Dunedin, 1980; *Through the King Country With the Camera, a photographer's diary*, Alfred Burton, Dunedin, 1885; 'Photographic Reportage of the New Zealand Wars', William Main, in *History of Photography, an international quarterly*, April 1981.

Chapter One. *We, the Navigators: the ancient art of land-finding in the Pacific*, David Lewis, Australian National University Press, Canberra, 1972; *Ancient Voyagers in the Pacific*, Andrew Sharp, Paul, Auckland and Hamilton, 1967; *Maori Origins and Migrations*, M. P. K. Sorrenson, Auckland University Press/Oxford University Press, Auckland, 1979; *The First New Zealanders*, Phillip Houghton, Hodder and Stoughton, Auckland, 1980; *The Great New Zealand Myth*, D.R. Simmons, Reed, Wellington, 1976; *The Prehistory of New Zealand*, Janet Davidson, Longman Paul, Auckland, 1984; *Two Worlds*, Anne Salmond, Viking, Auckland, 1991.

Chapter Two. *The New Zealand Wars: a history of the Maori campaigns and the pioneering period*, James Cowan, two volumes, Government Printer, Wellington, 1922–23; *The Origins of the Maori Wars*, Keith Sinclair, New Zealand University Press, Wellington, 1957; *A Show of Justice: racial 'amalgamation' in nineteenth century New Zealand*, Alan Ward, Auckland University Press/Oxford University Press, Auckland, 1973; *The Shadow of the Land: a study of British policy and racial conflict in New Zealand, 1832–1852*, Ian Wards, Government Printer, Wellington, 1968; *New Zealanders at War*, Michael King, Heinemann, Auckland, 1981; *Cork of War: Ngati Toa and the British mission, a historical narrative*, Ray Grover, John McIndoe, Dunedin, 1982; *The New Zealand Wars and the Victorian Interpretation of Racial Conflict*, Auckland University Press, 1986; *The Treaty of Waitangi*, Claudia Orange, Allen Unwin/Port Nicholson Press, Wellington, 1987.

Chapter Three. *The Maori Population of New Zealand 1769–1971*, D. Ian Pool, Auckland University Press/Oxford University Press, Auckland, 1977; *Maori Houses and Food Stores*, William J. Phillipps, Dominion Museum, Wellington, 1952; *Traditional Maori Clothing: a study of technological and functional change*, S. M. Mead, Reed, Wellington, 1969.

Chapter Four. *Politics of the New Zealand Maori: protest and co-operation, 1891–1909*, John Williams, University of Washington Press, Seattle, 1969; *Ask That Mountain: the story of Parihaka*, Dick Scott, Heinemann/Southern Cross, Auckland, 1975; *Education and Identity: a study of the New Zealand Maori Graduate*, Thomas K. Fitzgerald, New Zealand Council for Educational Research, Wellington, 1977; *Mihaia: the prophet Rua Kenana and his community at Maungapohatu*, Judith Binney *et alia*, Oxford University Press, Wellington, 1979; *The Autobiography of a Maori*, Reweti Kohere, Reed, Wellington, 1951; *Man of Two Worlds: Sir Maui Pomare*, J. F. Cody, Reed, Wellington, 1953; *Te Rangi Hiroa: the life of Sir Peter Buck*, J. B. Condliffe, Whitcombe and Tombs, Christchurch, 1971; *Ratana: the Man, the Church, the Political Movement*, J. McLeod Henderson, Reed/Polynesian Society, Wellington, 1972; *Te Puea*, Michael King, Hodder and Stoughton, Auckland, 1977; *Kotahitanga, the Search for Maori Political Unity*, Lindsay Cox, Oxford University Press, Auckland, 1993.

Chapter Five. *Maori Schools in a Changing Society: a historical review*, J. M. Barrington and T. H. Beaglehole, New Zealand Council for Educational Research, Wellington, 1974; *Challenge for Health: a history of public health in New Zealand*, F. S. Maclean, Government Printer, Wellington, 1964; *Challenge and Response: a study of the development of the Gisborne East Coast region*, W. H. Oliver and Jane M. Thomson, East Coast Development Research Association, Gisborne, 1971; *Integration or Identity? cultural interaction in New Zealand since 1911*, M. P. K. Sorrenson, Heinemann, Auckland, 1977; *Amiria: the life story of a Maori Woman*, Amiria Stirling and Anne Salmond, Reed, Wellington, 1976; *Te Ao Hurihuri*, Michael King (ed.), Hicks Smith/Methuen, Wellington, 1977.

Chapter Six. *A New Maori Migration: rural and urban relations in northern New Zealand*, Joan Metge, Melbourne University Press, Melbourne, 1964; *The Maori and New Zealand Politics*, J. G. A. Peacock (ed.), Paul, Auckland and Hamilton, 1965; *The Maori in the New Zealand Economy*, G. V. Butterworth, Department of Industries and Commerce, Wellington, 1967; *Tihe Mauri Ora*, Michael King (ed.), Methuen, Wellington, 1978; *Race Against Time*, Hiwi Tauroa, Human Rights Commission, Wellington, 1982; *Ka Whawhai Tonu Matou*, Ranginui Walker, Penguin, Auckland, 1990.

Photograph sources (ATL indicates the Alexander Turnbull Library, Wellington; and AM the Auckland Institute and Museum. Other sources are described in full):

Page 7 Taranaki Museum; 8 (left) William Main, AM; 9 (left) ATL, AM; 10 (left) AM, Gwen Howe; 11 (both) AM; 12 (upper left) F. O. Bradshaw, (right) Ngai Tahu Archive, (below) AM; 13 (left) ATL, National Museum; 14 (both) AM; 15 (both) AM; 16 ATL; 17 (upper left) ATL, (middle and right) AM, (lower) National Museum; 18 (left) ATL, AM; 19 AM; 20 (upper) ATL, AM; 21 (left) ATL, (right) AM, (below) National Museum; 22 (both) AM; 23 (all) ATL; 24 (both) ATL; 25 (left) AM, Alan Baldwin; 26 (both) ATL; 27 (upper) ATL, AM; 28 (upper) Auckland City Art Gallery, ATL; 29 (upper) AM, ATL; 30 ATL; 31 (both) AM; 32 (upper) AM, ATL; 33 (upper left) Ngai Tahu Archive, (right) AM, Gwen Howe; 34 (upper) AM, Meri Taka; 35 (upper) ATL, Ans Westra, Ans Westra.

Page 52 (both) AM; 53 (upper) ATL, AM; 54 (both) ATL; 55 (both) ATL; 56 (upper left) ATL, (upper right) AM, ATL; 57 (both) AM; 58 (upper left) AM, (right) National Museum, AM; 59 (upper) Canterbury Museum, ATL; 60 (upper left) Auckland Public Library, (right) Rotorua Museum, ATL; 61 (both) Gisborne Museum; 62 (upper) ATL, Ngati Tahu Archive; 63 (all) AM; 64 (upper) ATL, AM; 65 (upper) AM, ATL; 66 (upper left) ATL, (right) AM, ATL; 67 (upper) ATL, AM; 68 (both) ATL; 69 AM; 70 National Museum; 71 National Museum.

Page 79 (upper) AM, ATL; 80 (both) National Museum; 81 (upper) National Museum, ATL; 82 (both) ATL; 83 (upper) ATL, AM; 84 (upper) AM, ATL; 85 (both) ATL; 86 (upper) AM, ATL; 87 (upper) AM, ATL; 88 National Museum; 89 (upper) ATL, National Museum; 90 (upper) AM, ATL; 91 (upper) ATL, (middle) AM, AM; 92 (upper) AM, Rotorua Museum; 93 ATL; 94 (upper) AM, (middle) ATL, AM; 95 (upper) Wanganui Museum, ATL; 96 (upper) Ngai Tahu Archive, AM; 97 (upper) ATL, AM; 98 AM; 99 (upper) Rotorua Museum, ATL; 100 (left) AM, (others) ATL; 101 (upper) AM, ATL; 102 (upper) ATL, National Archives; 103 (both) ATL; 104 (both) AM; 105 (upper) AM, ATL; 106 (both) ATL; 107 (both) Ngai Tahu Archive; 108 (both) National Museum; 109 (left) Rotorua Museum, ATL; 110 Canterbury Museum; 111 (upper) ATL, (others) Henare Ngata; 112 F. O. Bradshaw; 113 (upper) Rotorua Museum, ATL; 114 (upper) Gisborne Museum, ATL; 115 (upper) Whina Cooper, Turongo House Collection; 116 (upper) AM, ATL; 117 (both) AM; 118 (both) ATL; 119 (both) ATL; 120 (upper) ATL, (middle) AM, Rotorua Museum; 121 (upper) ATL, (middle) Rotorua Museum, Wanganui

Museum; 122 (upper) Gisborne Museum, (others) Henare Ngata; 123 (all) Henare Ngata; 124 Auckland Public Library; 125 (both) ATL; 126 (all) ATL; 127 Norman Nicholls; 128 Ngai Tahu Archive; 129 (both) ATL; 130 Turongo House Collection; 131 ATL; 132 Nelson Museum; 133 (upper) Ngai Tahu Archive, ATL; 134 (upper) AM, ATL; 135 (both) AM; 136 (both) AM; 137 (upper) AM, ATL; 138 (upper) Gwen Howe, Ngai Tahu Archive; 139 (both) ATL; 140 (upper) Ngai Tahu Archive, ATL; 141 ATL; 142 (upper) ATL, (middle) Whina Cooper, ATL; 143 Heeni Wharemaru; 144 (both) AM; 145 (both) Rotorua Museum; 146 (upper) AM, Rotorua Museum; 147 (upper two) Ngai Tahu Archive, ATL; 148 AM; 149 (upper) Gisborne Museum, Bert Roth; 150 (upper two) Henare Ngata, ATL; 151 ATL; 152 (upper) Rotorua Museum, ATL; 153 (both) AM; 154 (upper) F. O. Bradshaw, Ngai Tahu Archive, 155 (all) ATL; 156 (both) ATL; 157 ATL.

Page 168 (upper) Gisborne Museum, Ngai Tahu Archive; 169 ATL; 170 Taranaki Herald; 171 (both) Taranaki Museum; 172 (left) National Museum, ATL; 173 (left) Turongo House Collection, AM; 174 (left) Canterbury Museum, ATL; 175 Auckland Public Library; 176 (left) Whina Cooper, Ngai Tahu Archive; 177 (upper) AM, Ngai Tahu Archive; 178 (both) ATL; 179 (both) ATL; 180 (upper) National Museum, ATL; 181 (both) ATL; 182 (both) ATL; 183 (upper) National Museum, ATL; 184 (upper) ATL, AM; 185 (both) ATL; 186 (upper) ATL, Whina Cooper; 187 (both) Whina Cooper; 188 (upper) Gisborne Museum, AM; 189 Turongo House Collection; 190 (both) R. G. H. Manley; 191 (upper) New Zealand Herald, R. G. H. Manley; 192 (both) ATL; 193 ATL.

Page 203 ATL; 204 (upper) ATL, Gisborne Museum; 205 William Main; 206 (upper two) AM, ATL; 207 (upper) Whina Cooper, Ngai Tahu Archive; 208 (both) ATL; 209 (upper) Barry Mitcalfe, AM; 210 AM; 211 (upper) ATL, Rotorua Museum; 212 (both) ATL; 213 (all) Ngai Tahu Archive; 214 (upper) Whina Cooper, Ngai Tahu Archive; 215 (both) Whina Cooper; 216 Ans Westra; 217 (upper) ATL, AM; 218 (upper) Te Uira Manihera, AM; 219 (upper) Ngai Tahu Archive, Henare Ngata; 220 Ngai Tahu Archive, Mairatea Tahiwi; 221 ATL; 222 (both) ATL; 223 (upper) ATL, Ngai Tahu Archive; 224 (both) Ngai Tahu Archive; 225 Northern Advocate; 226 (upper) AM, Whina Cooper; 227 Rotorua Museum; 228 (upper) Ngai Tahu Archive, ATL; 229 (upper) ATL, M. B. Couch; 230 Ngai Tahu Archive; 231 (upper) Canterbury Museum, ATL; 232 (upper) ATL, Whina Cooper; 233 (upper) ATL, Ngai Tahu Archive; 234 (upper) Rotorua Museum, Whina Cooper; 235 (upper) Heeni Wharemaru, Whina Cooper; 236 (upper) AM, Rotorua Museum; 237 (upper) Turongo House Collection, ATL; 238 (upper) Ngai Tahu Archive, Beryl Te Wiata; 239 ATL; 240 ATL; 241 (both) ATL; 242 (both) ATL; 243 (both) ATL; 244 (both) Turongo House Collection; 245 ATL; 246 ATL; 247 Queen Elizabeth II Army Memorial Museum.

Page 255 Kirby Wright; 256 (both) Marti Friedlander; 257 (upper) Ans Westra, Marti Friedlander; 258 (upper) Ans Westra, Whina Cooper; 259 (upper and lower left) Robin Morrison, Michael King; 260 (upper) Ans Westra, John Miller; 261 (upper) Ans Westra, Robin Morrison; 262 (upper) Pacific Films, Ans Westra; 263 (both) John Miller; 264 (upper) National Publicity Studios, John Miller; 265 (both) ATL; 266 ATL; 267 Kirby Wright, John Miller; 268 (upper) Marti Friedlander, Kirby Wright; 269 (upper) Evening Post, Marti Friedlander; 270 (left) Allan Baldwin, Marti Friedlander; 271 (upper) New Zealand Herald, Auckland Star; 272 John Miller; 273 Robin Morrison; 274 (upper) Auckland Star, Robin Morrison; 275 (upper) Auckland Star, John Miller; 276 Ans Westra; 277 (upper) Gil Hanly (New Zealand Listener), New Zealand Listener; 278 (both) Bruce Connew (New Zealand Listener); 279 (upper) Rotorua Daily Post, Bruce Connew (New Zealand Listener).

It has often been difficult to identify people and places in many of the photographs selected for this book. Sometimes little or no information was supplied by the photographer, sometimes what information had existed was lost, sometimes the information given was contradictory. I would invite people who can help with identifications or who can correct errors to write to me c/- the publisher, Private Bag 34901, Birkenhead, Auckland.

Index